MOSQUITO
SUPPER CLUB

MOSQUITO SUPPER CLUB

CAJUN RECIPES FROM A DISAPPEARING BAYOU

MELISSA M. MARTIN

Photographs by Denny Culbert

ARTISAN | NEW YORK

Library of Congress Cataloging-in-Publication Data

Names: Martin, Melissa (Chef), author. | Culbert,
Denny, photographer.
Title: Mosquito Supper Club : Cajun recipes from a
disappearing Bayou /
  Melissa Martin ; photographs by Denny Culbert.
Description: New York : Artisan, a division of
Workman Publishing Co.,
  Inc., 2020. | Includes index.
Identifiers: LCCN 2019050290 |
ISBN 9781579658472 (hardcover)
Subjects: LCSH: Cooking, Cajun. | Cooking,
American—Louisiana style. |
  Mosquito Supper Club. | LCGFT: Cookbooks.
Classification: LCC TX715.2.L68 M328 2020 | DDC
641.59763—dc23
LC record available at https://lccn.loc
.gov/2019050290

Design and map by Nina Simoneaux

The recipe for Garlic Crabs with Parsley and Lemon
(page 85) originally appeared in *Garden & Gun* maga-
zine in slightly different form.

Artisan books are available at special discounts
when purchased in bulk for premiums and sales
promotions as well as for fund-raising or educational
use. Special editions or book excerpts also can be
created to specification. For details, contact the
Special Sales Director at the address below, or send
an e-mail to specialmarkets@workman.com.

For speaking engagements, contact speakers
bureau@workman.com.

Published by Artisan
A division of Workman Publishing Co., Inc.
225 Varick Street
New York, NY 10014-4381
artisanbooks.com

Artisan is a registered trademark of Workman
Publishing Co., Inc.

Published simultaneously in Canada by Thomas
Allen & Son, Limited

Printed in China

First printing, March 2020

10 9 8 7 6 5 4 3 2 1

For my mom,
Maxine M. Martin,
who made feeding six kids
her full-time job

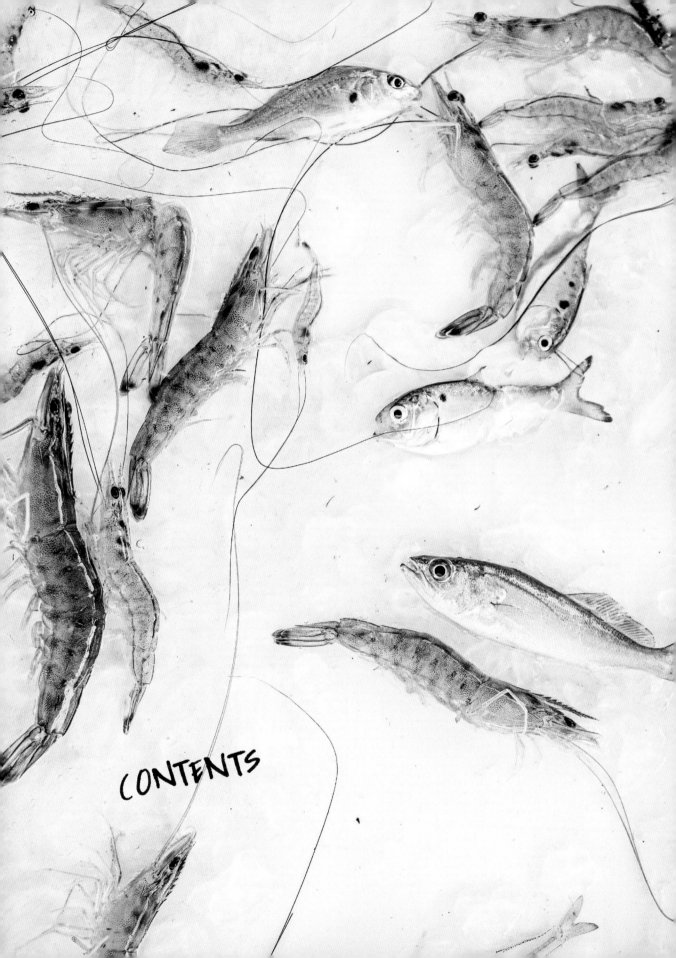

CONTENTS

INTRODUCTION

The first thing I think when someone refers to the states below the Mason-Dixon Line is "that's the north." As a child in one of the southernmost parts of Louisiana, I didn't understand the concept of the American South. To me, everything above Baton Rouge was the north. I grew up with leftover gumbo in the fridge and an oil rig drilling just outside my window. I didn't know it was special to eat cold crabs for breakfast and be surrounded by water and bayous, ibis and pelicans, receding land and dying cypress trees. I also didn't know I was Cajun.

I was born and raised in South Louisiana in Terrebonne Parish. *Terre bonne* means "good earth" in French, and situated as it is on delta soil, the parish is aptly named. The Terrebonne my dad remembers growing up in sounds like a fairy-tale land: cypress- and oak-lined waterways; squirrels jumping from tree to tree overhead; egrets, cranes, and herons hiding in hues of green, blue, and emerald. Now the 100 million migratory birds that use South Louisiana as a wintering habitat lack landing pads in Terrebonne Parish. Most of the cypress and oak trees that are still standing are stripped to bare branches, and the majority of the islands and bayous that encompassed the barrier waters have become lakes. Terrebonne Parish is hanging on to the coastline for dear life.

Louisiana is losing more good earth than any other place on the planet. Louisiana's coast, a thick, ever-changing blanket of marsh, is disappearing, and our wetlands and bayous are disappearing along with it. A whole list of places in South Louisiana that once held history are now covered in water. Before Cocodrie and Chauvin—the lands on which my grandparents, parents, siblings, and I were born and raised—join that list, I want to make sure we put the Cajun food I grew up with and the people responsible for it on record. It's imperative that the small fishing villages that push out so much seafood, tradition, and culture be recognized and remembered before time and tides take their toll.

Louisiana has already lost a landmass the size of Delaware. Unless the Mississippi River is diverted and allowed to flow into areas dependent on sediment, the delta lands, swamps, marshes, and bays on which our ancestors settled will disappear, submerged in the Gulf of Mexico. In the next twenty-five years, if the water continues to rise at the current rate, a majority of Terrebonne Parish could be gone, and New Orleans could become a seaside town.

A Brief History of Cajuns

"Cajun" is derived from the Acadian word for the French descendants of Acadiana. In Louisiana, we have many remnants of Acadian life, especially in our foodways. But before Cajuns could exist, Acadian life was cultivated by French settlers who took a risk to move or migrate to North America.

In the early 1600s, French explorers sailed to the New World in the hopes of gaining a monopoly on the fur trade. They landed in the Bay of Fundy and settled in the Canadian Maritimes. They did not show up to an empty country. When French settlers arrived in what would become Acadia, they met the Mi'kmaqs, one of Canada's many indigenous peoples, and the relationship they built with the tribe was instrumental in their survival. The French, who in time became known as Acadians, brought their cooking and agricultural skills to the region, where they lived simple lives and built an uncomplicated cuisine using minimal ingredients. This is a cuisine still served today in the Canadian Maritimes, and its influence is seen on tables in South Louisiana.

The *Grand Dérangement*

At the same time that French settlers were arriving in Acadia, the American South was being colonized, and the American slave trade had begun, dispersing enslaved Africans all over the southern United States. Native lands were being appropriated by strangers, and immigrants were flooding North America.

In the mid-1700s, the Seven Years' War between the French and the English put the French settlers in Acadia in a raw position, and as a consequence, the English demanded that the Acadians bend the knee to the British Crown. They refused, despite the fact that the region was, at the time, a British colony, so the Crown ordered them to be expelled. More than eleven thousand people were exiled from Acadia, and half of them died from consequences directly related to the trauma of the expulsion. (On December 9, 2003, 248 years later, a proclamation delivered by a representative of Queen Elizabeth acknowledged the forced exile of the peaceful Acadian people and designated July 28 "A Day of Commemoration of the Great Upheaval"— without, however, explicitly apologizing.)

Over the years, many Acadian exiles made their way south into America, and by the early 1800s, more than four thousand Acadians had settled in South Louisiana. In 1785, along with Catholic missionaries, two thousand French settlers arrived by ship from France. The Spanish, who were at that time ruling in Louisiana, welcomed the French and many other immigrants and sent them to live in the countryside. These settlers built communities alongside the American Indian tribes who had been inhabiting Louisiana since at least 700 BCE. Together, these groups—as well as people of Spanish, Basque, Croatian, German, Irish, Portuguese, African, Creole, Cuban, and Pacific Island descent, among others, who also migrated to the area—lived along the bayous

and waterways in semi-isolation for more than 175 years, sharing their respective skills and practices and intermarrying. Cajun folks and what we know as the Cajun way of life are the result of this intermingling of nations and peoples and the cultures and traditions they brought to South Louisiana and shared with their new neighbors.

American Indians are the beginning of everything in North America, in South Louisiana, and in what we know as Cajun country. They extended their friendship to French settlers so long ago on the Canadian shores and then again centuries later in South Louisiana. Cajuns are products of their

hospitality. A new culture, new traditions, and a new cuisine were born in the bayous and swamps of South Louisiana.

Tales from the Bayou

The word *bayou* is likely derived from the Choctaw word *bayok*. Physically, it refers to a body of water, which could be a slow-moving stream, a swampy marsh inlet, a river arm, or even some former paths of the Mississippi River. Bayous can be mammoth or tiny. The bayous are a braided network of waterways that push sediment across South Louisiana and form delta land. Communities settled on these passageways, building their homes on the banks and their livelihood on the water. Louisiana's bayous are a thoroughfare into history, an artery to the heart of the Cajun life I know.

The bayou and its Cajun settlers are often misunderstood, a condition not helped by how horribly Cajuns are portrayed on television and in films (Adam Sandler's 1998 movie *The Waterboy*, for example, is not an accurate depiction of Cajun people). But this inaccurate portrayal is not limited to the screen: Cajun food and culture are misrepresented on menus, in recipes and spice concoctions, and by businesses across the globe—as if in a word one could brand three hundred years of culture and tradition!

In South Louisiana, we have Cajun music, the Cajun language, and Cajun food, an evolving cuisine in which the ingredients and dishes differ from parish to parish, bayou to bayou. The people I grew up around are hardworking. They can erect a home without blueprints and rebuild it after a storm. They don't sit in despair and wait for help; they take action. (I suggest you read up on the Cajun Navy.) The people of the bayou have a bone-deep understanding of the water and its passages, the changing of the seasons, and the weather. They know the names of all the fish swimming in our waters, the birds gracing our skies, and the flora and fauna holding South Louisiana together. They live by the moon, and they have a distinct passion and joy for living. Cajuns became Cajuns because of many other nations, which means you can be Italian Cajun, German Cajun, Portuguese Cajun, and so on. Our traditions and cultures are shared among all our people; we are all hybrids of one another.

The Cajun community I belong to is rooted in the work of fishermen. I feel fortunate to have been raised in the seafood industry. To get to Terrebonne Parish, you leave the city limits of New Orleans and head south, along Highway 90 and then down Louisiana 56. The highway winds along the bayous through Houma, then Chauvin, Robinson Canal, and finally Cocodrie, which dead-ends at the Gulf of Mexico. As you make this journey, you can really feel the earth being stripped away. Cocodrie and the other towns bordering the Gulf of Mexico aren't the bustling centers of the industry that they used to be. Many fishing villages have been turned into destinations for sportfishing, but many working-class fishermen are still there, holding on to a life passed down to them through generations. Although the land has been depleted, there are still a handful of folks living in Cocodrie, where my parents grew up, but most folks have moved up the bayou to higher ground, places like Chauvin, where I was raised.

Chauvin is on Bayou Petit Caillou, a slow-moving fork of water that stretches due south and spills into the Gulf of Mexico. Those of us who live there have a complicated relationship with water: it ebbs and flows around everything in South Louisiana; it gives and it takes. Water is our lifeline and our dark shadow. Homes and businesses line the banks of the bayou. Yet when seen from above, the land is completely surrounded by water, and Chauvin is barely recognizable as a place of habitation. One might wonder how a community could exist inundated by so much water. But it is a community grounded in the convergence of salt water, brackish water, marsh, land, people, and traditions, and is one of the oldest and most influential culinary places in the country.

A Cook's Journey

Growing up on the bayou was an insular experience. I was immersed in the culture—we didn't leave the bayou very often. It was an eye-opening experience when I left home to study English literature at Loyola University in New Orleans. I struggled with my harsh Cajun accent and dialect, and I was confused by what the cafeteria was calling food. Nothing had flavor, and everything seemed so far from the cooking I knew. I began looking for real food with real ingredients, the kind I had eaten growing up. I realized how hard it was to find the kind of seafood and produce I remembered from home, ingredients with integrity. I got involved with the Crescent City Farmers Market in New Orleans and began to form relationships with fishermen and farmers, people who felt familiar to me. I started cooking with 100 percent farmers'-market ingredients and piecing together work in the culinary field.

After Hurricane Katrina devastated our region, everything I owned could fit into a couple of suitcases. I was a single mother with a five-year-old son, and I was at a crossroads in my life. But I welcomed being upended by the storm—I had no other choice but to open my mind (and my palate) to new experiences.

I followed my winemaker friend Sarah Vandendriessche to Napa, a culinary mecca, to take a mental and physical break from New Orleans. I worked as a harvest intern at her husband Christopher's winery, White Rock Vineyards, and stayed with them in their impossibly perfect tiny house on the Silverado Trail. Christopher loaned me a copy of *Cooking by Hand* by Paul Bertolli, and I read it from cover to cover through tears in a room that was only big enough to hold a full-size mattress. I was in heaven. Bertolli's words triggered an awakening in me, and that book, with its black-and-white photos and essays on seasonality and the simplicity of a meal anchored by time, patience, and real ingredients, changed the way I thought about the food and the place where I grew up.

I extended my stay in Napa Valley to learn as much as I could in West Coast kitchens. I credit Michelin-star chef Kelly McCown and Sarah Walz of Rubicon for having the patience and humor to train a young cook on the proper practices for preparing food in a professional kitchen. I wrestled my way through a year with these seasoned chefs and absorbed everything I could. We had a lot of laughs at my expense, and I made a lifetime of memories.

In Napa, I began to see how the dishes that land on a dinner table are truly the sum of all their parts—the work of farmers, fishermen, and millers that colors a cook's palette, whether that meal is served in a home kitchen or in the finest restaurant. Food (and eating it) is our common denominator, and all ingredients have a story. For me, that story always returns to the tiny fishing village where I was raised. And at some point, I knew I had to fly south and cook with the ingredients I knew best.

Cooking in New Orleans

A question New Orleanians are asked often is "Where can we get good Cajun food?" My answer would be "Do you know someone from down the bayou? Someone whose house you can go to?" That's where you find real Cajun food. You can eat incredible Cajun food throughout South Louisiana on any given day—but it's being prepared by busy, industrious women tucked away in home kitchens.

Every recipe in this book, I learned from a woman. Those of us who grew up on the bayou know that women run the kitchens. I am at the mercy of their knowledge, wisdom, and strength, and I've been fortunate to be on the receiving side of their kitchen mastery. Women are the backbone of the tiny village in which I was raised, and they are the masters of sustaining and ensuring the survival of bayou communities.

The Cajun food I ate growing up wasn't loud or flashy—no *bam!*—and it was not consumed with copious amounts of beer or alcohol. We ate simple, whole foods, and we ate with the seasons. We ate a cuisine rooted in the hard work of fishermen and the palates and grace of mothers and wives commanding their stoves.

I opened Mosquito Supper Club because I wanted people to learn about the real Cajun food I grew up with. And I wanted to present that food in the context in which we eat it on the bayou—with a woman in charge of the menu *and* the stories. I wanted to bring this simple Cajun food out of home kitchens and onto a restaurant table for folks from around the world to enjoy. I wanted to cook with Louisiana seafood and local produce; I wanted to forage for blackberries when they were in season and process okra when it was abundant and serve them both in ways that feel familiar to me. I wanted to bring the best of the bayou to the table and shine a light on what was happening to the place where I grew up and the people who live there.

Bittersweet Louisiana

When I was a kid, we were accustomed to dealing with hurricanes and flooding. When a storm was imminent, we moved our possessions as high as we could and waited for the water to topple the levees. When we were sure the water would keep rising, we'd leave our home for a place where the water couldn't reach us. Sometimes we even boarded our family's houseboat on Bayou Petit Caillou and just rose right along with the water. We kids thought it was an adventure.

At one time, my homeland had dense marsh, wetlands, and barrier islands that helped absorb a hurricane's intensity. Our islands are now underwater, and our marshes and wetlands are a jagged mess or have wholly disappeared into the Gulf of Mexico. Now even small Category 1 hurricanes, storms that in the past would give us little cause for concern, cause flooding, and places like Bayou Cook, Jacko Bay, Lake Barre, Last Island—barrier islands, fishing villages, dense marsh—have disappeared. They are gone.

When you imagine the outline of Louisiana, you probably think of the iconic boot shape, but that notion is out of date, and continuing to depict the state this way is a joke. Louisiana's borders have been irrevocably altered, and the state is now a misshapen boot, a spiderweb of land trying to stay afloat as the Gulf of Mexico encroaches. The new map of Louisiana shows a delta in distress.

Deltas are meant to be in flux, to naturally grow and subside, but South Louisiana's delta is contending with too many adversaries: the damming of the Mississippi River, the oil industry's negligence, and the government allowing the misconduct to happen.

Over a seven-thousand-year period, the Mississippi River drained most of the continent between the Appalachians to the east and the Rockies to the west, eventually creating the United States' delta region, which includes South Louisiana. The river naturally jumped courses, meandering across South Louisiana and depositing soil as it went. This soil built the delta, and when the Mississippi flooded every spring, flush with snow from the north and the spring rains, the soil it left behind rebuilt the land along the river's banks. Delta soil—referred to as "chocolate gold"—is fertile and magic. The Mississippi River levee system was the first of many dire alarm bells for Louisiana, robbing the delta of the natural sediment the river delivered each year.

Then came the oil industry. South Louisiana has been contending with the quest for this fossil fuel since 1901, when the first successful well was drilled in the state. After that, the industry wasted no time in cutting canals through our marshes and drilling everywhere they thought oil might be lurking. Permits issued by the state mandated that after drilling was complete, the oil companies restore our swamps to how they had found them. But to this day, no one has ever enforced this requirement, and in the span of a hundred years, more than fifty thousand permits have been issued for oil exploration in Louisiana. The industry has dredged more than ten thousand miles of canals, exposing Louisiana's interior to the Gulf of Mexico and creating severe saltwater intrusion that kills marshes. One canal, the Mississippi River Gulf Outlet (MRGO), washed out 618,000 acres of marshland, an area three times the size of all five of New York City's boroughs combined. In 2005, Katrina's twenty-five-foot storm surge overflowed through the MRGO and flooded St. Bernard parish.

Louisiana loses a football field's worth of land every hundred minutes—that's sixteen miles of lost barrier islands, swamps, and ground each year. In the past two hundred years, we have destroyed an ecosystem that took seven thousand years to build, and 36 to

60 percent of the total lost can be attributed to the oil industry.

Our marshes are breeding grounds for shrimp, oysters, crabs, fish, and more seafood—these creatures not only make up a large part of our diet in South Louisiana but also comprise our traditional industries. Louisiana is responsible for 50 percent of the United States' wild shrimp crop, 35 percent of the nation's blue crabs, and 40 percent of the nation's oysters. Louisiana also provides a home for 90 percent of all estuary-dependent gulf marine species from Florida to Texas.

The environmental and physical scope of the region has changed. Only when fishermen started noticing lakes widen and bayous and marshes disappearing did we realize that Louisiana was sinking. A $100 billion energy infrastructure is at risk from rising sea levels and land erosion. Ninety percent of the nation's offshore energy is from Louisiana's coast, as is 20 percent of the nation's natural gas. Louisiana's refineries make up almost 20 percent of the nation's refining capacity. This is not just a problem for bayou Cajuns. This is a problem for our entire country.

Losing land means water is creeping at Louisiana's back door. The federal government has built massive levee protection systems to try to reroute water or hold it out of communities. However, the levee system leaves some communities—Cocodrie, Lafitte, Plaquemines, and Isle de Jean Charles, to name a few—defenseless against storms and the rising sea. Isle de Jean Charles, the small town portrayed in the movie *Beasts of the Southern Wild*, is home to a mix of American Indian and Cajun peoples who represent the heart of Louisiana. But Isle de Jean Charles is nearly gone—98 percent of its land has been eroded in the past sixty-five years, and what

The iconic Louisiana boot shape is being lost to the Gulf of Mexico. The areas in light blue indicate land already gone and at-risk wetlands.

LAKE PONTCHARTRAIN

NEW ORLEANS

GULF OF MEXICO

HOUMA

CHAUVIN

COLODRIE

was once an abundant fishing village is now just a narrow two-mile-long strip of land surrounded by an expanse of open water and dead trees. The residents of Isle de Jean Charles are the first climate refugees in the United States, and the loss of their culture and traditions will be huge. Isle de Jean Charles is a vision of the future for all villages outside the levee protection system.

It is time to recognize the problem and the risk: when this land disappears, it takes with it a portion of our nation's safety and food supply, and a long legacy of culture and traditions. If we narrow our focus from the world to North America, then to Louisiana, then to the state's tiny bayou parishes, we can illustrate a universal threat to communities bound by culture and tradition. A tradition paying homage to fishermen, farmers, hunters, and trappers.

To be Cajun is to be so many things. I tell the stories in this book to recognize the challenges and to shine a light on all that is good. And to lead a call to every one of us to recognize that our environment is in dire straits, and in South Louisiana, our homes and Cajun culture are at risk of another expulsion. We must learn from the past and recognize how it shaped us. This cookbook is how I distilled my life as a Cajun woman and how I choose to tell it. After all, the best part of life is our stories and how we pass them on.

THE CAJUN LARDER

Keeping a pantry and freezer stocked with key ingredients is the way we create our everyday meals in Terrebonne Parish. You'll find our staples in this list. The recipes I cook honor the foods I grew up eating, but I have adjusted some ingredients to modernize the dishes, create a more sustainable meal, or bring in more nutrition. For example, if the ladies down the bayou used bouillon cubes in a dish, I update the recipe to include homemade chicken stock. The same goes for frying batters; most folks I know use Zatarain's Fish Fri mix, but it's easy enough to make your own. And with grain mills being resurrected all over the country, I recommend using freshly milled flours instead of commercial white flour because the freshly milled varieties are packed with flavor and nutrition; most mills offer online ordering, so you can have these flours delivered straight to your door.

At Mosquito Supper Club, we're always chasing the best possible local ingredients. That means going to the farmers' market and buying ingredients directly from farmers and fishermen. We set up relationships with butchers we trust, and we are always trying to tighten the net of how and where we source. You, too, should look for the best-quality products, the most sustainable ingredients, and the ones grown or bred or caught closest to you. Cooking with these principles is the norm for Cajuns down the bayou.

Dry Storage

BAY LEAVES

We put a bay leaf in almost every dish in this cookbook. There are many different types of bay trees. I use bay laurel. I'm always foraging the city of New Orleans looking for a bay tree, and I'm thrilled when the farmers at the Crescent City Farmers Market bring in branches that we can dry and use.

BEANS

White beans, red beans, lima beans—beans are a staple in the Cajun pantry. My mom swears by Camellia Brand beans; Rancho Gordo is another great producer (see Resources, page 359). I like to use non-GMO and heirloom varieties, and recently at my local market, I've been able to buy shucked fresh beans. They are so fresh, I usually use them in salads and they never see heat.

CANE SUGAR

I use only Louisiana raw cane sugar in any recipe that calls for sugar. Louisiana is a sugar state, so we have access to high-quality unbleached and unrefined sugar to bake with, cook with, and stir into our coffee or tea.

CANE SYRUP

Cane syrup is made from juicing cane stalks and boiling down the cane juice. It is bitter and sweet at the same time. Steen's (see Resources, page 359) has been producing cane syrup in Abbeville, Louisiana, since 1910. Its yellow can is iconic in the Cajun pantry. We use the syrup in many desserts, our Steen's Butter (page 297), and vinaigrettes.

CANE VINEGAR

We need a steady supply of vinegar for pickling okra, beets, and peppers, and my preference is cane vinegar. Recently, Steen's (see Resources, page 359) added cane vinegar to its product line, and you'll see it called for in some of the recipes in this book. If you don't have access to cane vinegar, you can use apple cider vinegar or distilled white vinegar as a substitute.

COFFEE

Dark coffee is always brewing in Chauvin. When I was a kid, I would sweeten it with condensed milk or PET evaporated milk and too much sugar. My mom's choice of coffee has always been Community Coffee, and I'm comforted by the scent of it brewing. It's not single-origin or tiny-batch coffee, but it jogs memories of my Cajun home.

CORNMEAL, CORN FLOUR, GRITS, AND CORNSTARCH

South Louisiana folks always have cornmeal, corn flour, and grits in the pantry. We are known for our fried food, so you always need some corn flour or cornmeal on hand to whip up a dredge for fresh shrimp, fish, or oysters. I use Bellegarde Bakery (see Resources, page 359) freshly milled coarse-ground cornmeal made from heirloom corn from Bayou Cora Farms in Baldwin County, Alabama, that has been grown by the same family since 1876. And I buy organic cornstarch from Whole Foods Market.

CRACKERS

Ritz, saltines, and Lance Captain's Wafers are always in our pantry, ready to be served alongside seafood boils.

EVAPORATED MILK

Bread custard (see page 320) was a staple dessert when I was growing up, and my mom always made it with PET brand evaporated milk. I still crave her custardy bread pudding, which she cuts into little slices and leaves out on the island in her kitchen. It's a good idea to have evaporated milk in your pantry in case you have a late-night craving for a Cajun snack of PET milk, sugar, and bananas.

FILÉ POWDER

Filé powder is ground dried sassafras leaves. It was traditionally used as a thickener for gumbo when okra wasn't in season and when folks wanted to add extra flavor. You can put a tiny bottle of filé powder on the table when you serve your gumbo for your guests to sprinkle in as they like.

FLOUR

We ate a lot of white flour in my childhood home. My mom made pancakes, biscuits, beignets, king cakes, monkey bread, rolls, and so many desserts with white flour, and white flour is also used to make a roux. When I use store-bought white flour, I prefer King Arthur brand, but nowadays, if a recipe calls for white flour, I try to use nutritious freshly milled flours to replace as much of it as I can without losing the heart and flavor of the recipe. Graison Gill started Bellegarde Bakery (see Resources, page 359) in New Orleans. It's been a welcome addition to the food scene, and I love using Bellegarde's freshly milled flours in place of white flour when I'm re-creating my mom's traditional breads and

desserts. I buy flour locally from Bellegarde.

HOT SAUCE

Original Louisiana Hot Sauce is my number one choice for adding flavor to a dish. It's produced in New Iberia, and it's made the same way it has been for the past eighty years. Louisiana Hot Sauce has a sweet, low heat I love for seasoning poultry or seafood, flavoring marinades, or dipping fried shrimp.

MUSTARD AND KETCHUP

When it comes to condiments, we make our own mayonnaise (see page 306) but buy our ketchup and mustard. If a recipe calls for ketchup, choose one without corn syrup or any artificial ingredients.

RICE

In South Louisiana, we eat rice with everything. I remember one of my brother's girlfriends making fun of us for our rice consumption. But the fact is, rice stretches food. It is present in many cultures where peasant or provincial food became the national cuisine. (I use the word peasant in a glorifying sense, no disrespect meant.) When you have hungry mouths to feed, rice is a savior. We eat rice in gumbo, jambalaya, étouffée, and stew, and we serve our beans over rice. I like Baker Farms (see Resources, page 359) popcorn rice from Gueydan, Louisiana. The rice is nutty and fills your house with the faint scent of popcorn while you're cooking it. But you can use any type of rice for these recipes; I prefer medium-grain varieties that are organic or natural.

SEASONINGS

The go-to seasonings in my Cajun pantry are cayenne pepper, kosher salt, fresh cracked black pepper, bay leaves, and Original Louisiana Hot Sauce (see opposite). Some people also use dehydrated onions or garlic for seasoning, but I stick to fresh.

At the end of each recipe, you should adjust the seasoning. "Seasoning" usually refers to the salt, black pepper, cayenne, and hot sauce that you have already put in the dish. Instructions to "adjust the seasoning" mean to make a judgment call based on the way you like things to taste. We all prefer a different level of saltiness or spiciness in our dishes. My recipes are on the mild side; make adjustments to fit your preference.

VANILLA

Always buy the real stuff.

Freezer

The Cajun larder includes what you keep in the freezer. Almost every home in Chauvin has the largest chest freezer available, and it's easy to find homes that have two of them! Inside, you'll find a lot of the same things: shrimp, gumbo crabs, crawfish, and a variety of fish; beans of all kinds; corn; blackberries; little bottles of filé powder; stocks; and leftover gumbo, stew, cooked beans, and more. If there's a hunter in the family, Cajun freezers will be stocked with deer sausage and all kinds of venison and boar cuts, too. Some people also keep alligator meat, turtles, squirrel, rabbit, duck, and other wild game.

CRAB

Crabs are plentiful in South Louisiana. Crabmeat is available through fish markets and online. Use only local crabmeat or meat from crabs caught in the United States. Use white meat and claw meat (it has so much flavor packed into it). Gumbo crabs are readily available in supermarkets and from fish markets. They keep well in the freezer.

CRAWFISH

We have as many crawfish boils as we can during the crawfish season and then peel the leftovers

and freeze them for making stews and étouffées during the summer, fall, and early winter.

FISH

It's a luxury to have a freezer stocked with fish. My parents have never purchased a fish in their lives, but they eat fish daily. We catch fish, fillet it, eat some fresh, and freeze the rest for suppers another time. But if catching your own isn't an option, buy fish local to wherever you are from a nearby fisherman or a trusted fish market—there's no need to eat a Louisiana fish if you're in New York or California.

POULTRY

Every time you purchase a chicken, you have an opportunity to turn back the clock on industrialization and to support families making their living by raising and growing good, sustainable food. So do your research and find a farmer who raises poultry and will sell to you directly, or look for one selling poultry at your local farmers' market or food cooperative.

Otherwise, choose the best possible option in your grocery store—that means chickens that are free of antibiotics and were fed quality ingredients and allowed to roam while they were alive. Quality chickens may cost a little extra, but they will be worth their salt in flavor, and you'll be supporting farmers trying to reinstate real food as our societal norm.

SALT PORK

You'll need salt pork for many dishes in this book. You can make your own (see page 239) or buy it (see Resources, page 359). I keep a healthy supply of salt pork in the freezer.

SHRIMP

Always buy fresh seafood when it's available. But seafood keeps well in the freezer, too. During shrimp season, folks in Chauvin buy five hundred pounds of shrimp, remove their heads, and freeze them for the year. We have a white shrimp season and a brown shrimp season (see page 62), and folks usually have both varieties in their freezers. We prefer inland shrimp that are caught in the bayous and lakes, the barrier waters of the Gulf of Mexico, rather than offshore shrimp, which are a little more bleached out from salt water. And of course we prefer shrimp from Lake Boudreaux, specifically from a long-gone Rabbit Bayou.

When buying shrimp, first seek out shrimp from local fishermen; if you aren't near a fishing town, try a farmers' market or local fish market. Otherwise, look for wild-caught shrimp from the United States and avoid nondomestic varieties. Try to buy small or medium shrimp, as they pack a lot of flavor.

Refrigerator

DAIRY

Look for local milk and buttermilk. Unfortunately, we have a shortage of local butter available in South Louisiana, so I use European salted butters, such as Plugrá. If you can find local butter, it will add terroir to any dish. And if you have a few minutes and some local heavy cream

on your hands, you can easily turn it into butter—just pour it into your mixer and blend on high and you're on your way.

EGGS

Always cook with local eggs. There is no easier way to start changing the way you eat than by simply buying local eggs. Find a good farmer who feeds their chickens well and allows them to roam freely. Chickens that eat a lot of great compost and natural feed produce delicious eggs—you'll know by their glowing yolks.

LEAF LARD

I use leaf lard in my rolls (see page 315) and some desserts. Leaf lard is rendered from the soft fat around a pig's kidneys and makes pie doughs extra flaky and rolls extra soft.

Produce

Use as many in-season fresh fruits and vegetables as you possibly can. Shop first at your local farmers' market, food cooperative, or grocer. Think on your toes and make substitutions in these recipes based on what's in season and available. For example, if you need green onions but there are spring onions popping up all over your yard, go ahead and swap in the spring onions.

When a vegetable or fruit is in season, "put away"—meaning can, preserve, pickle, or otherwise process for long-term storage—as much as you can. Put away corn and tomatoes, okra and blackberries, fresh beans and peas if you can. Make marmalade. Pickle everything. Put away vegetables like green beans that are harder to come by in the winter months. When the market is looking bleak in the winter, you'll be happy you made some plum jam to spread on hot buttered bread.

If you can, plant an herb garden. It is healthy and therapeutic to always have fresh herbs at your disposal. When it gets cold, bring the plants inside and sit them by a sunny window, or create a greenhouse outside. Preserve fresh herbs from your garden by hanging them upside down in bunches and letting them dry; then use them throughout the year in soups and stews.

BLACKBERRIES, FIGS, AND SATSUMAS

Perfect for in-season desserts, making quick compotes, or freezing.

GARLIC

We Cajuns don't cook with a lot of garlic, but I learned to use it from my grandmother. She told me she learned about garlic from some Italian ladies in New Orleans, and after that it slipped into her recipes when she could get her hands on some.

OKRA

Find okra in the summertime and enjoy it, then put some away to make a gumbo or two during the year.

ONIONS, BELL PEPPERS, AND CELERY

Louisianans swear by this mixture, known as the "holy trinity" (although we never referred to the mix by that name in my home when I was growing up), and use it as the base for every one-pot dish, especially the ones paired with seafood. Onions especially make up a large part of all our one-pot dishes.

PARSLEY AND GREEN ONIONS

We garnish almost every Cajun dish with flat-leaf parsley and green onions. As chef John Folse once said, if you go into a kitchen in Louisiana and there isn't a perfect pile of diced parsley and green onion on the counter, you should just grab your purse and get out of there.

PECANS

We grow pecan trees on the bayou, and as a kid, I thought it was loads of fun to fill buckets with pecans and then sit around, talking and cracking them. Use them for all kinds of sweet treats (see pages 328, 346, 349, and 350).

TOMATOES, POTATOES, AND CORN

We keep potatoes in stock to make quick stews, soups, and fried-potato po-boys. Corn is always on hand to make as a side dish to fried fish or to add to soups. Tomatoes from the garden (or put up from the garden) are used for salads, soups, and gumbos, or to neutralize the acidity in our smothered okra.

Pots and Pans

I am a minimalist; I don't believe in having anything in my kitchen that I don't use. I'm not much into gadgets or things that plug in. But I believe in having the essentials, which includes lots of wooden spoons and a heavy-bottomed pot. I cook in Lodge or Cajun cast-iron, Le Creuset enameled cast-iron, or Magnalite aluminum pots. You should decide which pot is best for you. The main pot you will need to make the recipes in this book is a heavy-bottomed pot

for slow cooking. These recipes will not work with flimsy pots. After that, consider investing in a great cast-iron skillet, Le Creuset Dutch oven, or Magnalite pot. And learn the nuances of each.

CAST IRON

My mom didn't cook much with cast-iron pans (cleaning them was probably one more step that she couldn't commit to while raising a large family), but I love cast iron. Cast-iron pots and pans take a bit longer to heat up than stainless-steel or other pots, but once cast iron is at temperature, it holds the heat, and that's a great thing when you're cooking. Cleaning cast iron doesn't take long: wipe out the pan, rinse it with water, dry it on the stove over high heat, and give it a quick polish with lard or canola oil.

MAGNALITE

Cajuns hold the Magnalite aluminum pot in great reverence. It came into popularity because it's easier to clean and lift than cast iron. I am nostalgic about my Magnalites. I have a soup pot from my grandmother that I still use. I had it sitting on my stove for years as a bit of comfort and a beautiful reminder of so many delicious meals. Magnalite pots are a true symbol of Cajun cooking.

TABLETOP FRYERS

While you can definitely deep-fry in a cast-iron pot (with a thermometer to test the oil temperature), a tabletop fryer is a smart investment. It doesn't require a lot of oil and makes it easy to maintain the oil's temperature.

SHRIMP

THE BAYOU IS LIKE A WATERY MAIN STREET

that runs through Chauvin, Louisiana, all the way to the Gulf of Mexico, and it reveals the history of our shrimp industry. Modern shrimp nets, booms, and paupières frame the sky. Boats in disrepair, half-sunken boats, and boats ready for shrimping can all be seen on the bayou, as can shrimp docks, processing plants, and abandoned industry of the past.

Paupières means "eyelids" in French, and when these nets are raised and lowered, they resemble blinking eyelids. Paupières were used for fishing, and, like many things on the bayou, are now almost extinct. In season, a few shrimpers still manually lower paupière nets into the water, and when the shrimp pass through Robinson Canal, the paupières catch delicious brackish sweet Louisiana shrimp.

Shrimpers once fished with paupières, seines, and cast nets. They fished with boats that could provide for a family and a community. They fished in pirogues, Lafitte skiffs, and modest wooden single-rig trawlers built locally, without the aid of blueprints, architects, or engineers. The same hands that made fishing nets repaired them. During the off-season, the bayou was lined with emerald-green nets stretched taut for repair and fishermen sewing their nets in solitude. Some of this pageantry is still alive on the bayou, but the traditions of a working fishing village are changing as a younger generation moves away from the bayou and traditional ways. You'll still find folks making a living on the water, but the industry is struggling.

My dad remembers a time when boat captains gauged the depth of the water using a weight tied to a string. A time when land and thick marsh were everywhere, and in the densest fog, you used intuition and a handheld compass when traveling Louisiana waters. Fishermen lived by the moon, fished by the tides, and inherently understood sustainability— fishing without overfishing. They took care of the environment that provided for their families and livelihoods. There was a time when you asked for permission if you wanted to go into another fisherman's home waters, but that time has passed.

The one thing that hasn't changed over the years is the food we prepare with shrimp. We boil shrimp whole in heavily seasoned vegetable stock with potatoes and corn, then use any leftovers in dip or to bind crab cakes. We make stock rich with the essence of shrimp heads that gets used in jambalaya and shrimp stew and spaghetti sauce. Delicate soft-shells are fried whole and consumed in their entirety. Any leftover catch is frozen to use all year round.

BOILED SHRIMP

SERVES 6

1½ bunches celery (about
11 stalks), cut into 4-inch
(10 cm) pieces

6 pounds (2.7 kg) yellow
onions, quartered

12 lemons (3
pounds/1.35 kg), halved

1 tablespoon cayenne
pepper, plus more as
needed

1 tablespoon whole black
peppercorns

5 pounds (2.3 kg) medium
head-on shrimp

½ pound (2 sticks/225 g)
unsalted butter

1 to 1½ cups (240 to 360 g)
kosher salt

12 ounces (340 g) small
red potatoes (about 6),
scrubbed

6 ears corn, husked

Crackers, for serving

Maria's Seafood Dip (page
306), for serving

The secret to boiling any seafood is a flavorful stock. Your stock should taste good *before* you add the shrimp. My mom claims that adding butter to the stock makes the cooked shrimp easier to peel—and I would venture to say it adds some flavor, too.

When you serve them with crackers, seafood dip, corn, and potatoes, it takes just a couple dozen shrimp to fill you up. If it's summer, serve some watermelon topped with a sprinkle of sea salt for dessert. Any shrimp you have left over can be used in another meal—maybe a shrimp omelet for breakfast or shrimp dip (see page 61) for a snack. You can also peel and freeze shrimp, then use them as a binder in crab cakes (see page 86). Try not to waste a single shrimp.

Fill a heavy-bottomed 4-gallon (15 L) stockpot halfway with water. Add the celery, onions, lemons, cayenne, and peppercorns to the pot. Bring the water to a boil over high heat, then reduce the heat to low and simmer until the vegetables are soft, about 1 hour. Taste the stock; it should have a subtle bright vegetable flavor and taste clean, with hints of onion and celery. If it's nicely flavorful, you're ready to boil the shrimp; if not, simmer for 30 to 45 minutes more, then taste again.

When the stock is ready, raise the heat to high and return it to a boil.

Rinse the shrimp briefly under cold running water and drain (don't overwash them—you don't want to rinse away all their flavor). Add the shrimp to the boiling stock and use a spoon to submerge them so they can release all their flavor. Let the liquid return to a boil, then boil the shrimp for 4 minutes.

Add the butter to the pot, stir and cook for 2 minutes more, then pluck a shrimp out of the stock and check for doneness. The shrimp should be bright pink and firm; if needed, cook for up to 2 minutes more, then turn off the heat. (They can get mushy quickly, so don't overcook them—from the time the stock returns to a boil after you add the shrimp, the total cook time should be no more than 8 minutes.)

Stir ½ cup (120 g) of the salt into the stock and let the shrimp soak for about 6 minutes. Taste the shrimp for flavor: your shrimp are done when they taste buttery and sweet, with hints of cayenne and the perfect amount of salt. At this point, you may need to add more cayenne or salt. Add cayenne to taste. Add another ¼ cup (60 g) of the salt and let the shrimp soak for 2 to 3 minutes more; repeat as needed. The amount of salt you use is relative: some folks want only a little, and some want a bit more. Finding the perfect balance is a matter of taste, but if your shrimp taste bland, they probably need a little more salt and a longer soaking time.

When you're happy with their flavor, use a strainer to transfer the shrimp to a large bowl, or set a colander over a large bowl and drain the shrimp in the colander, then transfer them to a large bowl (reserve the stock).

Return the stock to the stove and bring it back to a boil. Add the potatoes and boil for 6 minutes, then add the corn to the pot and boil the vegetables together for 4 minutes more, until the potatoes are tender. Strain the potatoes and corn and discard the stock. Transfer the potatoes and corn to a bowl.

Thoroughly prepare to feast: Cover a table with newspaper. Have your crackers out and ready to eat and small bowls of seafood dip for each person. Have plenty of paper towels or napkins ready to go. (Once you get your hands dirty peeling, you won't want to be grabbing supplies.) Pour the shrimp, corn, and potatoes right out onto the center of the table and enjoy.

How to Peel a Shrimp

Peeling shrimp is second nature to folks on the bayou, but I realize that's not the case for everyone. So here is a simple guide to peeling a raw or boiled shrimp.

1

2

3

1. Hold the tail of the shrimp in one hand and the head in the other. Twist the head and tail in opposite directions to remove the head. (Save the head for later.)

2. Use your fingers to crack and peel the shell off the tail and then remove the tail itself. (Discard both.)

3. Run a sharp knife along the top vein of the tail to remove and discard the digestive tract of the shrimp. This is called deveining or sand backing.

FRIED SOFT-SHELL SHRIMP

SERVES 4 TO 6

Peanut oil, for frying

1 pound (455 g) U-15 soft-shell shrimp (see Note)

4 large egg yolks

2 tablespoons hot sauce, preferably Original Louisiana Hot Sauce, plus more for serving

1 tablespoon yellow mustard

2 cups (360 g) cornmeal, preferably freshly milled

1 cup (130 g) cornstarch, preferably organic

2 teaspoons cayenne pepper

1 tablespoon kosher salt, plus more as needed

1 teaspoon cracked black pepper, plus more as needed

Soft-shell shrimp are a delicacy. Like crabs and crawfish, shrimp molt and shed their shells. After shedding, their new shells are soft, and this is when—to the human palate—they are divine and you can eat the shrimp whole: shells, heads, and all.

You need only egg yolks for this recipe—save the whites for another use, perhaps in your morning omelet or in pecan macaroons (see page 328) for a midday snack. Use freshly stone-milled cornmeal to dredge the shrimp before frying and cornstarch to make the coating extra crispy, too. Serve the shrimp with pickles and rice and beans or a cucumber and tomato salad (see page 281).

Fill a large heavy-bottomed pot with 4 inches (10 cm) of peanut oil and heat the oil over medium-high heat to 375°F (190°C). (Alternatively, use a tabletop fryer; see page 25.)

Gently rinse the shrimp under cold running water and pat dry.

In a shallow bowl, whisk together the egg yolks, hot sauce, and mustard. In a separate shallow bowl, combine the cornmeal, cornstarch, cayenne, salt, and black pepper.

Now back to the shrimp. To properly dredge the shrimp, designate one hand your wet hand and the other your dry hand. Use your wet hand to dip a shrimp in the egg yolk mixture, being sure to coat it evenly and letting any excess drip off, then place it in the cornmeal mixture. Use your dry hand to coat the shrimp evenly with the cornmeal mixture, then place it on a baking sheet. Repeat to dredge the remaining shrimp.

When the oil is hot, add the shrimp in two rounds (6 to 8 shrimp at a time) and fry until golden brown, about 3 minutes on each side. Use a slotted spoon to transfer the shrimp to paper towels or brown paper bags to absorb excess oil.

Give the shrimp a sprinkling of salt and black pepper, then serve immediately, passing the bottle of hot sauce at the table.

NOTE: *Soft-shell shrimp are hard to come by because shrimpers have to pick them out of their drag by hand and carefully chill them. They are delicate and easily fall apart while the shrimp are being dragged in and iced during trawling. Since getting fresh soft-shell shrimp means being right at the source, you will probably have to buy them frozen (see Resources, page 359). Put frozen shrimp in a bowl of cool water and thaw in the refrigerator. Use immediately once they're thawed, or add ice to the bowl to keep the shrimp extra cold. Handle defrosted soft-shell shrimp gently, as the heads sometimes want to slip off after thawing.*

VARIATION ────────────────────────────

Fried Spiders

When you peel the shell off shrimp heads and fry the remaining body and attached legs, they're known as "fried spiders," because that's what they look like when they come out of the oil. You can do this with jumbo shrimp.

The Patois of Shrimping

SHRIMPERS AND FISHERMEN have their own language. They use CBs and radios to talk to each other, from trawler to trawler, using the names of their boats to identify themselves. "The *H and H* to the *Heidi Marie*, come back" is a common call heard on the waves. A question might follow: "Are the shrimp giving?" Here's a glossary of common shrimping terms.

Giving means the shrimp are emerging from their hiding places. Shrimp hide away deep in marsh grass estuaries while they grow to adult size. Then they start an age-old journey of moving toward open water—in South Louisiana's case, that's toward the Gulf of Mexico. Their movement is predicted by the tides and controlled by the moon. Shrimpers make sure they are on the water three days before the full and new moons and three days after, as this is when, hopefully, the shrimp are giving.

Trawlers are boats that fishermen use to fish or shrimp ("I'm a fisherman; this is my trawler"). *Trawler* is also the term a fisherman uses to describe what he does for a living ("I'm a trawler; this is my catch").

A **trawl** is a net used to catch shrimp. A fisherman may also identify himself as a *shrimper*. A **skimmer** is a lighter modern net used to catch shrimp.

To **drag** means to pull nets through water to catch shrimp.

Lafitte skiffs are smaller vessels fishermen use to navigate estuaries, lakes, bays, and bayous.

A **trip** is when you shrimp from sundown to sunup. Most shrimpers sleep during the day. A trip could be one day or two weeks or longer, depending on how big your boat is and how much ice you can stow to keep the shrimp fresh. Shrimpers who fish for weeks on end are usually working in the Gulf of Mexico. Some boats have flash-freezing equipment, so the fishermen can freeze their haul and box it up aboard their vessels.

A **champagne** unit of measurement is about 70 pounds (32 kg) of shrimp if it's full.

SHRIMP BOULETTES

SERVES 6

¾ cup (110 g) coarsely chopped green bell pepper

2 tablespoons coarsely chopped green onion

¼ cup (25 g) coarsely chopped celery

2 tablespoons coarsely chopped fresh flat-leaf parsley

1¼ pounds (565 g) peeled and deveined small or medium shrimp (see page 33)

1 teaspoon kosher salt, plus more as needed

⅛ teaspoon cracked black pepper, plus more as needed

⅛ teaspoon cayenne pepper, plus more as needed

1 tablespoon plus 1 teaspoon hot sauce, preferably Original Louisiana Hot Sauce, plus more as needed

Peanut oil, for frying

Shrimp boulettes, or fried shrimp balls, might remind you of Thai fish cakes or Vietnamese shrimp on sugarcane. The shrimp is ground up and fried without any flour or cornmeal (shrimp is sticky enough to bind the vegetables together, so you don't need to add any filler). Eat the boulettes as a snack with hot sauce, or put some on a roll with bitter greens, cocktail sauce, or spicy mayo to turn them into a sandwich. Either way, they are a great way to eat small fresh shrimp.

In a large bowl, combine the bell pepper, green onion, celery, parsley, shrimp, salt, black pepper, cayenne, and hot sauce and toss to distribute the ingredients evenly. Using an old-fashioned meat grinder or a food processor, grind the mixture together. If using a food processor, work in small batches and pulse until smooth, then transfer to a bowl. In either case, after grinding, you should not see any vegetables; the boulette mix should be a homogenous paste.

Fill a large heavy-bottomed pot with 4 inches (10 cm) of peanut oil and heat the oil over medium-high heat to 375°F (190°C). (Alternatively, use a tabletop fryer; see page 25.)

Using two spoons or a small (#100) cookie scoop, form a ball of the boulette mix no bigger than the diameter of a quarter and carefully drop it into the hot oil. Fry this tester boulette for about 6 minutes, until golden brown on the outside. Transfer the boulette to a paper towel or a brown paper bag to drain excess oil and let it cool. Taste the boulette: Does the mix need more salt? More pepper or more heat? Add salt, black pepper, cayenne, or hot sauce to your liking—I like boulettes to have a slight vinegary taste, and hot sauce gives them that flavor. There is no one perfect formula. You have to taste your mix every time.

Once you've adjusted your mix, drop about 15 balls at a time into the hot oil and fry until golden brown, about 6 minutes. Transfer the boulettes to paper towels or brown paper bags to drain and cool briefly, then serve.

The boulette mix will keep, covered, in the refrigerator for 2 days. If making ahead of time, add the salt right before frying to keep the mix from getting watery.

The Count

AFTER SOUTH LOUISIANA was debilitated by two hurricanes in 2005, my family members needed to concentrate on cleaning out their homes and rebuilding. I was a young single mom and my house in New Orleans was still flooded from Katrina, so I went to help my aunt work her shrimp dock in Pointe-aux-Chênes. I was responsible for counting the shrimp.

Most fishermen's homes had been destroyed, but they still needed to make a living. So they navigated their boats around hurricane debris in the water and continued to fish. In the mornings, I'd make eye contact with overtired fishermen who'd been up all night and let them know the "count" of their shrimp. This was a dreadful task. Tired shrimpers are at the mercy of the docks, and the docks are at the mercy of the market.

Based on the market, dock owners decide what a shrimper will be paid for their catch, and that price is based on the count: the number of shrimp per pound. A three-pound sample of the fisherman's catch is weighed out and counted, and that number determines how much the dock pays for the catch. But the thing about the count is that you don't catch shrimp that are all the same size, so if small shrimp sneak into the baskets with large shrimp, they bring the count up and the value down.

Shrimpers are also pulling in their shrimp with a lot of bycatch—crabs, catfish, croakers, flounders, squid, and anything else unable to avoid being snagged by the net. For every pound of shrimp, fishermen sometimes have to deal with up to four times that weight in bycatch. Bycatch has to be picked out when the nets are pulled in; some, like crabs and squids, are bound for home, but most of it goes back into the sea.

The shrimp are then separated by size to be graded. If all the large shrimp are separated, they will be graded as large and will result in higher payment. But this grading takes a lot of time, and some fishermen just don't have the extra hands or hours to meticulously separate their catch. When all the shrimp is iced together and sold together, its price is driven down. Prices at the dock fluctuate from day to day, and even at $2.75 a pound, shrimpers have a really hard time making a living.

SHRIMP COUNTS AND PRICES AT THE DOCK

SIZE	COUNT (SHRIMP PER POUND)	PRICE PER POUND IN AUGUST 2019 IN COCODRIE
Tiny/Small	80/90 40/50	$0.75 $1.20
Medium	36/40 31/35	$1.35 $1.55
Large	26/30	$1.75
Extra-Large	16/20	$2.60
Jumbo	10/15	$2.75

FRIED SHRIMP PO'BOYS

1 pound (455 g) small or medium shrimp, peeled

Peanut oil, for frying

4 large egg yolks

1 tablespoon hot sauce, preferably Original Louisiana Hot Sauce, plus more for serving

1 tablespoon yellow mustard, plus more for serving

2 cups (360 g) cornmeal, preferably freshly milled

1 cup (130 g) cornstarch, preferably organic

1 teaspoon cayenne pepper

2 teaspoons kosher salt

¼ teaspoon cracked black pepper

2 soft baguettes or loaves of French bread, split lengthwise

Mayonnaise (store-bought or homemade; see page 306), ketchup, shredded iceberg lettuce, tomato slices, and dill pickle slices, for serving

Some folks grew up eating hamburgers or pizza, but on the bayou, we eat po'boys: French bread stuffed with fried seafood. Po'boy is short for "poor boy," because it was a sandwich to feed poor workers. The classic hard-time po'boy is the French fry po'boy, served with roast beef debris or gravy; it was widely eaten when folks couldn't afford other fillings. A po'boy is just a sandwich. I like my po'boys stuffed with seafood.

Fried seafood po'boys can be filled with anything that swims. The most popular options are oysters, fish, crawfish, soft-shell crabs, and shrimp. Any shrimp will do for this recipe, but smaller shrimp pack much more flavor than the larger varieties. Buy shrimp graded 26/30 or 40/50 (which means 26 to 30 or 40 to 50 shrimp per pound, respectively). Traditionally, the bread should be an oversize soft French baguette, but you can use your favorite bread, if you'd like.

To devein and butterfly the shrimp, run a sharp knife gently along the top of the shrimp to remove the black stripe running down the center, slicing just deep enough to allow the shrimp to open up like a book or a butterfly (do not fully cut through the shrimp or into the tail). My mom calls this technique sandbacking, or removing the sand.

Fill a large heavy-bottomed pot with 4 inches (10 cm) of peanut oil and heat the oil over medium-high heat to 375°F (190°C). (Alternatively, use a tabletop fryer; see page 25.)

In a shallow bowl, whisk together the egg yolks, hot sauce, and mustard. In a separate shallow bowl, combine the cornmeal, cornstarch, cayenne, salt, and black pepper.

To properly dredge the shrimp, designate one hand your wet hand and the other your dry hand. Use your wet hand to dip a shrimp in the egg yolk mixture, being sure to coat it evenly and letting any excess drip off, then place it in the cornmeal mixture. Use your dry hand to coat the shrimp evenly with the cornmeal mixture, then place it on a baking sheet. Repeat to dredge the remaining shrimp.

When the oil is hot, add a dozen shrimp and fry until golden brown, about 3 minutes. Use a slotted spoon to transfer the shrimp to paper towels or brown paper bags to absorb excess oil. Repeat to fry the remaining shrimp.

You're going to have to choose your own adventure here when it comes to assembly. I coat the cut sides of the bread with some homemade mayonnaise, a touch of yellow mustard, and a touch of ketchup, then layer on some shredded iceberg lettuce, 2 slices of tomatoes seasoned with salt and cracked black pepper, a lot of pickles, and the fried shrimp and douse it all in hot sauce. To be completely honest, I also like to dip each bite of my po'boy in ketchup. Lord knows why, but that's how I like to eat it.

SHRIMP BEYOND THE BAYOU

The journey shrimp make to end up on your dinner table is long and complex. When I was growing up on the bayou, shrimp went from the water to an ice chest to our dinner table, from my family's hands to my mother's kitchen. If you didn't grow up as lucky as we were, the journey is different. Before most shrimp ever get into the hands of the consumer, it has been fished and sold, processed at a dock and sold, processed at a factory and sold, sold again to larger seafood purveyors, then sold one or two more times.

Some factories freeze shrimp whole. If done correctly, freezing maintains the shrimp's flavor and freshness. At other factories, the shrimp are peeled and rinsed many times, which alters their flavor profile. Those factories box up a tasteless protein.

Consumers must choose what price they want to pay for shrimp. Restaurants, chefs, large-scale grocers and other purveyors, and regular shoppers make decisions about what they believe a shrimp is worth. Without knowledge of the realities of the industry, people often make these decisions hastily and choose the cheapest option to save a dime. With cheap imported shrimp flooding the market, not many people want to pay a higher price for top-quality domestic shrimp. Why choose wild-caught American shrimp when the farmed foreign stuff is so much less expensive? These decisions force dock owners to pay fishermen less for their catch—the dock can't buy shrimp at top dollar if they have no one to sell it to. And it is increasingly harder for a shrimper to make a living.

The system is broken. But we can help fix it if we commit to paying the right price for high-quality, sustainably fished wild American shrimp.

SHRIMP JAMBALAYA

SERVES 6 TO 8

½ cup (120 ml) canola oil or leaf lard (115 g, if using lard)

2½ pounds (1.2 kg) yellow onions, finely diced

⅓ cup (40 g) finely diced celery

½ cup (70 g) finely diced green bell pepper

3 bay leaves (see Note)

2 pounds (910 g) peeled and deveined medium shrimp (see page 33)

1 tablespoon kosher salt

¼ teaspoon cracked black pepper

¼ teaspoon cayenne pepper

1 tablespoon hot sauce, preferably Original Louisiana Hot Sauce

4 cups (780 g) medium-grain white rice

5 cups (1.2 L) unsalted chicken stock (page 304), shrimp stock (see page 305), or water

¼ cup (13 g) finely chopped fresh flat-leaf parsley, for garnish

¼ cup (20 g) finely chopped green onions, for garnish

White Beans (page 253), for serving

Pickles (see pages 300–303), for serving

If I could choose my last meal, it would be shrimp jambalaya, white beans, and fried seafood, all served on one plate. I can't get enough of these three dishes, especially when they come with a summer salad of cucumbers and tomatoes and pickled okra.

Jambalaya is a dish of West African, Spanish, French, and American Indian origins, to name a few. Each culture has a story of how the dish came to be; some of those stories are linguistically plausible, while others are tall tales. We believe rice came to North America via Africa. Ham is called *jambon* in French and *jamón* in Spanish, and *aya* is the African word for rice. Combining those two is most likely how we came to the word *jambalaya*. On the bayou, we eat everything with rice, and in jambalaya, it takes center stage.

Of all the dishes in the Cajun canon, jambalaya is the trickiest. You have to pay attention to it and make some judgment calls as it cooks. Start with room-temperature onions that have not been refrigerated. Your onions cannot be mushy; they need to be fresh and crisp. You'll know they're fresh by the tears in your eyes when you dice them. Cook the onions for a long, long time. Caramelize them, then take them past caramelization to a point where they are so dark, you might think you should throw them out and start over. But stay with it. As the onions break down and get darker (see the photo on page 81), they get sweeter and sweeter.

This is how I make the simple shrimp jambalaya I grew up on. If you like, you can add meat to a jambalaya: salt pork, smoked sausage, or andouille. You can make jambalaya with oysters and crabmeat and crawfish. You can make a duck confit jambalaya; you can save leftover chicken and make a chicken-and-sausage jambalaya. Use this recipe as a base to create your own.

Warm a heavy-bottomed 12-quart (11 L) Dutch oven over medium heat for 3 minutes, then add the oil and heat for 1 minute. Add the onions to the pot and stir, stir, stir. This starts the very long process of browning the onions. Cook the onions for 1 hour to 1 hour 30 minutes, depending on how hot your stove runs, watching them very closely and stirring every 2 minutes. If the onions start to stick too much, add a little bit of water or stock to loosen them, then stir to incorporate the browner onions and scrape up any stuck-on bits from the bottom of the pot. Stir, stir, stir. If you're worried about burning, lower the heat. You really don't want to walk away from the pot at any point. This is your time with your onions. All the other steps will be easy. Stir, stir, stir until the onions are deeply caramelized and resemble dark chocolate in color.

Add the celery, bell pepper, and bay leaves to the pot and stir. Cover, reduce the heat to low, and cook for 15 minutes, stirring every 5 minutes.

Meanwhile, put the shrimp in a large bowl and season with the salt, black pepper, cayenne, and hot sauce. Set aside to marinate at room temperature while the vegetables cook.

Add the rice to the pot with the vegetables and stir to combine. Raise the heat to medium and cook, uncovered, letting the flavors mingle and marry, for 5 minutes. Add the shrimp and stir to incorporate them.

Add the stock and bring to a boil, then reduce the heat to low and simmer until the liquid has almost completely evaporated or looks like little puddles of water, 8 to 10 minutes. When you're at the point of puddling—this is a judgment call based on temperature, pot size, and your stove—put the lid on the pot and reduce the heat to its lowest setting. From here, the cooking time is going to be 45 minutes total, and you can't remove the lid the entire time. This is a tough, long 45 minutes. But trust yourself. You'll want to peek, but don't.

Set a timer for 20 minutes. When it goes off, turn off the heat and let the jambalaya sit, covered, for 25 minutes before you lift the lid. (If you live with a lot of people, you might want to make a note and place it near the stove: "Please do not lift the lid off the pot." This lets everyone know you did not stir onions for over an hour just to have someone uncover the pot and ruin your dish.)

After 45 minutes, uncover the pot and stir the jambalaya. There may be a little burnt rice on the bottom—this is called the "grat" or "gratin." It's some folks' favorite part of the jambalaya.

Serve the jambalaya garnished with the parsley and green onions, with white beans and pickles alongside.

NOTE: *I like to leave the bay leaves in the final recipe. They're not meant to be eaten, but it makes for a beautiful, rustic presentation.*

The Blessing
of the Fleet

THE SPRING INLAND season begins the year for shrimpers; it's the reset button to start anew. The occasion is marked by the Blessing of the Fleet, a parade of boats on the bayou held annually in parishes across South Louisiana just after Easter. This custom traces its roots back to a centuries-old Catholic tradition in the Mediterranean, most likely brought to South Louisiana by the Portuguese.

In Chauvin, the Blessing of the Fleet begins with an early-morning shrimpers' Mass. The shrimpers and their families adorn the hulls and cabins of their boats with flags and decorations, and the procession of boats parades down Bayou Petit Caillou. A Catholic priest rides in the lead boat and blesses each boat with a prayer for a safe and prosperous season. After a boat receives its blessing, it joins the boats ahead on Lake Boudreaux. The whole community lines the bayous, watching the procession and celebrating in a day of food, dancing, and festivities. The boats tie up to one another, and people jump from boat to boat to enjoy the Cajun food offered by each family.

My family has always celebrated the Blessing of the Fleet, but we've watched it change over the years. What was once a parade of hundreds of boats has dwindled as fishermen hang up their trawls to work in other industries, mostly the oil industry. The blessing is now more about remembering than it is about celebrating, and the gathering no longer has the intensity and gravity it once did. You'll hear locals telling newcomers to the blessing, "It's not like it used to be" and "There used to be so many more boats." Still, the nostalgia of the blessing comforts and unites a small bayou town in anticipation of the May shrimping season that follows.

LUCIEN'S SHRIMP SPAGHETTI

SERVES 6 TO 8

½ cup (120 ml) canola oil

2¼ pounds (1 kg) yellow onions, finely diced

1½ tablespoons kosher salt

1 garlic clove, minced

½ cup (75 g) finely diced celery

½ cup (70 g) finely diced green bell pepper

5 cups (1.3 L) canned tomato sauce (from three 14.5-ounce/410 g cans; see Note)

5 teaspoons sugar

2½ pounds (1.2 kg) peeled and deveined small or medium shrimp (see page 33)

½ teaspoon cracked black pepper

Pinch of cayenne pepper

1 tablespoon hot sauce, preferably Original Louisiana Hot Sauce

1 pound (455 g) spaghetti, cooked as directed on the package (see Note)

2 tablespoons finely chopped fresh flat-leaf parsley, for garnish

2 tablespoons finely chopped green onion, for garnish

Grated Parmesan cheese, for serving (see Note)

Shrimp spaghetti is to bayou kids what spaghetti and meatballs is to kids in the rest of the United States. This was my son Lucien's favorite meal, which he would eat for breakfast, lunch, or dinner. It's a near perfect meal—simple, sweet, perfectly balanced—and it'll feed a big family or a crowd of friends. The recipe draws from the Creole cooking technique of smothering tomatoes long and slow. This version is made with store-bought sauce, but you can certainly make your own tomato sauce and cook it down in the same manner. Homemade tomato sauce tends to be thinner, so you might have to thicken it a bit with tomato paste to get the right consistency.

Warm a wide, heavy-bottomed 15-quart (14 L) Dutch oven or stockpot over medium-high heat for 2 minutes, then add the oil and heat for 30 seconds. Add the onions—you should hear a sizzle when they hit the oil—and season with the salt. Stir well to coat the onions with the oil, then cook, stirring often, for about 25 minutes, until the onions are soft and golden (they should not have a lot of color at this point).

Add the garlic and cook, stirring occasionally, for 5 minutes. Reduce the heat to medium-low, add the celery and bell pepper, and cook, stirring occasionally, until soft, about 45 minutes.

Now you're going to add the tomato sauce ½ cup (120 ml) at a time. Each time you add tomato sauce, add ½ teaspoon sugar. (Scandalous, I know.) So, let's begin. Add ½ cup (120 ml) of the sauce and ½ teaspoon of the sugar, stir, and heat until the sauce is simmering and bubbling but not boiling, then simmer for 15 to 20 minutes. Repeat this process until you've added all the sauce and all the sugar, then reduce the heat to its lowest setting and cook, stirring every 10 minutes, for 45 minutes more.

Meanwhile, put the shrimp in a large bowl and season it with the black pepper, cayenne, and hot sauce. Let it marinate on the counter while the sauce simmers.

When the sauce has simmered for 45 minutes, add the shrimp and 4 cups (1 L) hot water to the pot and stir to combine. Raise the heat to medium-high to bring the tomato sauce back up to a simmer, then reduce the heat to maintain a simmer and cook for 20 minutes, or until the sauce has thickened to the consistency of pizza sauce and no longer looks watery. Turn off the heat and let everything sit together for 30 minutes to allow the flavors to marry.

Serve the sauce over the cooked spaghetti, garnished with the parsley and green onion and topped with Parmesan.

NOTES: *Buy canned tomato sauce (not pasta sauce) with no added sugar or salt. This is important, because canned tomatoes are often racked with sugar and sodium. Try to buy organic, if possible. I like making this recipe with organic Muir Glen tomato sauce; my mom uses Del Monte sauce.*

If you'd like one less pot to wash, cook the spaghetti right in the sauce the way some Cajuns do: 8 to 10 minutes before the sauce is done, crack the spaghetti in half and add it to the pot along with ¼ cup (60 ml) water. The pasta's starch helps to thicken the sauce. Cover the pot and simmer the noodles in the sauce for about 15 minutes.

When I was growing up, there was no real cheese in the grocery aisles down the bayou—only the "Parmesan cheese" that came in a green can. We all know that what comes out of that green can isn't true cheese, so get a nice chunk of the real stuff and smother your spaghetti with freshly grated Parmesan.

BROWN SHRIMP SEASON

The May shrimping season is brown shrimp season. Brown shrimp are a coveted sweet shellfish that breed predominantly in inland estuaries and soak up the diverse flavors of the brackish waters. They are bottom-feeding omnivores and eat algae, worms, microscopic animals, and organic debris. The way they taste is the result of an organic estuary composting system. Just as a person learns the terroir of a glass of wine or the nuances of different oyster grounds, on the bayou, we can pinpoint the environment where the best shrimp come from.

SHRIMP STEW

SERVES 6 TO 8

½ cup (120 ml) canola oil, or ½ cup (115 g) unsalted butter or lard

½ cup (65 g) all-purpose flour

3½ pounds (1.6 kg) yellow onions, finely diced

1 tablespoon plus ½ teaspoon kosher salt, plus more as needed

½ cup (70 g) finely diced green bell pepper

⅓ cup (40 g) finely diced celery

1 bay leaf (see Note, page 46)

4 pounds (1.8 kg) peeled and deveined medium or small shrimp (see page 33)

½ teaspoon cracked black pepper, plus more as needed

½ teaspoon cayenne pepper, plus more as needed

1 tablespoon hot sauce, preferably Original Louisiana Hot Sauce, plus more as needed

4 cups (1 L) unsalted chicken stock (page 304) or shrimp stock (see page 305)

¼ cup (13 g) finely chopped fresh flat-leaf parsley

¼ cup (20 g) finely chopped green onions

Cooked rice (see page 209), for serving

Pickles (see pages 300–303), for serving

A stew and an étouffée are very similar. My family makes a brown stew consisting of a quick roux (see page 179), onions, green bell pepper, celery, and seafood. If you add a tomato and a pot lid to this mix, you could call it an étouffée. A stew is made in a similar way to a gumbo that starts with a roux (which can be made with oil, butter, lard, or any other fat), but in the end, there is less liquid, so stews have a thicker consistency than gumbo.

Some folks add boiled eggs to their stew to stretch the pot. Some folks use sausage or salt pork in their stews, too. But when I cook seafood, I want the seafood flavor to stand out and not be upstaged by pork products. Serve the stew over cooked rice, with a side of something pickled, perhaps some fried seafood, and a green salad.

Warm a heavy-bottomed 6-quart (6 L) Dutch oven over medium heat for 2 minutes, then add the oil and heat for 30 seconds. Add the flour and cook, stirring continuously with a wooden spoon, for 15 to 20 minutes, until the roux is a little darker than café au lait, closer to the color of peanut butter. Don't walk away—focus on stirring your roux.

Add the onions, season with a dash of salt, and stir to combine. (Be careful to avoid splattering the roux when adding the onions—this is when folks sometimes burn themselves.) Cook, stirring occasionally, until the onions are soft and translucent, about 20 minutes.

Add the bell pepper, celery, and bay leaf to the onions and stir to combine. Reduce the heat to low, cover, and let the vegetables smother (see Note) together until very soft, with no bite remaining, about 20 minutes, stirring once halfway through to make sure nothing is burning and to ensure even cooking. Taste a piece of bell pepper and a piece of celery—if they're ready, there should be no more crunch to them.

Meanwhile, put the shrimp in a large bowl and season with the salt, black pepper, cayenne, and hot sauce. Set aside at room temperature to marinate while the vegetables cook.

Add the shrimp to the vegetables and stir to combine. Cook for 5 minutes, then add the stock and stir. Bring the liquid to a boil over medium-high heat, then reduce the heat to maintain a simmer and cook

for 30 minutes to let the flavors marry. You want to reduce the liquid by a quarter or a half depending on how thick you want your stew.

Taste the stew: Does it need more salt or pepper? Add some. Does it need more heat? Add cayenne. Does it need acid? If so, add more hot sauce. Adjust the seasoning to your liking, then stir in the parsley and green onions.

Serve the stew over rice, with pickles alongside.

NOTE: *In French,* étouffer *means "to smother," which is how I describe the process of cooking onions, bell pepper, celery, and tomato over the lowest possible heat in a covered pot. Smothering traps all the flavors inside the pot, slowly softening the vegetables and concentrating their flavors.*

THE BENEFITS OF FROZEN SHRIMP

Freezing fresh shrimp is one of the best ways to ensure that you can eat it all year long. When my family brings in five hundred pounds of shrimp, we immediately wash them, remove their heads, and freeze them. This maintains the shrimp's freshness and flavor. Shrimp should be a beautiful silver color when they are frozen. If you mess with the process by adding solutions, salt, corn syrup, or sugar, then you mess with the integrity of the product. The best way to freeze shrimp is to buy an ice chest packed with fresh shrimp from a shrimper during shrimp season. Once you've got them home, lightly wash the shrimp, remove their heads, and pack them into quart or gallon freezer bags. Freeze them for up to six months so you have delicious shrimp available to enjoy anytime. You can freeze some of the heads, too, for stocks. To defrost, pull a bag of frozen shrimp out of the freezer before you want to cook a dish and place in a bowl of cold water until it's thawed, or take it out the night before and place the bag in a bowl in the refrigerator. If you don't have access to fishermen, then visit a fishmonger and ask for the best domestic option. There are some great online resources, too (see page 359).

Dancing the Shrimp

WHEN I WAS a young girl in a dance troupe that performed in South Louisiana, I learned the *tinikling*, one of the oldest dances in the Philippines. In this traditional Filipino folk dance, dancers imitate swift, elegant tinikling birds by gracefully sliding between bamboo poles, balancing like the birds moving through reeds and grasses. The dance was assimilated into the Cajun culture I knew, but I didn't know what the dance meant or that it was from the Philippines until I was much older. Even as a child, I was unknowingly shifting in and out of many worlds; my Cajun upbringing was influenced by the knowledge and traditions of many other cultures.

As early as the late 1700s, Filipino immigrants were part of Louisiana's shrimping industry. At that time, folks paddled pirogues out into bayous and bays, catching shrimp with seines and cast nets to feed their families and sell or trade. Wooden anchored platforms where shrimp could be brought in and processed were soon erected in the bays and estuaries. Chinese and Filipino immigrants taught Louisianans how to preserve shrimp by drying them so they could be easily stored and transported.

During the late nineteenth century, there were more than twenty-one shrimp-drying plants run by Chinese and Filipino immigrants in South Louisiana. Both groups dominated the shrimp industry for over a hundred years. They built stilt homes in the wetlands that were connected by platforms—long, wide, wooden walkways that stretched for acres. On these platforms, their surfaces grooved like a washboard, shrimp that had been quickly boiled were spread out to dry and dehydrate naturally in the Louisiana sun. In times of rain, the shrimp were raked into large mounds and covered with huge tarps; after the rain, they were raked out once again to dry in the sun.

After the shrimp were dried, the time came for "dancing the shrimp." Community members would wear canvas shoes and dance on the shrimp-covered platforms to break up the shells. Once the shells were loosened, the south wind would blow them off the shrimp. The shelled

dried shrimp were then packaged for consumption. In 1965, Hurricane Betsy destroyed most of these stilt communities. They were never rebuilt. Instead, most members of the Filipino and Chinese communities assimilated to life in New Orleans.

My family learned how to dry shrimp from information passed down in the Chinese and Filipino communities. During my childhood, we called my aunt Earline's shrimp dock "the platform," even though the process had moved ashore many decades before. On the inland dock, the shrimp were boiled, then spread out to dry under the sun's heat. The health department argued that this wasn't a safe way of preserving the shrimp and shut down the outdoor drying operations. They mandated that shrimp be dried in newer electric dryers, which are essentially industrial dehydrators. Many folks on the bayou could not understand these regulations. Folks had to either upgrade to electric dryers or give up on the industry. There are a couple of dried shrimp facilities still present on the bayou.

Refrigeration revolutionized the seafood industry. Shrimp no longer needed to be dried. Fresh shrimp could be moved longer distances and stored for longer intervals. What was left of the shrimp-drying industry dwindled further as folks gained access to fresh seafood. Docks could buy shrimp and sell it on ice to markets farther away. And this was great—until foreign imports knocked the wind out of the domestic shrimping industry.

DRIED SHRIMP

MAKES 4 CUPS (192 G)

3 pounds (1.35 kg) shell-on small shrimp

¼ cup (60 g) kosher salt

You can find dried shrimp at almost any gas station or grocery store along the bayou. They are a snack as easily accessible as potato chips. My dad calls the shrimp used to make dried shrimp "seabobs." These shrimp are so small that you can really only prepare them dried. They are impossibly hard to peel. But they have so much flavor packed into their tiny shells.

Drying shrimp in the old tradition is a slow process. It takes three or four days and starts with boiling shrimp and laying them out in full sun during the peak summer months when the temperature reaches the high eighties or nineties. After about three days outside in direct sunlight, the shrimp are crispy and dry.

While the sight of shrimp drying is beautiful, the traditional method is time consuming; using a dehydrator can speed the process. In a dehydrator, low heat and a continuous flow of air remove moisture from foods.

You can dehydrate shrimp with or without their heads and shells on. Try grinding up dehydrated shrimp and using them to add umami to stews, gumbos, and salads, or snack on them whole.

Wash the shrimp in cold water in a large bowl by agitating the shrimp with your hands while running cold water over them. Empty the water frequently by dumping the shrimp into a colander every few minutes and repeating the process until the water runs clear.

In a heavy-bottomed pot large enough to accommodate 3 pounds (1.35 kg) of shrimp, bring 2 cups (480 ml) water and the salt to a boil over high heat until the salt is dissolved.

Once the salt is dissolved, add the shrimp. Bring to a boil, then lower the heat to medium, keeping the shrimp simmering. Stir the shrimp into the salt water, stirring often until the shrimp are cooked and fully pink. This will take about 10 minutes. The shrimp will release water, and there will be a lot more water in the pot. Once the shrimp are cooked, leave them in the pot with the heat off and let cool completely. The shrimp will steep in the water and absorb more of the salt this way.

Once the shrimp have cooled completely, after about 6 hours, place a large colander over a large bowl and drain the shrimp for about an hour. Stir them every 10 minutes or so to make sure all of the liquid drains.

Continued →

If you have a dehydrator, you can dry the shrimp in batches until they are dry and crispy. Start the shrimp at 145°F (63°C) for 6 to 8 hours. Leave space between each shrimp on the dehydrating trays, so as not to overcrowd them. The shrimp are done when the shells turn papery and come off easily and the shrimp can be snapped in half.

Once the shrimp are dehydrated, remove the heads and shells, if desired (see Note). Working in small batches, put the shrimp in a ziplock bag and lightly tap them with a rolling pin. The shells and heads should release easily. You can eat the shrimp as is, or use a mortar and pestle or food processor to grind the shrimp into a powder for seasoning dishes later.

Store dried shrimp in an airtight glass container in the refrigerator for 6 months or up to a year in the freezer.

NOTE: *It is not necessary to remove the heads and tails. All parts of the shrimp are edible, but traditionally, these shrimp were stored and sold without the heads and tails.*

SHRIMP DIP

MAKES 3 CUPS (1 KG)

½ pound (225 g) peeled (see page 33) boiled shrimp

2 (8-ounce/226 g) packages cream cheese, at room temperature

1 tablespoon diced onion

1 tablespoon diced celery

1 teaspoon kosher salt, plus more as needed

½ teaspoon cracked black pepper, plus more as needed

⅛ teaspoon cayenne pepper, plus more as needed

1 teaspoon hot sauce, preferably Original Louisiana Hot Sauce

Juice of 2 lemons

2 tablespoons finely chopped fresh flat-leaf parsley

2 tablespoons finely chopped green onion

Ritz crackers or other crackers, for serving

Shrimp dip is great for parties on the bayou—or anywhere. I wish there were a better name for it, something clever and catchy, cool and hip. But it's just shrimp dip. Make this dip when you have leftover boiled shrimp; it gives you an excuse to eat buttery Ritz crackers or Lance Captain's Wafers.

In a food processor, combine the shrimp, cream cheese, onion, celery, salt, black pepper, cayenne, hot sauce, and lemon juice and pulse until the shrimp are finely ground and the mixture is creamy (see Note).

Transfer the mixture to a serving bowl and fold in the parsley and green onion. Taste and adjust the seasoning.

Spread on Ritz crackers or another cracker of your choosing. Store any leftover dip, covered, in the fridge for up to 1 week.

NOTE: *If you want to add liquid to make the dip extra creamy, add a tablespoon or two of evaporated milk.*

Shrimping by
the Moon

SHRIMPING IN INLAND waters is controlled by the Louisiana Department of Wildlife and Fisheries as a measure of sustainability. Lines drawn on the department's maps regulate where you can shrimp and at what times of year, and high fines (and a bit of public humiliation) are imposed on those who disobey these regulations.

Brown shrimp season runs in the spring, and white shrimp season starts in the midst of summer's heat, usually in August, and runs into fall. Department regulators test the waters to determine the size and multitude of the shrimp in both seasons, then release shrimping dates to the fishermen. It's a game of hurry up and wait. When the date and time are released, you and your boat have to be ready to fish.

Running a boat is running a business on the water. That business involves constant boat upkeep and maintenance, dealing with commercial fishing licenses and environmental compliance, and taking the time to retail your shrimp, if you don't want to sell it at the shrimp docks. Shrimpers have been voicing complaints about the industry since the late 1970s, about the time they started competing with foreign importers. This is why most shrimpers now hold two jobs—if they haven't left the industry altogether. Others have sought out ways to change the industry and the chain of distribution.

My cousin Heidi and her husband, Lance, are from a long line of inland shrimpers, and both shrimp part-time. Each season, in addition to their full-time jobs—she works as a cook and he as a welder—they skim for shrimp from dusk till dawn on Lake Boudreaux, in the barrier waters of the Gulf of Mexico, and then retail them.

A night for Heidi and Lance goes like this: After stocking up on fuel and ice, they set out at sunset on the *Heidi Marie*, a Lafitte skiff, to skim on Lake Boudreaux. With their skimming nets lowered into the water, one of them drives the boat, following patterns passed down through generations. After thirty minutes or so, when the nets start to feel full, they raise them into the boat, open the tied-off bottoms over a picking table to release their haul, and pick out all the bycatch, the other seafood that's

caught in the nets. They separate the shrimp into different sizes for grading, pack them in ice in champagnes or an ice hole, clean the boat down, and repeat, all night long. Other shrimpers share in this waltz, passing each other on their boats, guided by the waxing and waning of the moon and the ebb and flow of the tides.

The catch is unpredictable. One day the shrimp might be small, sixty to seventy per pound. The prices are extremely low, and at that rate, the catch won't even pay for the fuel for the trip. Shrimping is part wit and intuition and part lottery; some shrimpers find their way to the best grounds for the night, while others head home hoping the shrimp will be giving on their next trip. Heidi and Lance say if there are no boats in the bayou, you know shrimp aren't giving.

THE SEAFOOD INDUSTRY IN LOUISIANA

Louisiana's seafood industry has enjoyed success since the late 1700s, producing more seafood than any other state in the United States except Alaska. Seafood is our last wild food, our last wild industry. And seafood is plentiful in Louisiana.

Yet according to the National Oceanic and Atmospheric Administration, which oversees American fisheries, the United States imports more seafood than it has at any other time in its history—80 percent of it. Most of the imported seafood that moves from country to country satisfies the world's notion of on-demand food availability and feeding ourselves frivolously. Though we may be meant to fish for food, we aren't meant to *overfish*.

Shrimp is the most-consumed seafood in the United States, and foreign shrimp is often purchased over domestic because of miseducation and the need for cheap and fast food. Purchasing foreign seafood when a domestic option is available sends reverberations through a culture, a community, and an industry, affecting fishermen's livelihoods. The purchasing of foreign shrimp affirms that it's okay to continue moving food around the world no matter what the human cost is. Yes, it's okay to buy the cheap imports. Yes, culture and traditions aren't important. Louisiana has about 6,000 shrimpers today, compared to 36,000 thirty years ago when imported shrimp began flooding the market.

I've experienced this "yes" sentiment over and over in my daily work. I have seen a company touting its Cajun and Creole food but using Egyptian crawfish. I have seen many restaurants make the decision to cut costs by using foreign crawfish, shrimp, soft-shell crabs, and fish instead of supporting the fishermen in their own backyards. Yet it's decisions like these that decimate the fishing industry.

As a consumer, it's easy to make changes. Say no to imported seafood, say no to fast food, and make the connection to what you're eating and where you are. Ask a restaurant the origin of its seafood. Dine at restaurants that can be trusted. When in Louisiana, eat seafood that is native to Louisiana.

CRAB

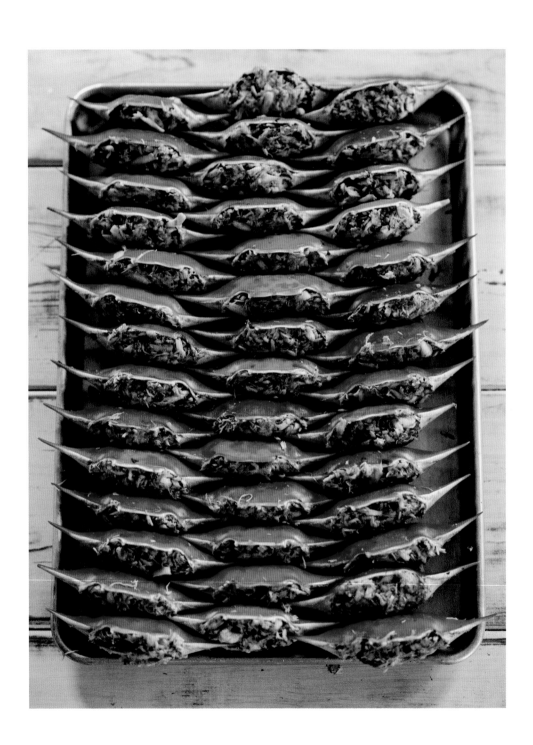

CRABS ARE THE SUMMER SUN HELD TOGETHER

by shell and seawater. They are poetry. You can steam crabs, stew them, boil them, roast them, or even grill them. They are versatile and tasty.

Summer in Louisiana means an abundance of crabs, and to me, there is no better way to eat them than simply boiled. To sit down to a table of boiled crabs is one of life's great slow, visceral experiences. You can't eat crabs quickly; it is a primal act with no shortcuts. It is work to catch them, work to prepare them, and work to eat them. But the result is sweet, succulent crabmeat. To eat crabmeat pried out by nimble fingers, with no condiments interfering, is to taste sunlight, summer, and the sea.

My family never buys crabs, but we eat them often. In the summer, my uncle Gordon, a retired shrimper, comes by weekly with platters of crabs. Heidi and Lance, his daughter and son-in-law, snag crabs as bycatch while skimming for shrimp (see page 62). Those crabs that measure up don't get tossed overboard with the rest of the bycatch—they make it home and get turned into meals.

On the bayou, a crab boil means cooking a couple bushels of crabs. Folks sit together to slowly break down crabs and make a meal of it. With crackers, corn, and potatoes on hand, too, it's hard not to fill up. Afterward, women gather around the table picking the meat from any leftover crabs or breaking them down for gumbos or stews. The crabmeat gets stored in the fridge or frozen to be used in cakes, patties, and bisques in the coming days or throughout the year. And the leftover shells can be used to make decadent crab butter (see page 77). Many crab dishes on the bayou evolved as ways to use leftover boiled crabs.

Crabmeat is a delicacy. Whether you start by boiling live crabs or buying a pound of cooked crabs from a reputable source, you are treating yourself to an exquisite meal. Gather some friends, put your phones far out of reach, have a real conversation, and settle in for a crab feast.

BOILED CRABS

SERVES 6 TO 8

1½ bunches celery (about 11 stalks), cut into 4-inch (10 cm) pieces

6 pounds (2.7 kg) yellow onions, quartered

12 lemons (3 pounds/ 1.35 kg), halved

6 bay leaves (see Note, page 46)

3 tablespoons cayenne pepper, plus more as needed

2 tablespoons whole black peppercorns

18 live large or medium blue crabs

¾ cup (1½ sticks/170 g) unsalted butter

1¾ cups (435 g) kosher salt, plus more as needed

12 to 16 ounces (340 to 455 g) small red potatoes (6 to 8), scrubbed

6 to 8 ears corn, husked and broken in half

Assortment of crackers, for serving

Maria's Seafood Dip (page 306), for serving

I'm a purist when it comes to boiled crabs; crabmeat should taste like crab, perfectly balanced, not overwhelmingly spicy. I boil crabs with onions, lemons, celery, and spices like cayenne, bay leaves, and black pepper, ingredients that enhance the crabs' deliciousness and sweet, subtle essence. Some folks add Old Bay or Zatarain's potent shrimp and crab boil seasoning liquid, which contains mustard seed, coriander, cayenne, bay leaves, dill, and allspice. If you want to add some to this recipe, go ahead—just don't add too much (a little goes a long way). There's really only one thing you can't change in this recipe: you need to start with live crabs. Give the crabs a good cool-water rinse to remove any debris or dirt, and keep them safe and alive until you're ready to boil them.

Fill a heavy-bottomed 4-gallon (15 L) stockpot halfway with water. Add the celery, onions, lemons, bay leaves, cayenne, and peppercorns to the pot. Bring the water to a boil over high heat, then reduce the heat to low and simmer until the vegetables are soft, about 2½ hours. Taste the stock; it should have a subtle bright vegetable flavor and taste clean, with hints of onion and celery. If it's nicely flavorful, you're ready to boil the crabs. Simmer the stock longer if the vegetables need to release more flavor.

Raise the heat to medium-high and return the stock to a boil. Take a deep breath and say a prayer thanking the bountiful sea for the crabs and the crabs for giving their lives. Then add the crabs to the boiling stock and use long tongs to press all the crabs underneath the liquid. Cover the pot and let the stock come back to a boil. Once it does, cook the crabs until they are bright red-orange in color, about 10 minutes.

Turn off the heat and add the butter and salt to the pot, stirring to melt the butter and dissolve the salt. Let the crabs soak in the stock for 15 minutes so they absorb flavor. Taste a crab by peeling one and trying the meat; if you think the meat needs more seasoning, add more cayenne and salt and soak for 5 to 10 minutes more, then taste again and repeat until the crabs are to your liking, up to 45 minutes total.

Using tongs, transfer the crabs to a platter. Bring the stock back to a boil over high heat. Add the potatoes and boil for 6 minutes, then add the corn and boil the vegetables together for 4 minutes more, until the potatoes are tender. Transfer the potatoes and corn to another platter and discard the stock.

Cover a table with newspaper, set out crackers and small bowls of shrimp dip, and have paper towels or napkins ready to go. Dump the crabs in the center of the table and serve the corn and potatoes alongside. Save all the crab peelings and shells to make crab butter (see page 77).

VARIATION

Crab Eggs on Crackers

When you crack open a blue crab, you may find a cluster of orange eggs—that means the crab was female. These eggs are a delicacy, like most fish eggs, and you can't let them go to waste. Try them with crackers or on crusty bread. If you don't eat them all, refrigerate them to enjoy later as a snack. They're also a great way to top deviled eggs or lump crabmeat salads, and crab eggs on a soft-boiled egg is splendid.

How to Eat a Crab

Louisiana natives grow up eating boiled seafood, so picking crabs and peeling shrimp and crawfish are second nature. We are pros, and scary fast at the task. But learning to pick crabs takes practice, and if you don't know how to pick a crab properly, you're going to waste a lot of meat—a sure way to go hungry at a seafood boil. Follow these steps to learn how to break down a boiled crab.

1. Working on a newspaper-covered table or over a large tray or baking sheet, hold the crab legs in your dominant hand with the crab's body hanging vertically.

2. With your other hand, grab the top of the shell, wrapping your fingers around the tip to create a hinge and a bit of resistance.

3. Pull the legs and shell apart. This should be easy.

4. Flip the crab over and remove the back flap. (This flap is called the apron, and it reveals the crab's gender: a long, skinny flap means the crab was male; a triangular, rainbow-shaped flap means it was female.)

5. Using your thumbs, apply pressure to the center of the crab's body so it cracks in half.

6. The soft, white, feathery bits you see are the crab's lungs—remove and discard them.

Continued →

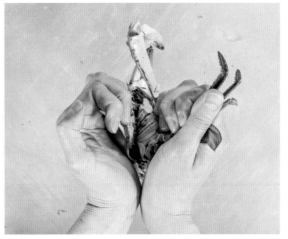

— 1, 2 —   — 3 —

— 4 —   — 5 —

— 6, 7, 8 —

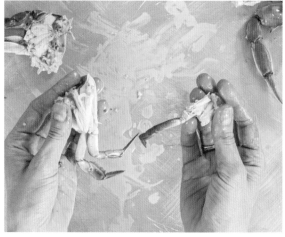

9

10

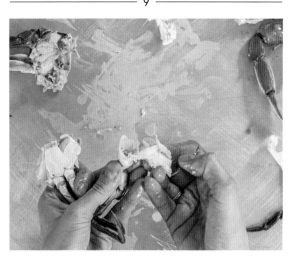

11

7. If you have a female crab, you might see some bright orange roe. Remove the roe and eat it—it's delicious—or save it for crab cakes (see page 86) or bisque (see page 101).

8. Remove the gooey parts in the middle (these are the liver and fat). You can allow them to pool in the bowl and use the fat to make crab butter (see page 77) or to add an extra bit of seasoning to many dishes. It has a rich umami flavor.

9. Remove the back swimming legs by carefully wiggling them away from the body in a half-circle motion. If done carefully, this will yield the jumbo lump part of the crab.

10. Remove the rest of the legs and claws.

11. The inside of the crab's body has meat tucked between pieces of cartilage. Use a sharp knife, a butter knife, or your fingers to delicately remove the crabmeat from these crevices.

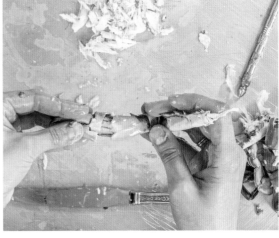

12

13

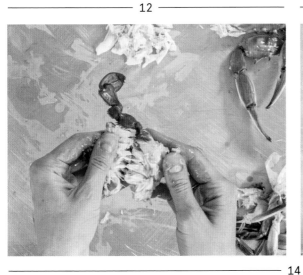

14

12. Use a nutcracker or crab cracker to crack the leg pieces and pull out any meat inside. Skinny crabs won't have a lot of meat. Large, heavy crabs will yield a bit in their legs. Try to extract every tiny bit. Growing up, we used our teeth to crack crab legs. I don't think my dentist would approve, but I still do this (try it at your own risk!).

13. Use the nutcracker to crack the claw at the knuckle area, near the pincer. Carefully remove the shell and slide the claw meat out.

14. Use all of your delicious crab. Save the peelings and make crab butter. If you are making it immediately, then forge ahead. If not, wrap and freeze the peelings to use at a later time.

CRAB BUTTER

MAKES 1 PINT (475 ML)

4 cups (8 sticks/910 g)
unsalted butter

1 pound (455 g) crab shells,
cartilage, and fat (the crab's
top shell isn't necessary)

Picking crabmeat is tedious, and there will always be some meat left in the shells. Using those shells to make crab butter is the perfect way to soak up every last drop of flavor.

One New Year's Day, I used this butter to teach my friend Cassandra to make jambalaya. The resulting dish was so rich and silky, we named it Sexy Jambalaya. It reminded me that crab butter can elevate the simplest things to new levels. Use it for making omelets, jambalayas, pastas, roux, and stews, or spread it on crackers for a snack—wherever you'd use butter, use this super-sexy flavorful crab butter instead.

In a wide, shallow, heavy-bottomed pot or flameproof roasting pan, melt the butter over low heat. Add the crab shells, cartilage, and fat and use a wooden or stainless-steel spoon to crush the shells and cartilage. With the heat set as low as possible, let the crab peelings and the butter marinate together for 1 hour. The crab parts will release all their flavor and infuse the butter. Taste the butter; when it has a full crab-forward flavor, it has steeped long enough and is done.

Set a sieve over a bowl and pour the contents of the pot into the sieve; let stand until all the butter has dripped into the bowl (this will take a while). Discard the solids.

Pour the strained butter into small airtight containers and label them with "crab butter" and the date. The butter will keep in the refrigerator for up to a month or in the freezer for up to a year.

Higgins
Seafood

CRABBERS CAN GET top dollar selling their live crabs to customers out of state, so it's an anomaly when you find a small family-run operation supporting a co-op of local crabbers. It's also an anomaly to find a local business that sells hand-picked crab. But Higgins Seafood is the anomaly, and is an essential supplier to about a dozen restaurants in New Orleans, including my own.

Higgins has been in business in Lafitte, Louisiana, for more than fifty years. They buy and sell fresh live and processed seafood. Crabs, shrimp, crawfish, catfish, soft-shell crabs, and practically anything else that swims can be found fresh or in their stocked chest freezers. You can get a bushel of live crabs or perfectly hand-picked crabmeat. You can get a tray of fresh soft-shell crabs or frozen ones. They will keep you in gumbo crabs and peeled shrimp, and you'll never find a gallon of better shucked oysters unless you shuck them yourself. Going to their tiny seafood shack in Lafitte is like going home to me.

The Higgins family works with roughly ten local crabbers, and their crab is the best you'll ever find. The boiling is done old-school, on propane burners in large pots. The crabs are seasoned perfectly, and, most important, the crab picking is done by hand. Hand-picking crabmeat means you're getting meat with the very best flavor and its integrity intact.

Hand-picking is tedious work. It's not an easy process, and it takes time, practice, and skill. It requires a labor force that wants to work as crab pickers. Today, as in the past, most of these pickers are women, and most are immigrants.

If you have access to Higgins Seafood crabmeat, then you are always on the verge of a fantastic dish. You can have a beer with Denny Higgins at almost any time of day and watch him boil or pick crabs. He'll talk about politics, evolution, religion, the weather, hurricanes—just about anything. Visiting Denny transports me to another time. The world pauses for a moment. This is slow food at its finest.

CRAB JAMBALAYA

SERVES 6 TO 8

½ cup (220 g) Crab Butter
(page 77) or ½ cup (115 g)
unsalted butter

½ cup (120 ml) canola oil

3 pounds (1.35 kg) yellow
onions, finely diced

⅓ cup (40 g) finely diced
celery

½ cup (70 g) finely diced
green bell pepper

1 bay leaf (see Note, page 46)

6 gumbo crabs, cleaned (see
Note)

1 tablespoon kosher salt

¼ teaspoon freshly ground
black pepper

¼ teaspoon cayenne pepper

1 tablespoon hot sauce,
preferably Original
Louisiana Hot Sauce

4 cups (780 g) medium-grain
white rice

5 cups (1.3 L) chicken stock
(page 304) or water

1 pound (455 g) lump
crabmeat

½ pound (225 g) crab claw
meat

¼ cup (13 g) finely chopped
fresh flat-leaf parsley

¼ cup (20 g) finely chopped
green onions

Cucumber and Tomato Salad
(page 281), for serving

Pickled Okra (page 300), for
serving

This crab jambalaya is a variation of the shrimp jambalaya on page 45. The steps to make that jambalaya repeat themselves here except for a couple of small changes. For this recipe, I like to use both crab butter and canola oil. I also add a few small gumbo crabs to enhance the flavor. Because picked crabmeat is so delicate, I add the lump meat at the very end.

Warm a heavy-bottomed 12-quart (11 L) Dutch oven over medium heat for 2 minutes, then add the butter and oil. When the butter has melted, add the onions and stir, stir, stir. This starts the very long process of browning the onions. Cook the onions for 1 hour to 1 hour 30 minutes, depending on how hot your stove runs, watching them very closely and stirring every minute. If the onions start to stick too much, add a little bit of water or stock to loosen them, then stir to incorporate the browner onions and scrape up any stuck-on bits from the bottom of the pot. Stir, stir, stir. If you're worried about burning, lower the heat. You really don't want to walk away from the pot at any point. This is your time with your onions. All the other steps will be easy. Stir, stir, stir until the onions are deeply caramelized and resemble dark chocolate in color.

Add the celery, bell pepper, and bay leaf to the pot and stir. Cover and cook over low heat for 15 minutes, stirring every 5 minutes.

Meanwhile, put the gumbo crabs in a large bowl and season with the salt, black pepper, cayenne, and hot sauce. Set aside to marinate at room temperature while the vegetables cook.

Add the rice to the pot with the vegetables and stir to combine. Raise the heat to medium and cook, uncovered, letting the flavors mingle and marry, for 5 minutes. Add the gumbo crabs and stir to incorporate them.

Add the stock and bring to a boil, then reduce the heat to low and simmer until the liquid has almost completely evaporated or looks like little puddles of water, about 8 minutes. When you're at the point of puddling—this is a judgment call based on temperature, pot size, and your stove—put the lid on the pot and reduce the heat to its lowest setting. From here, the cooking time is going to be 45 minutes total,

and you can't remove the lid the entire time. This is a tough, long 45 minutes. But trust yourself. You'll want to peek, but don't.

Set a timer for 20 minutes. When it goes off, turn off the heat and let the jambalaya sit, covered, for 25 minutes before you lift the lid. (If you live with a lot of people, you might want to make a note and place it near the stove: "Please do not lift the lid off the pot." This lets everyone know you did not stir onions for over an hour just to have someone uncover the pot and ruin your dish.)

After the 45 minutes is up, uncover the pot. Add the lump crabmeat, claw meat, parsley, and green onions and stir the jambalaya.

Enjoy this rich, silky rice dish with a cucumber and tomato salad and pickled okra.

NOTE: *A cleaned crab is a live crab that has had the top shell, gills, and back flap removed. Ask your fish market or seafood purveyor for fresh cleaned crabs, or ask if they'll clean some crabs for you if they're not already on hand.*

Crab Glossary

Boxes and bushels: Boxes of crabs are called bushels, and bushels contain 60 to 110 crabs, depending on their size.

Brown crabmeat: This is meat from the claws. Brown crabmeat has a distinctly different flavor from white crabmeat. Think of it like the dark and white meat of poultry. Both are equally delicious.

Busters: Also known as red liners, these are crabs that are about to molt (shed their shells).

Crab roe: Crab roe, or eggs, are a delicacy usually enjoyed only by folks who peel their own crabs.

Crab traps: These are baited with fish parts. Fishermen pull the traps out of the water to collect their catch. They attach float balls to find their traps and identify which ones are their own. It is a serious faux pas to check someone else's crab traps.

Gumbo crabs: These are crabs that are raw but have been broken down. The top shell, gills, and back flap are removed, then the crabs are usually frozen. The eggs are left in for extra flavor. You can use boiled crabs in gumbos, but if you can procure raw gumbo crabs, your dish will be more flavorful.

Jumbo lump crabmeat: This meat, from the back swimming legs, is the prize of a crab, the filet mignon. This is the whitest, most delicate, most mouthwatering meat on the crab. It's also the most expensive, because it takes precision when peeling to not disturb or break up the large chunks of meat. If you're boiling crabs at home, carefully remove the back swimming legs and pull out this delicious crabmeat lollipop.

Lump crab: The smaller white pieces of broken-down lump and pieces from the fins are less expensive but are still packed with flavor. This

includes the lump and the regular meat. After buying lump and regular crabmeat, pick through it for shells before using it in a recipe.

No. 1 crabs: These male blue crabs measure 6¼ inches (about 16 cm) and up from tip to tip (the "tips" are the spiky points on the side of the crab, above the legs). These crabs will command almost any amount of money on the market.

Soft-shell crabs: These are crabs that have just molted (shed their shells). See page 105 for more.

GARLIC CRABS WITH PARSLEY AND LEMON

SERVES 2 TO 4

Leaves from 1 small bunch flat-leaf parsley

12 garlic cloves, peeled

Zest and juice of 1 lemon

6 boiled large or medium blue crabs, halved and cleaned of their gills and lungs (see Note, page 81)

1 teaspoon kosher salt

½ teaspoon cracked black pepper

¼ teaspoon cayenne pepper

2 tablespoons hot sauce, preferably Original Louisiana Hot Sauce

3 bay leaves (see Note, page 46)

½ cup (120 ml) canola oil

½ cup (1 stick/115 g) unsalted butter

Crusty bread or cooked rice (see page 209), for serving

In Louisiana, when temperatures start rising to sweltering highs and the brackish water heats up, it's peak crab season. From June to September, you can open just about any icebox on the bayou and find a tray of boiled crabs. We eat them for breakfast, lunch, and dinner. There are endless ways to eat leftover boiled crabs. You can eat them cold, stew them, throw them in gumbo, or roast them like this, with garlic and lemon. The crabs are already cooked, so you are just warming them through and creating a delicious sauce that will be partially baked on. You'll need lots of crusty bread or rice to soak up the buttery, garlicky jus.

Preheat the oven to 450°F (230°C).

On a cutting board, combine the parsley, 6 of the garlic cloves, and the lemon zest. Finely chop them together, transfer to a bowl, and set aside.

Put the crabs in a large bowl and season with the salt, black pepper, cayenne, and hot sauce. Add the bay leaves.

Warm a large cast-iron skillet or ovenproof sauté pan over medium-high heat for 3 minutes, then add the oil and the remaining 6 garlic cloves. Cook until the garlic becomes fragrant, then use a slotted spoon to transfer it to a plate; set aside.

Working in batches to avoid crowding the skillet, add the crabs to the hot oil and cook until starting to brown on the bottom, about 3 minutes, then flip and cook until starting to brown on the second side, about 3 minutes more. Transfer the crabs to a roasting pan and repeat to brown the remaining crabs.

Add 2 tablespoons of the butter to the skillet and let it melt. Return the crabs to the skillet and turn them to coat evenly with the butter. Transfer the crabs and the reserved garlic to the roasting pan and place the pan in the oven. Roast, flipping once after 3 minutes, until the crabs are golden, about 6 minutes total.

Remove from the oven and add the remaining 6 tablespoons butter and the parsley-garlic mixture to the pan. Toss until the crabs are evenly coated. Season with the lemon juice and serve with crusty bread or rice.

LOUISIANA LUMP CRAB CAKES

MAKES 8 CRAB CAKES

For the Crab Mix

2 tablespoons unsalted butter

2 pounds (910 g) yellow onions, finely diced

¼ cup (45 g) finely diced celery

¼ cup (35 g) finely diced green bell pepper

1 bay leaf (see Note, page 46)

1 cup (240 ml) heavy cream

1 pound (455 g) boiled or steamed crabmeat (see page 70)

½ cup (130 g) peeled (see page 33) boiled shrimp

2 tablespoons finely chopped green onion

2 tablespoons finely chopped fresh flat-leaf parsley

1 teaspoon kosher salt, plus more as needed

¾ teaspoon cracked black pepper, plus more as needed

¼ teaspoon cayenne pepper, plus more as needed

2 tablespoons hot sauce, preferably Original Louisiana Hot Sauce, plus more as needed

½ lemon, plus lemon wedges for serving

For Dredging and Panfrying

2 cups (360 g) fine cornmeal, preferably freshly milled

1 tablespoon kosher salt

½ teaspoon cayenne pepper

Clarified butter (see Note) or canola oil

My aunt Christine taught me how to make crab cakes over the phone. And what I learned is that you can use leftover boiled shrimp as a binder instead of bread crumbs. When you grind shrimp in a food processor, it becomes sticky, and just a small amount will hold crabmeat and smothered vegetables together well enough to form into patties.

A seasonal salad made with cucumber and tomato (see page 281) or corn on the cob is the perfect accompaniment for crab cakes. Because crab patties freeze well, you can make dozens at once to eat for weeks to come. We stuff the same crab mix inside crab shells (see page 91), adding a bit of rice here and there to stretch the mix. We also use it to stuff large butterflied shrimp (see page 92), which we then dredge in cornmeal and fry as a special treat.

You'll need a pound of crabmeat for this recipe. If you have a reputable supplier for picked crabmeat, the meat should be good enough that you can buy regular lump, not more expensive jumbo lump, and you won't have to pick crab for hours.

Make the crab mix: Warm a heavy-bottomed Dutch oven or a cast-iron skillet over medium heat for 2 minutes, then add the butter. When it has melted, add the onions and cook, stirring occasionally, until soft and translucent, about 20 minutes.

Add the celery, bell pepper, and bay leaf and cook, stirring occasionally, until the vegetables are very soft with no bite remaining, about 20 minutes. Taste a piece of bell pepper—if the vegetables are ready, there should be no more crunch to it.

Add ½ cup (120 ml) of the cream, stir, and reduce the heat to low. Cook until most of the cream has reduced, about 8 minutes, then add the remaining ½ cup (120 ml) cream and simmer until the liquid has completely reduced and thickened to the consistency of a paste, 20 to 30 minutes. (It's important to reduce the liquid as much as possible, or the mix will be watery.) Turn off the heat, transfer the mixture to a large bowl, and let cool.

While the mixture is cooling, put your crabmeat in a large bowl and use your fingers to carefully pick through it and remove any crab shells:

Take a little crab at a time and lightly rub it between your fingers—you should be able to feel bits of shell. Go through the meat before using.

Pulse the shrimp in a food processor until finely ground. Add the ground shrimp to the cooled onion mixture and stir well. Add the crabmeat, green onion, and parsley. Season with the salt, black pepper, cayenne, and hot sauce and a squeeze of lemon juice and stir to combine. Taste the crab mix and adjust the seasoning to your liking.

You can make the crab cakes at once or transfer the crab mix to an airtight container and refrigerate for 6 to 12 hours. Be sure to taste again and adjust the seasoning, gently stirring in any additions.

Dredge and fry the crab cakes: Put the cornmeal in a shallow bowl and season with the salt and cayenne.

Dip a ½-cup dry measuring cup into the cornmeal to lightly dust the cup. Fill the cup with the crab mix and tap the portion out into your hand. Coat the disk of crab mix liberally with the cornmeal on both sides and use your fingers to press and turn the disk in your hand, forming it into a hockey puck that is a little wider than the measuring cup and about half as thick as its depth. Be sure to flatten both the top and bottom for even cooking. Be liberal with the cornmeal so the crab mix doesn't stick to your hands as you form the cakes. With practice, you'll be able to form them with a few quick turns of your hands and fingers. Set the crab cake aside on an oven tray or a large plate and repeat with the rest of the crab mix. Each crab cake should weigh a tad under 4 ounces (115 g).

Warm a large heavy-bottomed nonstick sauté pan or a well-seasoned cast-iron skillet over medium-high heat for about 2 minutes, then fill the pan with clarified butter to a depth of ¼ inch (6 mm)—it should come one-quarter of the way up the crab cakes when you add them to the pan. When the butter is shimmering, carefully place a few crab cakes in the pan in a single layer; don't crowd the pan. The crab cakes should sizzle when they hit the butter. (Be careful not to burn yourself, as the butter will be hot.) Sear the crab cakes for 2 to 3 minutes on each side, until they're crispy on the edges and golden on the top and bottom, with a slight crust forming around the whole thing. Use a fish spatula to remove the crab cakes from the pan and place on a paper towel–lined pan or plate to blot any excess oil. Serve immediately with a lemon wedge.

NOTE: *To make clarified butter, bring a pound of butter to a boil in a medium saucepan over medium heat; the butter will boil, then start to foam. The foam is milk solids and proteins; let the foam sink to the bottom and then eventually disappear. At this point, adjust the heat to medium-low and allow the butter to brown slightly and clear up again. The milk solids will fall to the bottom of the pan. Strain the butter through cheesecloth into a glass container, discarding the solids. Clarified butter will keep for a year in the refrigerator or freezer, and you can keep it at room temperature too.*

VARIATION ─────────────────────────────

Crab Patties

Crab patties are perfect for making sandwiches. Growing up, we'd make a couple dozen crab patties and freeze them to have on hand for a quick sandwich any time of day. Just form the crab mix into a flat disk, like a hamburger patty, instead of into a hockey puck shape, and use slightly less clarified butter or canola oil to fry them. For sandwiches, slather a hamburger bun or two thick slices of toasted bread with homemade mayo (see page 306) and top it with a thick slice of tomato seasoned with salt and pepper, then place a fried crab patty on top of the tomato, close the sandwich, and enjoy.

FRIED STUFFED CRABS

**MAKES 12 STUFFED
CRABS**

2 cups (360 g) cornmeal,
preferably freshly milled

1 tablespoon kosher salt

½ teaspoon cayenne pepper

1 recipe Crab Mix (see page
86)

12 crab shells, the top shell
of the crab with inside
debris removed (optional;
see headnote)

½ cup (120 ml) clarified
butter (see Note, page 89),
melted butter, or canola oil,
for frying

Cooked rice (see page 209),
for serving

Lemon wedges, for serving

The best time to make stuffed crabs is after a crab and shrimp boil. Save all the leftover seafood, pick out all the meat for the mix, and keep the shells to fill with the stuffing. If you can't get your hands on shells, look for the crab-shaped aluminum pans and use those instead.

If you're short on the meat and want to stretch the mix, you can add 1 cup (195 g) cooked rice. Stuffed crabs freeze well. There's nothing like a fresh one, but if you have extras, freeze them for another day. Serve stuffed crabs with rice and a side salad.

Put the cornmeal in a shallow bowl and season with the salt and cayenne.

Stuff the crab mixture into the crab shells (do not overstuff them, and try to keep the crabmeat level for easier cooking), then dip the tops in the cornmeal to coat.

Warm a large heavy-bottomed nonstick sauté pan or a well-seasoned cast-iron skillet over medium-high heat for about 3 minutes, then pour the clarified butter into the pan. When the butter is shimmering, carefully place the stuffed crabs in the pan, stuffing-side down; don't crowd the pan. Cook until golden brown, about 3 minutes. Flip the crabs over and cook for 3 minutes more to ensure that the filling is heated through. Transfer to a platter and repeat to cook the remaining stuffed crabs.

Serve the stuffed crabs with rice, a salad, and lemon wedges alongside.

CRAB-STUFFED SHRIMP

MAKES 12 STUFFED SHRIMP

12 jumbo shrimp, peeled (see page 33), with tails still attached

¼ cup (130 g) Crab Mix (see page 86)

Peanut oil, for frying

4 egg yolks, beaten

1 tablespoon heavy cream

½ teaspoon yellow mustard

½ teaspoon hot sauce, preferably Original Louisiana Hot Sauce

2 cups (360 g) cornmeal, preferably freshly milled

1 cup (130 g) cornstarch, preferably organic

½ teaspoon kosher salt

½ teaspoon cracked black pepper

⅛ teaspoon cayenne pepper

Stuffed shrimp is another way to use crab mix. Down on the bayou, we are partial to the taste of small and medium shrimp. But when jumbo shrimp come in, we like to butterfly them, stuff them with crab mix, and fry them for a special treat. Stuffed shrimp are easy to master, and they freeze well, too.

Using a sharp paring knife, slice each shrimp along its back ridge, leaving the tail on. Remove the vein (see the photo opposite, top right). Do not slice all the way through—just make a slice deep enough to open the shrimp like a book. Flatten it out by pressing down on it with your hands.

Hold a shrimp in your hand, opened up like a little book, and fill the inside with 1 teaspoon of the crab mix, packing it in firmly. Close the shrimp around the filling (it won't close completely). Repeat with the remaining shrimp and crab mix.

Fill a large heavy-bottomed pot with 4 inches (10 cm) of peanut oil and heat the oil over medium-high heat to 350°F (180°C). (Alternatively, use a tabletop fryer; see page 25.)

In a medium bowl, whisk together the egg yolks, cream, mustard, and hot sauce. In a shallow bowl, whisk together the cornmeal, cornstarch, salt, black pepper, and cayenne. Carefully dip a stuffed shrimp in the egg mixture, coating it well and letting any excess drip off, then dredge it in the cornmeal mixture, coating it completely. Set the cornmeal-dredged shrimp on a baking sheet. Repeat to dredge the remaining shrimp.

Working in batches to avoid crowding the pan, carefully add the stuffed shrimp to the hot oil and fry until golden brown, 3 to 4 minutes. Remove to a paper towel–lined oven tray or plate and serve immediately as a snack.

LOUISIANA CRAB CLAWS, TWO WAYS

The claws are the best part of the crab. You have to work for the meat in them, but when you get a claw that slides perfectly out of its shell, well, you're in luck. I am fortunate to get my crab from Higgins Seafood (see page 78), which provides us with perfectly peeled claws for the restaurant. You can buy cooked crab claws from your local seafood shop or counter. Serve them one of two ways: with warm drawn butter and just a squeeze of lemon, or marinated in vinegar.

Crab claws are a perfect summer snack. Eat them with crusty bread and a side of watermelon.

CRAB CLAWS IN DRAWN BUTTER

MAKES 4 CUPS; SERVES 8 AS A SNACK

1 pound (455 g) cooked crab claws with the finger part attached (see Note), preferably from Louisiana crabs, peeled and at room temperature

Juice of 1 lemon

½ teaspoon kosher salt, plus more as needed

⅛ teaspoon cracked black pepper, plus more as needed

¼ cup (60 ml) clarified butter (see Note, page 89)

1 tablespoon finely chopped fresh flat-leaf parsley, for garnish

1 tablespoon finely chopped green onion, for garnish

Put the crab claws in a medium bowl and season with the lemon juice, salt, and pepper.

In a small saucepan, warm the clarified butter over medium-low heat, then pour it over the claws. Gently mix, then adjust the seasoning to taste. Garnish with the parsley and green onion.

CRAB CLAWS MARINATED IN CANE VINEGAR

**MAKES 5 CUPS; SERVES 8
AS A SNACK**

1 tablespoon chopped onion

1 teaspoon cane vinegar,
preferably Steen's (see
Resources, page 359), or
sherry vinegar

Juice of 2 lemons

½ teaspoon Worcestershire
sauce

1 tablespoon plus 1 teaspoon
finely chopped green onion

1 tablespoon finely chopped
fresh flat-leaf parsley

2 teaspoons hot sauce,
preferably Original Louisiana
Hot Sauce, plus more as
needed

¾ teaspoon kosher salt, plus
more as needed

¼ teaspoon cracked black
pepper, plus more as needed

1 pound (455 g) cooked
crab claws with the finger
part attached (see Note),
preferably from Louisiana
crabs, peeled and at room
temperature

In a small bowl, soak the chopped onion in the cane vinegar. Let sit for
5 minutes.

In a large bowl, stir together the onion, lemon juice, Worcestershire, green
onion, parsley, hot sauce, salt, and pepper. Add the crab claws and
gently toss until well coated. Set aside to marinate for 1 hour.

Taste and adjust the seasoning. Serve at room temperature.

NOTE: *To make these recipes, ask your fishmonger for cracked crab fingers, or if you're
having a crab boil, put some of the crab claws away. The crab finger, or claw, is the
large pincer with the shell removed around the meat and the pincer still attached so
you can hold on to it while sliding the crabmeat off through your teeth.*

CHAUVIN CRAB STEW

SERVES 6 TO 8

½ cup (110 g) Crab Butter (page 77) or other fat (see headnote)

½ cup (65 g) all-purpose flour

3 pounds (1.35 kg) yellow onions, finely diced

2 garlic cloves, finely chopped

½ cup (70 g) finely diced green bell pepper

½ cup (55 g) finely diced celery

1 bay leaf (see Note, page 46)

12 small or medium cleaned crabs (3 pounds/1.35 kg)

1 tablespoon plus 2 teaspoons kosher salt, plus more as needed

1 teaspoon cracked black pepper, plus more as needed

¼ teaspoon cayenne pepper, plus more as needed

¼ cup (60 ml) hot sauce, preferably Original Louisiana Hot Sauce, plus more as needed

6¼ cups (1.5 L) chicken stock (page 304) or water

Lemon juice (optional)

¼ cup (13 g) finely chopped fresh flat-leaf parsley

¼ cup (20 g) finely chopped green onions

Cooked rice (see page 209), for serving

Making a crab stew means getting your hands dirty. The roux and crab will form a savory-sweet sauce, delivering comfort in each bite. The taste of the sea will linger in the stew, and you and your guests will linger over the meal, picking each crab until all the sweet meat is removed.

If you've got crab butter, use it to make the roux. Otherwise, make your roux with oil, butter, lard, or any other fat. For the liquid, chicken stock is great, but water will do just fine in a pinch. It's best to use small or medium cleaned crabs (see Note, page 81), but if you can only get boiled ones, that will work, too. If you know a crabber who will sell you crabs off the boat, even better.

Crab stew is perfect with crusty bread. But in Chauvin, it's always served over cooked rice, with a side of something pickled and a crisp green salad.

Warm a heavy-bottomed 6-quart (6 L) skillet or Dutch oven over medium heat for 2 minutes, then add the crab butter. When it has melted, add the flour and cook, stirring continuously with a wooden spoon, until the roux is a little darker than café au lait, closer to the color of peanut butter, about 30 minutes. Don't walk away—focus on stirring your roux. Put on an audiobook or just meditate as you stir.

Add the onions. (Be careful to avoid splattering the roux when adding the onions—this is when folks sometimes burn themselves.) Cook, stirring occasionally, until the onions are soft and translucent, about 20 minutes.

Stir the garlic into the onions and cook for a couple of minutes, until the garlic is fragrant. Add the bell pepper, celery, and bay leaf, then stir everything together. Reduce the heat to low, cover, and let the vegetables smother together until very soft, with no bite remaining, about 20 minutes, stirring once halfway through to make sure nothing is burning and to ensure even cooking. Taste a piece of bell pepper and a piece of celery—if they're ready, there should be no more crunch to them. If they still have a lot of bite, cook the vegetables for 6 to 8 minutes longer, then test again.

Meanwhile, put the crabs in a large bowl and season with the salt, black pepper, cayenne, and hot sauce. Toss to coat them evenly. Set aside to marinate at room temperature until the vegetables are soft.

Continued →

Add the crabs to the vegetables and stir to combine. Raise the heat to medium and cook for 5 minutes. Add the stock and stir. Raise the heat to medium-high and bring the contents of the pot to a boil, then reduce the heat to maintain a simmer and cook for about 20 minutes, until the liquid has reduced by one-quarter to half, depending on how thick you want your stew.

Taste the stew: Does it need more salt or pepper? Add some. Does it need more heat? Add cayenne. Does it need acid? Perhaps more hot sauce or a squeeze of lemon? Adjust the seasoning to your liking, then stir in the parsley and green onions.

Serve the crab stew over rice. Use your hands to pluck out the crabs and get to the sweet crabmeat.

SHE-CRAB BISQUE

SERVES 4 TO 6

¼ cup (55 g) Crab Butter (page 77) or other fat such as oil, butter, or lard

¼ cup (30 g) all-purpose flour

2 pounds (910 g) yellow onions, finely diced

1 cup (110 g) finely diced celery

2 cups (115 g) finely chopped green onions, greens and whites kept separate

3 bay leaves (see Note, page 46)

6 female crabs (1½ pounds/ 680 g) with eggs, shells, gills, and lungs removed, broken in half

8 cups (2 L) chicken stock (page 304) or store-bought unsalted stock

2½ teaspoons kosher salt

1 teaspoon cracked black pepper

Pinch of cayenne pepper

2 cups (480 ml) heavy cream

1 pound (455 g) picked lump or jumbo lump crabmeat

1 small bunch flat-leaf parsley, stems separated and finely chopped, leaves kept whole

Freshly grated nutmeg

Crusty bread, for serving

Bisque—whether made with crab, shrimp, crawfish, or corn—is one of the only soups my family makes with cream. Bisque is derived from our French friends and can be found in lots of fine New Orleans restaurants. And while bisque is cream-based, this bisque is not heavy, because most of the liquid is stock. A little bit of cream and a delicious roux bring the bisque together. If you want a lighter version, skip the roux. If you want it thicker, add more roux and simmer it into the base.

This bisque—packed with so much flavor, especially if you ask your seafood purveyor for female crabs full of eggs—is the perfect meal for a chilly winter day, but not too heavy for high summer. I love dishes that require you to eat with your hands, too, so this recipe features whole crabs that you need to pick apart with your fingers. Cook it for adventurous eaters who love crabs.

Warm a heavy-bottomed soup pot over medium heat for 2 minutes, then add the crab butter. When it has melted, add the flour and cook, stirring continuously with a wooden spoon, until the roux is the color of condensed milk, about 10 minutes.

Add the onions and stir them into the roux. (Be careful to avoid splattering the roux when adding the onions—this is when folks sometimes burn themselves.) Cook, stirring occasionally, until the onions are soft and translucent, about 20 minutes. Add the celery, green onion whites, and bay leaves and cook until the celery is soft, 15 to 20 minutes.

Add the crabs and stir. Reduce the heat to low, cover, and let everything smother together for 10 minutes.

Add the stock. Taste the soup and season with the salt, black pepper, and cayenne. Raise the heat to medium and bring the soup to a simmer, then reduce the heat to maintain a simmer and cook for 45 minutes more.

Warm the cream and stir it into the soup, then add the crabmeat, parsley stems, and a few gratings of nutmeg and stir to incorporate. Warm on low heat for an additional 2 minutes.

Ladle the bisque into bowls and garnish with the parsley leaves and green onion greens. Serve with crusty bread.

SOFT-SHELL CRABS

SERVES 6

Peanut oil, for frying

6 large egg yolks

2 tablespoons hot sauce, preferably Original Louisiana Hot Sauce

2 tablespoons heavy cream

3 cups (540 g) cornmeal, preferably freshly milled

2 cups (255 g) all-purpose flour

1 cup (130 g) cornstarch

1 tablespoon kosher salt

¼ teaspoon cracked black pepper

¼ teaspoon cayenne pepper

6 soft-shell crabs, cleaned (see page 106)

Butter, for serving

Lemon wedges, for serving

Coarsely chopped fresh flat-leaf parsley, for serving

Soft-shell crabs are blue crabs that have recently shed their hard outer shells in a process known as molting (see page 105). When I was a kid, I loved playing in the soft-shell crab tanks at the shrimp dock. I'd watch, intrigued, as the crabs molted, walking backward out of their protective shells and becoming totally defenseless. It's a natural wonder, and as an adult, I still find the process fascinating.

The key to enjoying soft-shell crabs is sourcing and prepping them. How easy it is to get your hands on live soft-shell crabs will depend on where you live. Find a good seafood market, or order them online (see Resources, page 359).

Fill a large heavy-bottomed pot with 4 inches (10 cm) of peanut oil and heat the oil over medium-high heat to 375°F (190°C). (Alternatively, use a tabletop fryer; see page 25.)

In a medium bowl, whisk together the egg yolks, hot sauce, and cream. In a shallow bowl, mix the cornmeal, flour, cornstarch, salt, black pepper, and cayenne.

Dip a crab in the egg mixture and allow any excess to drip off, then dredge it in the cornmeal mixture, making sure it is completely coated. Be sure to coat under the flaps of the top shell and in the nooks and crannies of the legs and claws. Place the cornmeal-dredged crab on a baking sheet. Repeat with the remaining crabs, keeping the dredged crabs in a single layer, not touching.

Carefully add 2 crabs to the hot oil (they have a lot of moisture in them and will pop when they touch the oil). Fry until golden brown, about 3 minutes per side. Transfer the crabs to paper towels or brown paper bags to drain. Repeat to fry the remaining crabs in batches of two, letting the oil come back up to temperature after each batch.

Serve each crab topped with butter, lemon, and parsley.

Panfried Soft-Shell Crabs

Instead of deep-frying these crabs, you can dredge them in a light dusting of cornmeal (no egg wash) and panfry them in ½ cup (120 ml) clarified butter or canola oil in a large, heavy-bottomed skillet. They're a tad bit lighter this way.

MOLTING, OR LETTING GO

Crabs are an incredible species. They shed their shells repeatedly over their lifetimes in a process known as molting, which allows the crab to grow. Molting normally happens in dim, shaded conditions. During molting, a crab will walk backward out of its shell, emerging twice the size as the empty shell it leaves behind—it is an eye-opening process to watch. The crab must free its entire body from its shell, even popping its eyes out of their protective covering. If the crab fails to completely release itself and let go, it will perish; its resistance to vital change will be its destruction. After its hard shell is shed, the crab has absolutely no defense mechanism, but its shell will quickly begin to harden.

Male crabs mate as many times as they want during their life span, but females mate only once, and only right after molting, when they have just shed their outer shell and their bodies are soft. After mating, the male crab stays on top of the female to protect her, knowing of the imminent danger she faces without her hard outer shell.

When a crab is about to molt, a tiny break or line in the shell is visible. A white line on the paddle fin indicates that the crab has about two weeks before it molts, a pink line indicates a week, and a red line indicates molting within a day or so. The crabs with red lines are called busters and can be sold to shedders.

Shedding crabs is the business of producing soft-shell crabs onshore. Shedders buy busters and place them in holding tanks until they shed their hard shells. In the 1990s, there were about three hundred businesses "shedding" soft shells. That number has dwindled to forty to fifty. After molting, the crabs must be removed from the tanks and sent to buyers immediately, before their shells harden. Some are frozen, packed in boxes, and shipped. Soft-shells garner a high price all over the country. The Atlantic market alone will buy every soft-shell crab locals can harvest for top dollar. Live soft-shells nestled together in trays arrive at restaurants all over New Orleans and around the United States.

How to Clean a Soft-Shell Crab

Every part of a soft-shell crab is edible—it just doesn't all taste good, so cleaning the crabs to remove those unappetizing bits is important. But unlike hard-shell crabs, soft-shell crabs are alive, defenseless in your hands, as you're cleaning them, so it's not an easy thing to do. At the restaurant, we do this as a team so we can mourn the crabs together. We apologize to them over and over, especially to the bigger guys that try to attach themselves to our hands with their soft claws. Once the crab is cleaned, it's ready for dredging and panfrying or deep-frying. Here is the best way to clean a soft-shell crab.

1. Hold the crab in your nondominant hand. Using sharp kitchen shears, make one clean cut across the crab's face to remove the eyes and mouth.

2. Pull up on the pointed end of one side of the top shell to lift it and expose the gills. Use the shears to remove and discard the gills, then do the same to the other side.

3. Flip the crab over and cut off and discard the apron (the flap in the middle of the shell).

4. You can cut the crab in half using kitchen shears or fry them whole.

5. Soft-shell crabs have a thick pink mass called a "sand sack"—you'll want to remove and discard this, too. Use your fingers to sweep the front part of the cavity where you cut the face off; if you find a sand sack, pull it out (sometimes you can find the sand sack, sometimes you can't—just do your best).

1

2

3

4

CRAB TRAPS

The crabbing industry came to Louisiana much later than oystering and shrimping. But not because crabs weren't plentiful. With almost eight thousand miles of brackish shoreline, Louisiana is a perfect habitat for crabs, especially blue crabs.

In the early nineteenth century, crabs were sold here and there to people waiting at shrimp docks but were mostly consumed by shrimpers, who caught them as bycatch, and other locals. Crabbing just wasn't a desirable way to make a living—it was hard work, and particularly miserable in the cold months. (The Isleños, who settled in South Louisiana from the Canary Islands, sang *décimas* about being frozen while checking crabbing lines in February.) But in the mid-1800s, New Orleans was growing, and fishermen recognized a niche market for crabs in the city's burgeoning restaurant scene. That new demand led folks to look at crabbing as a way to supplement their income.

Crabbing methods haven't modernized much. Fishermen work out of motorized flat-bottomed boats. They bait their traps with fish parts, leave them overnight, and return for their bounty the next day. The crabs are packed in bushels, then sorted at the docks, graded, and packed for shipment. The whole dance replays itself the next morning.

But it's never that simple. Crabbers are exposed to the wrath of nature and do the backbreaking work of pulling heavy traps from the water and unloading them in extreme heat, rain, wind, and cold. They contend with environmental and natural disasters, closures of crabbing regions, and shortages of crabs. Despite these hardships, a fisherman with a good catch and some knowledge of running a small business can carve out a decent life as a full-time crabber. With the demand for crab increasing through the years, some fishermen turned to crabbing as their main source of income, and for good reason: the industry went from paying a measly 20¢ a bushel for crabs to paying $300 in the last 100 years.

When the Atlantic Coast's crab population started dwindling in the late 1990s due to habitat decline and overfishing, buyers offered to pay top dollar for crabs from Louisiana. Today, Louisiana remains the United States' leading supplier of blue crabs. Our docks process and sell over 45 million pounds of crab each year, which is more than $50 million annually. Refrigerated trucks move up and down the bayou, bringing live crabs north to the Eastern Seaboard and elsewhere around the country. Crabs that aren't sold live are sent to factories that process and sell the meat. Louisiana fulfills a serious want for crab, pushing our waters to satisfy a nation's cravings.

OYSTERS

MY MOM AND DAD MET BECAUSE OF OYSTERS.

They're from a small town, so they were already crossing paths at elementary school. But my dad remembers seeing my mom on her dad's dock while his parents bought oysters from her father. He was probably only eight years old, but he was smitten with the beautiful girl. It would take him years of growing up before he made the bold move to ask her father for a job on his oyster boat. The rest is history.

My love affair with oysters started in Chauvin, Louisiana, with the oysters my father shucked for us. The first time I ate an oyster that wasn't plucked from the brackish waters on which I grew up and wasn't shucked by my father, I was in my late twenties, at Hog Island Oyster Bar in San Francisco.

Oysters are marvelous living beings. They aren't gender-fixed, and move between being male and female throughout their lifetimes. "He is she and she is he," said food writer M. F. K. Fisher of oysters. Oysters have a quick wild streak as babies and teens, then they find a hard rock and settle into stability for their adult life. If they don't settle, they'll perish. Oysters are filter feeders and get their food by taking in water and filtering it through their bodies—sometimes filtering up to fifty gallons a day. This natural process feeds the oysters but also purifies the ecosystem around them. Their growth and survival are indicators of a marine system's health.

In the same way a great wine from Piedmont, Napa, or Alsace has clearly distinguishable terroir, flavors unique to the area in which the grapes were grown, the flavor of an oyster reflects the waters in which it grew. When you eat an oyster, it's like jumping into the ocean, tasting the salt water on your lips, the seaweed and algae, the brackish marsh or the frigid Nova Scotia coast. To eat a Gulf oyster, an Olympian oyster, a Breton Sound oyster, or a Prince Edward Island oyster is to travel by tasting the waters of the world.

My family members were oyster fishermen, so when oysters were in season, we ate them daily. Hearty oyster soups, filling oyster spaghetti, simple fried oysters over rice, and overstuffed oyster po'boys all had a place on our dinner table, along with simple and perfect raw oysters eaten straight from the shell. My grandmother jokes that the only thing we didn't make with oysters was preserves!

VELMA MARIE'S OYSTER SOUP

SERVES 8 TO 12

1 tablespoon canola oil

½ pound (225 g) salt pork, homemade (see page 239) or store-bought, diced

4 pounds (1.8 kg) yellow onions, finely diced

4 large ripe tomatoes (2 pounds/910 g), cored

1 cup (135 g) finely chopped garlic

½ teaspoon cracked black pepper, plus more as needed

⅛ teaspoon cayenne pepper, plus more as needed

12½ cups (3 L) oyster liquor (see Note), or fish stock (page 228) or chicken stock (page 304)

2 pounds (910 g) shucked salty oysters, drained

Kosher salt, if needed

½ pound (225 g) small or medium pasta shells, cooked as directed on the package

¼ cup (13 g) finely chopped fresh flat-leaf parsley, for garnish

¼ cup (20 g) finely diced green onions, for garnish

My mom gave me my grandmother's Magnalite soup pot when I was going through a rough time; seeing it daily helped ground me in my life's work, procuring ingredients and cooking. It is the pot my grandmother cooked her oyster soup in, a memento of a life lived. The battered pot reminds me of her patience and kindness, her wit and fierceness, and her ability to marry ingredients. Her grandfather, father, and husband were oyster fishermen. This is a soup to feed a large family and hungry workers. It is a fishermen's soup and, for me, a prayer.

My grandmother's oyster soup tastes of salt pork and briny oysters, of sweet tomatoes and alliums. Like the mussel and fish stews of France, Italy, Spain, and Portugal, it marries tomatoes and seafood in a broth. It resembles a tomato-forward bouillabaisse and smells like the oyster beds of Louisiana. The salt pork comes from our Acadian salt-curing roots; it mellows the acidity of the tomatoes and mingles perfectly with the salt from the sea.

To make this soup, I ask farmers at the Crescent City Farmers Market to save me their "seconds"—those ripe red tomatoes that are bruised or too soft. They're perfect for soup and sauces, and you can often buy them at a discount. Core them and put them in the pot otherwise whole to break down. Call it superstition, but I think letting whole tomatoes break down slowly enhances the flavor. The soup's taste is also dependent on the oysters' salty, briny liquor, so you really want to procure as much as you can to make this soup. The best way to do this is to shuck your own oysters and reserve all the drops of liquor from the shells, or ask a seafood purveyor to save you the precious liquid. If you can't shuck your own, then forge ahead with fish or chicken stock. It's important to hold off on salting the soup until the very end, as the pork and oysters pack loads of salt.

Warm a large heavy-bottomed soup pot over medium-high heat for 2 minutes, then add the oil and heat for 30 seconds Add the salt pork and cook, turning as needed to brown it on all sides, about 12 minutes.

Add the onions and cook, stirring occasionally, until soft and translucent, about 20 minutes.

Add the tomatoes, garlic, black pepper, and cayenne and stir well. Reduce the heat to low, cover, and let everything smother together, stirring every 15 minutes, until the tomatoes are completely broken down and fall apart easily when you press on them with a spoon, about

45 minutes. (The timing may be a little shorter or longer depending on the size of your tomatoes.)

Add the oyster liquor and raise the heat to medium. Bring the soup to a boil, then reduce the heat to low and simmer for 45 minutes, letting all the flavors marry; the soup will be salty from the oyster water and salt pork and sweet from the tomatoes and onions. Be careful to not boil down the soup too much.

Just before serving, add the oysters to the soup and raise the heat to medium. Bring the soup to a brisk simmer and cook for 5 minutes, then turn off the heat. Taste the soup: Does it need salt, pepper, or heat? The cayenne is essential to the taste. Not too much, but a tiny bit of sweet cayenne heat makes it perfect. Add the cooked pasta shells and stir to combine.

Ladle the soup into bowls and garnish with the parsley and green onions. Reheat the leftovers and enjoy them with crusty country bread.

NOTE: *To get your hands on oyster liquor (also known as oyster water), look for a supplier of raw oysters, an oyster factory, or an oyster bar. Make friends with the supplier or shucker and ask if they will save some oyster liquor for you. If you can't get your hands on the liquor, a tip from Captain Johnny, my oyster purveyor, is to take 6 shucked oysters and blend them with 1 quart (1 L) water, adding 1 teaspoon kosher salt, then strain the liquid and use it in place of the oyster liquor. Taste your oyster liquor: If it's not salty, add a teaspoon of salt to bring the brininess up (if that doesn't do it, add up to 2 teaspoons more).*

OYSTERS AND PRESERVATION

Oyster reefs are a natural defense against coastal erosion. Efforts are being made to restore the Terrebonne Parish oyster beds, which once ranked highest in oyster production in Louisiana. In recent years, as a result of oil industry activity, the damming of the Mississippi River, and successive natural disasters, too much saltwater intrusion—and sometimes too much fresh water—has caused a steady decline in the oyster beds and their output. The fight to rebuild and sustain the oyster beds, which include the ground on which my grandparents farmed oysters, is perpetual. Today, my dad fishes where the oyster reefs are being rebuilt. He's told me that it seems like a million cane reeds have been erected marking where culch (recycled oyster shells) and seed oysters are being dumped, and the beds should be productive in about five years.

OYSTER GUMBO

SERVES 4 TO 6

1 tablespoon canola oil

½ pound (225 g) salt pork, homemade (see page 239) or store-bought, cut into cubes

3 pounds (1.35 kg) yellow onions, finely diced

2 tablespoons kosher salt, plus more as needed

4 garlic cloves, finely chopped

1 medium tomato, cored and diced

1½ cups (170 g) diced celery

1½ cups (270 g) diced green bell peppers

8 cups (2 L) oyster liquor (see Note, opposite), strained

4 pounds (1.8 kg) shucked salty oysters

1 teaspoon cracked black pepper

¼ teaspoon cayenne pepper

¼ cup (13 g) finely chopped fresh flat-leaf parsley, for garnish

¼ cup (20 g) finely chopped green onions, for garnish

Crusty bread, for serving

"Thin" gumbos—those made without roux—are starting to fall out of circulation on Cajun tables as our way of life changes and the older generation takes their traditions with them. This simple oyster gumbo is one attempt to hold on to a way of life that is disappearing.

The preparation is a lot like making French onion soup because it starts with caramelizing a mess of onions and then adding the rest of the ingredients in the final steps. This simple gumbo can be the base for further additions, such as smoked sausage or seafood. Make sure you serve it with crusty bread.

Warm a large heavy-bottomed soup pot over medium heat for 2 minutes, then add the oil and heat for 30 seconds. Add the salt pork and cook, turning as needed to sear it on all sides, about 12 minutes. Add the onions and a dash of salt. Reduce the heat to medium-low and cook, stirring often, until the onions are caramelized, about 1 hour.

Add the garlic, tomato, celery, and bell peppers and cook, stirring often, until fragrant, about 5 minutes. Add the oyster liquor, bring to a simmer, and cook for 30 minutes over medium-low heat.

Add the oysters, salt, black pepper, and cayenne. Raise the heat to medium to bring the soup back to a simmer and cook for 5 minutes.

Serve the gumbo garnished with the parsley and green onions, with crusty bread alongside.

Early Oyster Farming

MY GRANDPARENTS' OYSTER farm in Cocodrie was a sea of brackish water rather than a field of soil, but oysters, like plants, have to be seeded, planted, raked, and harvested.

My grandfather's oyster beds were quite a way from his home. So during the oyster season, the cold months from October through February, he and the other fishermen had to move to camps in the middle of the water to work their beds. Originally, these camps were primitive shacks that kept the fishermen out of the elements and gave them a place to sit or sleep after a hard day of fishing. Some were floating cabins, and others were built on stilts in the water or on oyster mounds. These outposts were not equipped with any luxuries and were a far cry from today's camps.

Fishermen would stand on flat-bottomed wooden boats or barges and pull oysters out of the water using long wooden tongs. It was backbreaking work. Fishermen would tong oysters out of beds and bring them into fenced areas where they were banked. Picture this like moving animals into a pen, except the animals need to be carried in. Fisherman banked oysters to protect them from predators like redfish, drum, and snails.

When the oysters grew large enough to sell, they were tonged from the banked area, culled, sorted, and put into wooden crates. Women joined men in the oyster camps to cook and help with the process of culling, or breaking apart clumps of oysters with a hammer and sorting them by size. The crates were loaded onto boats, and the fishermen made the long journey up the bayou to Houma, Louisiana, to sell the oysters. The boats were either paddled or cordelled, towed along with ropes by men or mules. A trip that now takes thirty minutes in a vehicle could take days by boat back then. Because oysters are so perishable, trips like these were necessary every time a fisherman had enough oysters to fill his boat, and the timing from harvest to market had to be impeccable.

OYSTER DRESSING

SERVES 6 TO 8

8 tablespoons (1 stick/115 g) unsalted butter

3 pounds (1.35 kg) yellow onions, finely diced

2 cups (300 g) finely diced green bell peppers

2 cups (240 g) finely diced celery

8 garlic cloves, finely chopped

4 cups (270 g) cubed country bread (cubes a little larger than 1 inch/2.5 cm)

2 pounds (910 g) shucked oysters

1 tablespoon kosher salt

½ teaspoon cracked black pepper

⅛ teaspoon cayenne pepper

½ teaspoon hot sauce, preferably Original Louisiana Hot Sauce

2 cups (390 g) cooked rice (see page 209), at room temperature

¼ cup (13 g) finely chopped fresh flat-leaf parsley, for garnish

¼ cup (20 g) finely chopped green onions, for garnish

Oyster dressing is rich and buttery. This version is tinged with hints of briny flavor and married with smothered vegetables. To make it, use a full-flavored rustic bread like a country loaf. Oyster dressing is typically served at holiday time with cooked fowl, but it's great eaten when oysters are plentiful and salty. You can also eat it all by itself or with a side of pickles and white beans. Be sure to dry the oysters really well so they don't add unnecessary liquid to the dressing.

Warm a heavy-bottomed pot or Dutch oven over medium heat for 3 minutes, then add 4 tablespoons of the butter. When it has melted, add the onions and cook, stirring often, until soft and translucent, about 20 minutes, then reduce the heat to medium-low and cook until the onions turn golden brown, about 25 minutes.

Add the bell peppers, celery, and garlic and cook, stirring often, until the vegetables are soft, about 20 minutes.

Meanwhile, in a large skillet, melt the remaining 4 tablespoons butter over medium heat. Add the cubed bread and toss in the butter.

Drain the oysters and dry them on paper towels or clean dish towels. (Save the oyster liquor for another recipe.) Cut the oysters into 1-inch (2.5 cm) pieces.

Add the oysters to the vegetables and season with the salt, black pepper, cayenne, and hot sauce. Reduce the heat to medium-low and cook, stirring often, for about 5 minutes, then remove from the heat. Add the rice and toasted bread and stir to combine. Place in a buttered baking or casserole dish and let cool, then cover with a dish towel or plastic wrap and refrigerate overnight to let all the flavors marry.

When you're ready to bake the dressing, preheat the oven to 350°F (180°C). Bake for 45 minutes, until the bread cubes are golden and the center of the dressing is warmed through.

Serve garnished with the parsley and green onions.

OYSTER BISQUE

SERVES 6 TO 8

3 tablespoons unsalted butter

2 pounds (910 g) yellow onions, finely diced

2½ teaspoons kosher salt, plus more as needed

8 garlic cloves, finely diced

¼ cup (30 g) finely diced celery

2 ounces (50 g) green onions, white and green parts separated and thinly sliced

4 cups (1 L) oyster liquor (see Note, page 116), strained

3 cups (720 ml) heavy cream

½ teaspoon cracked black pepper, plus more as needed

⅛ teaspoon cayenne pepper, plus more as needed

1 teaspoon hot sauce, preferably Original Louisiana Hot Sauce, plus more as needed

1½ pounds (680 g) small red or Yukon Gold potatoes (see Note), scrubbed, quartered if large

2 pounds (910 g) shucked oysters

2 ounces (55 g) flat-leaf parsley, stems and leaves separated and finely chopped

Crusty bread or saltines, for serving

Bisque is perfect to eat on a chilly day, and this one comes together quickly. Unlike most Cajun dishes, oyster bisque doesn't require a really long cook time. Even though the bisque is astonishingly simple, it is still full-flavored, with hints of the sea from the oysters. Heavy cream makes this bisque rich, but milk will do just fine instead. The potatoes—small red ones or Yukon Golds—add body to the soup, and their starch thickens it slightly. When feeding a large family, potatoes are indispensable for filling everyone up. So are crusty bread or buttered saltines to eat with this creamy, hearty bisque.

Warm a heavy-bottomed soup pot over medium heat for 3 minutes, then add the butter. When it has melted, add the onions and a dash of salt and cook, stirring occasionally, until the onions are soft and translucent, 15 to 20 minutes.

Add the garlic, celery, and green onion whites and cook, stirring often, until fragrant, about 5 minutes. Add the oyster liquor and cream and season with the salt, black pepper, cayenne, and hot sauce. Bring to a simmer and cook for about 10 minutes, until the celery has lost most of its bite. Add the potatoes and cook until they are tender and easily pierced with a sharp paring knife, about 10 minutes more. Add the oysters and simmer for 5 minutes. Add the parsley stems and stir to combine.

Taste and adjust the seasoning.

Ladle the soup into bowls, garnish with the parsley leaves and green onion greens, and serve with bread or saltines alongside.

NOTE: *Try to find a farmer in your area who grows potatoes and buy several pounds. Stored in a cool spot in your home, they'll keep for months.*

FRIED OYSTERS ON TOAST

SERVES 2

Peanut oil, for frying

1 cup (180 g) cornmeal, preferably freshly milled

½ cup (65 g) cornstarch, preferably organic

1 teaspoon kosher salt, plus more as needed

½ teaspoon cracked black pepper, plus more as needed

Pinch of cayenne pepper

1 pound (455 g) shucked oysters, drained

2 slices thick-cut bread, preferably from a country loaf or Texas toast

1 tablespoon homemade mayonnaise (see page 306)

Tomatoes, lettuce, pickles, and (optional) mustard or hot sauce, for assembling the toast

When you have some oysters on hand, this a simple and delicious dish to make. All you need to do is fry cornmeal-dredged oysters until crunchy and serve on thick-cut toast with perfectly ripe tomato slices and homemade mayo—simplicity at its best.

Fill a large heavy-bottomed pot with 4 inches (10 cm) of peanut oil and heat over medium-high heat to 375°F (190°C). (Alternatively, use a tabletop fryer; see page 25.)

In a small bowl, combine the cornmeal, cornstarch, salt, black pepper, and cayenne.

Dredge the oysters in the cornmeal mixture and carefully add them to the hot oil (they have a lot of water in them, which can make the oil pop and burn you). The oysters will make a lot of noise at first and then calm down—keep your face and appendages away from the pot as the oysters talk. Listen for the moment when they quiet down; that's when they are done. Don't overfry them. As soon as they are quiet, carefully lift them out of the oil using a spider or tongs and place them on paper towels to absorb the excess oil.

Toast the bread. Spread some homemade mayo on the bread and top with thick-sliced tomatoes seasoned with salt and pepper, some crisp iceberg lettuce, pickles, and fried oysters. You can add mustard, if you like, and a touch of hot sauce. Serve open-faced.

VARIATION

Fried Oysters and Rice

Fry the oysters as described above. Put the oysters in a clean bowl and toss them with 2 tablespoons unsalted butter and a couple dashes of hot sauce. Serve the oysters over warm cooked rice, with parsley and green onions sprinkled on top.

OYSTER SPAGHETTI

SERVES 6 TO 8

10 ounces (280 g) salt pork, homemade (see page 239) or store-bought

2 tablespoons canola oil

3½ pounds (1.6 kg) yellow onions, finely diced

1 small head garlic, finely diced

8 large ripe tomatoes (4 pounds/1.8 kg), cored

2 teaspoons kosher salt

½ teaspoon cracked black pepper

¼ teaspoon cayenne pepper

4 pounds (1.8 kg) shucked oysters, drained

1 pound (455 g) spaghetti, cooked as directed on the package (see Note)

¼ cup (13 g) finely chopped fresh flat-leaf parsley, for garnish

¼ cup (20 g) finely chopped green onions, for garnish

Oyster spaghetti sauce is made with the same ingredients as oyster soup (see page 115), but without the extra liquid. It's a rich and complex dish. This sauce is a testament to what can be done when the same ingredients are treated slightly differently. You should always have dry spaghetti on hand because it makes a fine and fast meal—if you have time to make your own pasta, then it will elevate the dish just a tad.

Put the salt pork in the freezer for 15 minutes (this makes it easier to slice). Cut the salt pork into a large dice.

Warm a large heavy-bottomed pot over medium heat for 2 minutes, then add the oil and heat for 30 seconds. Add the salt pork and cook, turning as needed to sear on all sides, about 12 minutes. Carefully drain the rendered pork fat from the pot and save for another use or discard. Leave the seared pork cubes.

Return the pot to medium heat. Add the onions and cook, stirring every 10 minutes, until caramelized, about 45 minutes.

Add the garlic and cook, stirring, for 5 minutes. Season the tomatoes with the salt and black pepper, then add them to the pot. Reduce the heat to low, cover the pot, and let the onions and tomatoes smother together for about 1 hour 30 minutes, lifting the lid every 20 minutes to give them a stir.

Uncover the pot and cook until the tomatoes have completely broken down and the sauce has thickened. Stir in the cayenne and oysters, then simmer for 10 minutes.

Serve the sauce over the spaghetti, garnished with the parsley and green onions.

NOTE: *If you're able to get your hands on a lot of oyster liquor (see Note, page 116), boil your pasta in it. You won't be sorry.*

Moving Oysters

THE OYSTER INDUSTRY hinges on transporting bivalves, a product so perishable that moving the harvest quickly is of utmost importance. The industry is part of a chain of movement from the marshes of South Louisiana to New Orleans and the rest of the country. The movement of oysters illustrates the intensity at which the industry sped up.

There were only a few ways to move product to market when my great-grandparents were harvesting oysters: paddling your boat to market forty miles away, hiring a mule to cordelle or pull the boat up the bayou, or using a sailboat. It was common to see sailboats tacking their way to markets, but if the wind didn't cooperate, sometimes fishermen had to dump their oysters back into the water to keep them fresh, thereby losing all the work of tonging them into the boat. By the 1920s, paddling, cordelling, and river sailboats were becoming passé with the invention of the engine. Oyster luggers with motors became the norm.

Before long, most oyster fishermen had their own engine-powered boats, which made going to market from the oyster beds quicker and easier. Fishermen could even work their beds during the day and come home at night, making oyster camps obsolete.

The advent of automobiles and refrigeration exponentially quickened the harvest-to-market pace and made the oystering industry what it is today. Fishermen no longer made the long trip to sell their oysters at market; trucks were waiting at docks to move sacks of oysters. Finally being able to ice and cool oysters for transport meant they could be held longer raw and didn't need to be immediately shucked, steamed, or smoked.

The transition from my great-grandfathers' generation of paddling a boat, or being cordelled by a mule, to sell off an oyster harvest, to the current state of the industry is nothing short of magnificent. It's funny for me to think of sailboats moving oysters on the bayous and lakes I grew up on. I never saw a sailboat until I left the bayou and moved away from home. Today at Mosquito Supper Club, the raw oysters we serve are harvested in the morning in South Louisiana; they're shucked and ready for our diners just a few hours later.

OYSTER BUTTER

**MAKES A LITTLE OVER
1 POUND (455 G)**

1 pound (4 sticks/455 g)
butter

½ pound (225 g) shucked
oysters, drained and patted
dry

1 tablespoon kosher salt
(see Note)

This butter goes a long way to add richness to any dish. Spread it on toast or crackers or use it to cook a simple omelet.

In a large saucepan, melt the butter over medium heat. Add the oysters and bring the butter to a simmer. Cook until the oysters pucker up and shrink, about 5 minutes. Turn off the heat and let cool.

Transfer the oyster butter to a food processor, add the salt, and pulse until smooth. Store the oyster butter in an airtight container in the refrigerator for up to 2 months.

NOTE: *Check your oysters for salt content before adding more by tasting the liquor on a freshly shucked raw oyster.*

How to Eat Oysters on the Half Shell

There is nothing quite as satisfying as eating oysters in the fall when the temperatures have dropped, the rain has slowed, and the oysters are holding salt. Gathering friends to shuck and eat oysters together is a perfect way to spend a lazy autumn day. Here's how to do it. You'll need oysters; crushed ice (optional); a shucking knife; dish towels; a container of water; a heavy-duty oyster glove (optional); an oyster tray, for serving (optional); and cocktail sauce (see page 307), lemon juice, horseradish, and mignonette (see page 307), for serving (optional).

1. Get a sack of oysters from a reputable source—check the tag for the harvest date to make sure the oysters were harvested within the week.

2. Once you've got them home, hose them off really well to remove any debris. Put the oysters in an ice chest and cover them with ice to keep them at peak chilled temperature.

3. When you're ready to shuck, work at a heavy table with a shucking knife and lots of towels for leverage and cleaning. Have a small container of water at hand, and dip your oyster knife into it after shucking each oyster to clean it. Unless you're an experienced shucker, wear an oyster glove on your nondominant hand, the one that will be holding the oyster as you shuck it. (Your hand will thank you for investing

| 1 | 2 |

in an oyster glove. It's important to wear one for safety.) Take a towel and fold it lengthwise into thirds. Then roll the towel almost completely, leaving enough space (1 to 2 inches/2.5 to 5 cm) for an oyster to rest.

4. Each oyster has one flatter shell and one cupped or rounded shell; the cupped shell is the bottom of the oyster and holds all the oyster liquor. The point at which the top and bottom shells are joined is called the hinge. Place an oyster with the cup side of the oyster on the towel and the flat side up.

5. Holding the oyster steady with your nondominant hand, slide the knife into the hinge of the oyster and use a twisting motion (like you're turning a key) to lever the shells apart. Then carefully run the knife

along the top shell to sever the adductor muscle and free the oyster from the shell; try not to puncture the oyster. Remove the top shell and toss it into the bayou or on the compost heap. Dip the tip of the knife in your container of water and wipe it clean with a kitchen towel.

6. Take the tip of the knife and slide it under the oyster, along the bottom shell, to release the oyster completely. At this point, many folks flip their oyster in the shell to check for any bits of shell or other debris. (This is known as the "Philly flip," for reasons that I don't know.) To flip or not to flip is completely up to you.

7. Dip your oyster knife in the water and repeat with the remaining oysters. Place each ready oyster on the tray on a bed of ice, if using.

8. After you've shucked each oyster, give it a sniff—if anything smells awry, discard the oyster. Make sure you do this; it's a good quality-control measure. After the smell check, the oyster is ready to eat.

9. Eat the oyster straight: just tilt the shell and knock back the oyster and its liquor. Or you can dress up your oysters by serving them with cocktail sauce, lemon juice, horseradish, and mignonette alongside.

NOTE: *I prefer oysters naked or with just a tad of lemon juice, but my dad and my friends in Louisiana eat them atop saltines with cocktail sauce and horseradish. It's the typical way on the bayou. These must be assembled one by one and eaten immediately. It's a local delicacy worth trying.*

BOWLS OF OYSTERS

When I was growing up, we ate oysters outside straight from a sack. Sitting under our gazebo, my dad shucked oysters with ease. He used an old-fashioned bayou knife to shuck the meat from the bill of the oyster (the front part of the shell, not the hinge side). He opened as many as we could eat raw, saving the shells to deposit back into the bayou, then he shucked the rest of the sack into a stainless-steel bowl, careful to not lose any of the oyster liquor. From there, my mom would fry freshly shucked oysters for sandwiches or to eat over rice with beans, or she would reserve them in the fridge to use in soup, gumbo, or jambalaya. A stainless-steel bowl filled with oysters and oyster liquor was a common sight in my mother's, aunts', and grandmothers' iceboxes from late October to February.

OYSTERS AND
THE STATE

As sedentary creatures, oysters can't move away from danger, unlike shrimp and fish that can adapt to other environments—oysters don't have that privilege. They bed down for life on healthy water reefs. There was a time when oysters were plentiful, when Louisiana's Delta was growing and not receding into the Gulf, when the Mississippi River flowed wild. South Louisiana was then a utopian vision, but with that utopia came consequences. We had too many resources, and folks wanted to privatize and capitalize on that: enter the state and oil.

A state system was put into place to allow the sustainable harvesting of oysters in Louisiana in 1902. Generations of fishermen who worked oyster beds were offered private leases for fifteen years by the state. The leases were renewable, so a family could keep a lease for generations. With those leases came adherence to new systems put in place by the Louisiana Department of Health and Hospitals and the Louisiana Department of Wildlife and Fisheries. The leases allowed fishermen to use public grounds for seed oysters and bring those oysters back to their private leases for bedding and harvesting.

Here's how it worked: The state maintained public beds that were for gathering seed only.

Seeds are oysters that are 1 inch (2.5 cm) to 3 inches (7.5 cm). Lease holders could take a seed and move it to a private leased bed and bed the seeds until the oysters had matured to 3 inches (7.5 cm) and larger. Then the oysters could be harvested and sold.

Non-lease holders were not permitted to fish for oysters for consumption or sale on public beds; they had to purchase oysters from a fisherman with a lease.

This privatization was quasi-sustainable and manageable for a growing commercial industry. But the damming of the Mississippi River led to too much salt water, which caused problems with the health of oysters; they need a steady supply of fresh water to dilute salinity. But too much fresh water will have the opposite effect. This *could* have come in the form of Mississippi River diversions, but diversions need to be approved, constructed, and tested, and another, larger problem loomed: the oil industry.

The leases that the state once protected were mowed over by oil drilling, dredging, and pipe laying. Pipes were laid all over the wetlands, wells were drilled, and canals were dug, allowing salt water to intrude on the marshes and eat away at the coast. Louisiana started sinking, and the wetlands started eroding. The oyster beds were polluted with

oil infrastructure and backwash, leaving oyster fishermen with little recourse.

The oil industry had pull, lining the pockets of local and state politicians, workers, and the state treasury. The only thing oyster fishermen could do was sue oil companies, and it was easier for oil companies to pay off the fishermen than to stop drilling or polluting. The environmental consequences and the magnitude of the destruction to Louisiana came later.

In 2005, two hurricanes caused further devastation. Hurricanes Katrina and Rita caused over $1 billion of damage to the oyster industry, including the destruction of public and private leases, wiping out the commercial infrastructure needed to market oysters and displacing workers who no longer had homes to return to.

Oyster beds represent a healthy ecosystem and thriving wetlands. The oyster industry is community driven, and oysters are woven tight into the larger fabric of Louisiana fishermen making their living from the natural resources around them.

The oyster fishermen of today are still trying to recover from both environmental and man-made disasters. In 2019, when the Mississippi River was at an all-time high, practically lapping at the tops of its levees, so much water had to be diverted from spillways that the oysters I usually serve were washed out and flavorless. Oysters are ephemeral, and their taste and survival are dictated by salinity levels. Louisiana waters are in flux, and fishermen are constantly adapting to this ongoing battle. It's something to consider the next time you enjoy a perfect Louisiana oyster.

CRAWFISH

CRAWFISH FARMERS AND CONNOISSEURS,

myself included, all have opinions about the best ways to acquire, prepare, and eat these crustaceans. We'll ask: Where do you buy crawfish? Farmed or wild? Is this spillway crawfish, Belle River, pond, basin, or ditch? Do you set traps yourself? Do you boil your own? What's your favorite restaurant that boils? And we'll share what we think is best: Buy medium crawfish—not large—because the tails will yield more meat and make a great stock. Add your salt after boiling, and soak your crawfish for at least an hour.

I grew up eating crawfish every year from February to late April when they were in peak season. Recently, when I was spending time on my houseboat in the Atchafalaya Basin, I was on a mission to eat at as many restaurants specializing in boiled crawfish in South Louisiana as I could. I concentrated my search on Breaux Bridge and the surrounding parishes, which are flooded with great crawfish *and* great restaurants. I'd judge what I loved about each restaurant.

We have our share of perfectly seasoned crawfish throughout New Orleans, too, and in Houma and beyond, but Breaux Bridge and the areas surrounding the basin are home to the heaviest crawfish production. When choosing your favorite crawfish house, it's about not just the boiled crawfish and their spice level but also the quality of the restaurant's seafood dip and the availability of crackers, potatoes, corn, and sausage.

From all my eating experiences, I've discovered that I prefer my crawfish boiled with only the usual vegetable stock (made of onions, garlic, and celery) and lemons, with the addition of corn and potatoes to round out the meal. I don't want my crawfish to taste like hot dogs, Vienna sausages, or anything pork-related, for that matter. But I know I'm in the minority. There are lots of folks who dump sausages into their boils, along with artichokes, citrus, pineapples, and whatever else the boil master wants to add to the pot. I also prefer my crawfish to not be covered with spice powder, but some restaurants are renowned for the ground spices they sprinkle over their crawfish before serving. It's a matter of taste, just like sucking the heads.

And that is a question: To suck the heads or not? My answer: When you're eating boiled crawfish, it's a sin not to suck the heads. There is a tiny, flavorful glob inside a crawfish head—it's not the brain—that's like the foie gras of a crawfish. This prized delicacy should not be wasted. We also use the heads for making stock (see page 305), for our étouffée (see page 148), and for bisque (see page 159).

Personal taste will dictate which crawfish you prefer, whether it be at a backyard boil or a local restaurant; farmed, spillway, pond, or ditch; extra spicy or mild.

BOILED CRAWFISH

SERVES 10 TO 15

6 pounds (2.7 kg) yellow onions, quartered

12 lemons (3 pounds/ 1.35 kg), halved

2 bunches celery (about 15 stalks), cut into 4-inch (10 cm) lengths

6 heads of garlic, halved

1 cup (50 g) cayenne pepper, plus more as needed

½ cup (140 g) whole black peppercorns

1 cup (50 g) paprika

8 bay leaves (see Note, page 46)

1 sack live crawfish (30 pounds/13.6 kg)

3 pounds (1.35 kg) kosher salt, plus more as needed

1 pound (4 sticks/455 g) unsalted butter

2¼ pounds (1 kg) small red potatoes (about 18), scrubbed

15 to 20 ears corn, husked and cut in half, depending on how many guests you have

Crackers, for serving

Maria's Seafood Dip (page 306), for serving

Gather some friends, find a backyard, and have a springtime crawfish boil. You'll need live crawfish, of course. Also seafood dip—a concoction of mayonnaise and ketchup—corn on the cob, potatoes, a roll of paper towels, and some beer. (Frosty beer never tastes better than with boiled seafood.)

Boiling crawfish is a journey in itself. The party is the gathering, but it starts with the prep, the long cook, and the time meandering outdoors around the steaming pot. It proceeds to the table, covered in newspaper, ready for a pile of steaming, spicy crawfish, and then time spent luxuriating around the table getting your hands dirty and your belly full.

Anyone—experienced chef or novice cook—can execute a stellar crawfish boil. Start by figuring out how much crawfish you'll need. Fifteen to 20 pounds is great for six to eight guests—if said people aren't from Louisiana. Most Louisiana natives will eat 5, 10, 15 pounds in one sitting. Assume 1 to 2 pounds for novices. You'll need a 60-quart pot with a double boiler to cook 30 pounds of crawfish. If you don't have a double boiler, you can always use a net to dip them out.

Once you have all your equipment and ingredients, you'll create a delicious stock in which to cook the crawfish. Crawfish tails absorb flavor from all the spices in the stock. The crawfish heads are filled with fat and rich liquor so spicy, it will make your sinuses run. This is part of the experience. Peel the crawfish, suck the heads, eat corn or a potato slathered in seafood dip, and repeat.

Set a 60-quart (60 L) stockpot with a steaming basket on a large outdoor propane burner (set the basket aside for now). Fill the pot halfway with water using a hose. Add the onions, lemons, celery, garlic, cayenne, peppercorns, paprika, and bay leaves. Bring the water to a boil over medium-high heat, then reduce the heat to low and simmer until the vegetables are soft, about 2 hours.

Meanwhile, get your crawfish ready. Crawfish have to be alive when you cook them, so be careful with the little crustaceans when you're handling and cleaning them. Empty the crawfish onto a table and sort through them, discarding any dead ones (if they aren't moving around, then they have probably expired). Transfer the crawfish to an ice chest or tub large enough that the crawfish won't be crowded and with enough space for you to add water to cover them. Use a hose to fill the ice chest or tub with water, then continue to run water through the tub

for about 15 minutes to clean the crawfish. If some of the crawfish make it to the top and escape, just wrangle them back into the water.

When the stock has simmered for an hour, ladle a bit of the stock into a cup, add a pinch of salt, and taste it: if you taste the vegetables and heat and citrus, then you're ready to boil the crawfish. Remember that the crawfish will be only as good as the stock.

Drain all the water from the ice chest by unscrewing the plug. If your ice chest doesn't have a plug or you rinsed the crawfish in a tub, use a long-handled net to carefully remove the crawfish. Place all the crawfish in the steamer basket.

Return the stock to a rapid boil over high heat. Submerge the steamer basket in the stock and allow the stock to come back up to a full boil. Once the stock has been boiling consistently for 5 minutes, turn the burner off. Add the butter and half of the salt, and stir to melt the butter and dissolve the salt. Let the crawfish soak for 15 minutes. Taste a crawfish: Does it need more salt? More cayenne? Stir in ½ cup (120 g) salt or ¼ cup (12.5 g) cayenne as needed, let the crawfish soak for 15 minutes, then taste again; repeat until the taste is to your liking. It usually takes 40 minutes of soaking for the crawfish to absorb flavors.

Cover your table with newspaper. When the crawfish have soaked up the flavors, ask someone to help you pull the heavy basket out of the pot, or just dip the crawfish out with a net or a substantial strainer and transfer them to the table for eating.

Bring the stock back to a boil over medium-high heat. Add the potatoes and cook for 8 minutes or until a fork pierces them, then add the corn and cook for an additional 4 minutes. Transfer the corn and potatoes to a platter.

Set out the crackers, small bowls of dip, and rolls of paper towels. Serve the crawfish right on the table with the potatoes and corn alongside. As you're eating, set aside some crawfish heads for stock (see page 305) or stuffed crawfish heads (see page 156).

How to Peel Crawfish

Peeling crawfish is easy—you just need to remove the head and then peel away the shell to find the tail meat, which is the true prize. Follow these simple steps, and then work on your speed.

1. Hold the head of the crawfish in one hand and the tail in the other.

2. Twist the head and tail in opposite directions—like when wringing out a towel. Put the head aside.

3. Squeeze the tail a bit to soften the shell around the tail; peel away the first and second parts of the shell.

4. Squeeze the back of the tail and pull the meat away from it; the meat should slide right out.

5. Remove the top layer of the crawfish tail if you want to get rid of the digestive tract.

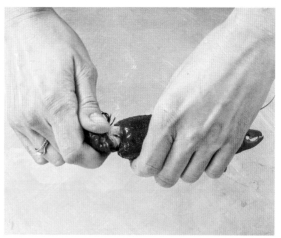

1

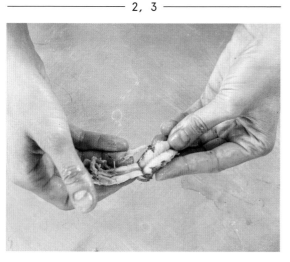

2, 3

4

5

CRAWFISH ÉTOUFFÉE

SERVES 6 TO 8

1 pound (4 sticks/455 g)
unsalted butter

2 pounds (910 g) yellow
onions, diced

1½ pounds (680 g) ripe
tomatoes

¼ cup (30 g) diced green
bell pepper

¼ cup (30 g) diced celery

2 garlic cloves, finely
chopped

½ cup (65 g) all-purpose
flour

4 cups (1 L) crawfish stock
(see page 305) or chicken
stock (page 304)

4 pounds (1.8 kg) crawfish
tails, with fat (see Note)

1 tablespoon plus 1 teaspoon
kosher salt, plus more as
needed

½ teaspoon cracked black
pepper, plus more as needed

½ teaspoon cayenne pepper,
plus more as needed

2 tablespoons hot sauce,
preferably Original Louisiana
Hot Sauce, plus more as
needed

Cooked rice (see page 209),
for serving

¼ cup (13 g) finely chopped
fresh flat-leaf parsley, for
garnish

¼ cup (20 g) finely chopped
green onions, for garnish

In French, *étouffer* means "to smother." An étouffée looks like a stew. It is thicker than a gumbo; it's eaten with a bit more rice than a gumbo, and it has a concentrated shellfish taste. It is sweet, with a touch of acid from the tomatoes, and *so* buttery. The crawfish give this étouffée a deep, rich profile, but not so rich that you can't have a second bowl. My favorite étouffée is from Kay Brandhurst, a fisherman's wife who sells shrimp at the Crescent City Farmers Market. She suspends crawfish and in-season Creole tomatoes in butter, and it is one of the most delicious things I've ever tasted. My version, a nod to Kay and her mean kitchen skills, uses a roux and crawfish stock to deepen the flavor.

Warm a 15-quart (14 L) heavy-bottomed pot over medium heat for 3 minutes, then add the butter. When it has melted, add the onions and cook, stirring often, until soft and translucent, about 35 minutes.

Add the tomatoes, stir, and reduce the heat to low. Cover and let the vegetables smother together for 30 minutes or until the tomatoes are completely broken down. Add the bell pepper, celery, and garlic and stir. Cover and cook, stirring occasionally, for 45 minutes more, until the vegetables are very soft, with no bite remaining. Add the flour and whisk until completely incorporated.

Add the stock and bring to a boil over high heat, then reduce the heat to low and simmer, stirring occasionally, until the mixture thickens enough to coat the back of a spoon, about 45 minutes. If you have crawfish heads from a boil, you can add them while simmering down the stock for extra flavor.

Put the crawfish tails and any fat from the bag in a large bowl and season with the salt, black pepper, cayenne, and hot sauce. Add the tails to the pot and stir to combine. Cook over low heat until the crawfish is heated through, about 5 minutes. Taste and adjust the seasoning.

Serve the étouffée over rice, garnished with the parsley and green onions.

NOTE: *If you're buying precooked crawfish tails, look for a package labeled "with fat" or "fat-on." If you're using home-boiled tails, make sure you reserve the heads, and throw some into the pot when simmering. You can serve them with the heads or remove them before serving.*

CRAWFISH STEW

SERVES 6 TO 8

½ cup (120 ml) canola oil

½ cup (65 g) all-purpose flour

3½ pounds (1.6 kg) yellow onions, finely diced

½ cup (70 g) finely diced green bell pepper

⅓ cup (40 g) finely diced celery

1 bay leaf (see Note, page 46)

4 pounds (1.8 kg) crawfish tails, with fat (see Note)

½ teaspoon cracked black pepper, plus more as needed

½ teaspoon cayenne pepper, plus more as needed

1 tablespoon hot sauce, preferably Original Louisiana Hot Sauce, plus more as needed

1 tablespoon kosher salt, plus more as needed

4 cups (1 L) chicken stock (page 304) or crawfish stock (page 305)

¼ cup (13 g) finely chopped fresh flat-leaf parsley

¼ cup (20 g) finely chopped green onions

Biscuits, homemade (see page 326) or store-bought, for serving

Pickles (see pages 300–303), for serving

When there is a little crawfish left over after a crawfish boil, we stir it into a stew. Like étouffée (see page 148), crawfish stew is thicker than a gumbo and suspends the crawfish in a gravy of smothered onions, green bell peppers, celery, and stock. It is also quicker to make than a gumbo, especially when you have a rich, delicious stock already at hand. The method for preparing stew and étouffée is practically identical except that a stew is cooked down with the lid off, doesn't have tomatoes, and uses oil instead of butter to make a roux. This results in a brown gravy rather than the étouffée's red gravy.

I like to make biscuits or hush puppies when I make stew; serving them together is like a Cajun ode to chicken and dumplings.

Warm a heavy-bottomed 6-quart (6 L) Dutch oven over medium heat for 2 minutes, then add the oil and heat for 30 seconds. Add the flour and cook, stirring continuously with a wooden spoon, for 15 to 20 minutes, until the roux is a little darker than café au lait, closer to the color of peanut butter. Don't walk away—focus on stirring your roux.

Add the onions to the roux and stir to combine. (Be careful to avoid splattering the roux when adding the onions—this is when folks sometimes burn themselves.) Cook, stirring occasionally, until the onions are soft and translucent, about 20 minutes.

Add the bell pepper, celery, and bay leaf to the onions and stir to combine. Reduce the heat to low, cover, and let the vegetables smother together until very soft, with no bite remaining, about 20 minutes, stirring halfway through to make sure nothing is burning and to ensure even cooking. Taste a piece of bell pepper and a piece of celery—if they're ready, there should be no more crunch to them. If they still have a lot of bite, cook the vegetables for another 5 minutes, then test again.

Meanwhile, put the crawfish in a large bowl and season with the black pepper, cayenne, hot sauce, and salt. Set aside at room temperature to marinate while the vegetables cook.

Add the stock to the vegetables and stir. Bring the liquid to a boil over medium-high heat, then reduce the heat to maintain a simmer and cook

for 25 minutes to let the flavors marry. You want to reduce the liquid by a quarter or half, depending on how thick you want your stew. Add the seasoned crawfish and simmer for 5 minutes longer.

Taste the stew. Does it need more salt or pepper? Add some. Does it need more heat? Add cayenne. Does it need acid? If so, add hot sauce. Adjust the seasoning to your liking, then stir in half of the parsley and green onions and save the rest for garnish.

Serve the stew garnished with the remaining parsley and green onions, with biscuits and pickles alongside.

NOTE: *Crawfish is sold in 1- to 2-pound (455 to 910 g) bags by markets and seafood purveyors, and comes packed in crawfish fat. When adding it to your recipe, be sure to squeeze all the fat out of the bags and incorporate it. Store-bought crawfish is sold unseasoned; if you use leftover boiled crawfish, you don't need to season it as much, so omit half of the salt, pepper, cayenne, and hot sauce.*

CRAWFISH HAND PIES

MAKES ABOUT 18 HAND PIES

3 cups Crawfish Étouffée (page 148) or Crawfish Stew (page 150)

All-purpose flour, for dusting

2 disks Leaf Lard Pie Dough (recipe follows)

1 large egg yolk

1 tablespoon heavy cream

Where other parts of the South have meat pies, in Louisiana, we have crawfish pies. All along the bayou, you can pick them up at gas station lunch counters. They're made using stewed local crawfish, encased in a savory lard dough and fried to flaky perfection. This is the Cajun hand pie.

These hand pies are best made with leftover étouffée or stew, but you can make either fresh to use just for filling the pies. I don't fry my pies, but I'm not opposed to it. I just like these baked ones the best.

Freeze the filling until it has the consistency of slurry, about 45 minutes. This will make it easier to fill the pies.

Meanwhile, on a lightly floured work surface using a lightly floured rolling pin, roll out one disk of dough to a ¼-inch (6 mm) thickness. Using an upside-down 5- to 6-inch (12 to 15 cm) bowl and a pizza cutter, cut out as many rounds of dough as you can. (Alternatively, use the pizza cutter to cut out 5- to 6-inch/12 to 15 cm squares.) Repeat with the remaining disk of dough. You should have 12 to 18 rounds of dough. Gather the scraps together and pat them into a disk. Wrap in plastic wrap and refrigerate. You can use these scraps to make more rounds (or squares) if needed.

In a small bowl, whisk together the egg yolk with the cream to make an egg wash.

Line a baking sheet with a silicone baking mat or parchment paper.

Hold one round of dough in the palm of one hand and use the warmth of your fingers on the other hand to gently press the dough while turning it counterclockwise, moving from the center of the dough to the edges. This will thin out the dough slightly and make it more pliable. Make one complete rotation, then lay the round on a flat surface. Repeat with 5 more rounds of the dough.

Place 1 tablespoon of the filling in the center of each thinned dough round. Use a pastry brush to brush the edges of the dough with the egg wash, then gently fold the rounds in half to create half-moons. Use a fork or the handle of a spoon dipped in flour to seal the edges. Use a sharp knife to cut a few slits in the top of each hand pie (this allows steam to escape during baking). Transfer the hand pies to the prepared baking sheet (there doesn't need to be a lot of space between them, so try to fit as many as you can on the same pan). Brush the tops with the egg wash. Repeat with the remaining dough rounds and filling. If you have extra filling, roll out the reserved dough scraps, cut out more rounds, and fill them.

Freeze for 15 minutes. (At this point, the pies can be wrapped well and frozen for up to 1 month, to be thawed and baked whenever you like.)

Preheat the oven to 425°F (220°C).

Bake the hand pies until the tops are a deep golden brown and the filling is bubbling out of the slits, about 25 minutes. Serve as an appetizer on a platter; this is finger food, so there's no need for a plate or forks and knives.

LEAF LARD PIE DOUGH

MAKES ENOUGH DOUGH FOR 18 HAND PIES

½ cup (120 ml) cold water

2½ cups (320 g) freshly milled whole wheat flour (see Note), preferably Ruby Lee (see Resources, page 359)

2 teaspoons kosher salt

½ cup (115 g) cold leaf lard, cut into ½-inch (1.5 cm) pieces and partially frozen (see Note)

½ cup (1 stick/115 g) cold unsalted butter, cut into cubes

I learned how to make piecrust from Julia Child's baking book, using her recipe as a guideline and changing it to include Crisco and butter. I like the texture of both all-butter dough and all-Crisco dough, but the Crisco batches have an airy nothing kind of taste. So I started using leaf lard in place of Crisco and fell in love with it. Leaf lard makes pie dough that flakes as well as dough made with Crisco, while also lending a rich flavor that is not bacon-forward. Lard is especially good for crawfish pies because it adds flakiness and an element of earthiness. Lard is extremely versatile and good in cookies, cakes, dumplings, and other pastries, too.

For this pie dough, be sure to start with cold leaf lard: cut it into pieces and freeze it until chilled before smudging it into the flour. It is also imperative that your water be ice-cold. I use hard whole wheat flour for its flavor, but any freshly milled flour will work.

Place the water in the freezer.

In a large bowl, combine the flour and salt. Add the leaf lard and butter and smudge them into the flour using your fingers, pressing the fat through the flour until the fat is combined with the flour. You're not looking for crumbled pieces of butter that resemble pebbles and sand but rather smudged pieces that you can see. Place the bowl in the freezer for 5 minutes.

Remove the flour mixture from the freezer. Add the water to the flour mixture 1 tablespoon at a time, using your fingers to lightly bring the wet and dry ingredients together and making sure each tablespoon is incorporated before adding the next. It is very important to hydrate the flour but not add too much water, so you may need only 4 tablespoons (60 ml) of the water (see Note). When the flour is hydrated and the dough comes together, stop adding water. The dough should look shaggy but not be dry, with streaks of lard and butter throughout. Form it into a large ball, then use a bench scraper or knife to cut the dough into two equal pieces and shape them into disks. Put the disks on a plate lined with a clean dish towel, then cover with a second clean towel and allow the dough to rest for at least 1 hour before using.

NOTES: *Leaf lard is available from your local butcher or online. I actually procured some great organic leaf lard from an Etsy seller once, but now I get my leaf lard from Piece of Meat butcher.*

You have a lot more play with whole wheat flour; it is more forgiving and harder to overwork than white flour, so you can really squeeze and manipulate it. The amount of water you use will vary depending on the weather. If it's humid and hot, you might need a little less water, and in drier places, you'll need more.

STUFFED CRAWFISH HEADS

**MAKES 40 STUFFED
CRAWFISH HEADS**

40 boiled medium crawfish
heads

2 pounds (910 g) boiled
crawfish tails with fat

1 teaspoon kosher salt, plus
more as needed

¼ teaspoon cracked black
pepper, plus more as needed

¼ teaspoon cayenne pepper,
plus more as needed

2 teaspoons hot sauce,
preferably Original Louisiana
Hot Sauce, plus more as
needed

½ cup (110 g) peeled (see
page 33) cooked shrimp

½ cup (70 g) finely diced
green bell pepper

¼ cup (30 g) finely diced
celery

2 tablespoons finely
chopped flat-leaf parsley

2 tablespoons finely
chopped green onion

Crawfish bisque is not complete without stuffed crawfish heads. The filling is reminiscent of almost all Cajun dishes, with its combination of smothered vegetables, crawfish, and shrimp. Because my hometown has a surplus of shrimp, I like to use shrimp as a binder in the filling instead of eggs and bread crumbs. These stuffed heads can be served as an appetizer, or they can be floated in Crawfish Bisque (page 159) just before serving. The stuffing is meant to be scooped out into the bisque or sucked out of the heads between spoonfuls of soup.

Making stuffed crawfish heads is a group project. Families get together and make the savory filling, then stuff it into the crawfish heads. They freeze the unbaked stuffed heads, then pull them out of the freezer during the year to bake as they need them.

Preheat the oven to 350°F (180°C).

Peel the boiled crawfish heads by removing the bottom cavity of the crawfish head. Insert your finger and pull down on the bottom segment, which will release the legs from the upper portion of the crawfish head. Discard the legs.

Put the crawfish tails in a large bowl and season with the salt, black pepper, cayenne, and hot sauce. Add the shrimp, bell pepper, celery, parsley, and green onion. Transfer to a meat grinder or food processor and grind until smooth. Taste and adjust the seasoning, if necessary.

Use your fingers to push the crawfish stuffing into the heads, stuffing in as much of the mixture as you can and placing the stuffed heads on a baking sheet as you go.

Bake until the filling is set and golden, about 25 minutes. If you would like to freeze the heads for later use, place them on a baking sheet and put them in the freezer; as soon as they are frozen, put them in a freezer-safe ziplock bag and label the bag. When you want to use the heads, thaw them before baking them in the oven.

CRAWFISH BISQUE

SERVES 8 TO 10

½ cup (1 stick/115 g) unsalted butter

½ cup (65 g) all-purpose flour

2 pounds (910 g) yellow onions, finely diced

⅓ cup (40 g) finely diced celery

¼ cup (35 g) finely diced green bell pepper

4 cups (1 L) crawfish stock (see page 305) or chicken stock (page 304)

2 cups (480 ml) whole milk

3 cups (720 ml) heavy cream

3 pounds (1.35 kg) crawfish tails (see Note) with fat (see Note, page 151)

1 tablespoon kosher salt, plus more as needed

¼ teaspoon cracked black pepper, plus more as needed

¼ teaspoon cayenne pepper, plus more as needed

1 tablespoon hot sauce, preferably Original Louisiana Hot Sauce

1 lemon wedge

Pinch of freshly grated nutmeg

Stuffed Crawfish Heads (page 156)

¼ cup (13 g) finely chopped fresh flat-leaf parsley

¼ cup (20 g) finely chopped green onions

My aunt Earline was responsible for the crab, shrimp, and crawfish bisques that my family ate. She would cross the bayou and bring us whatever dish she was creating in her kitchen. Recently during a hurricane it was air-fried chicken wings, but when I was a kid, I remember her steaming bowls of crab and corn bisque; crawfish bisque with stuffed heads; and simple, delicious shrimp bisque. This crawfish bisque is rustic, filled with chopped vegetables and stuffed crawfish heads. It's better after it sits awhile, which allows the flavors to marry.

Warm an 8-quart (8 L) heavy-bottomed pot over medium heat for 2 minutes, then add the butter. When it has melted, add the flour and cook, stirring continuously with a wooden spoon, for about 15 minutes, until the roux is the color of condensed milk.

Add the onions and stir them into the roux. (Be careful to avoid splattering the roux when adding the onions—this is when folks sometimes burn themselves.) Cook, stirring occasionally, until the onions are soft and translucent, about 30 minutes.

Add the celery and bell pepper and cook, stirring occasionally, until the vegetables are soft, about 20 minutes. Add the stock, milk, and cream and stir to combine. Bring to a simmer over medium heat and cook until the flavors marry, about 40 minutes, reducing the heat to maintain a simmer. You want the broth to be infused with vegetable flavor.

Put the crawfish tails and any fat from the bag in a large bowl and season with the salt, black pepper, cayenne, and hot sauce. Let marinate for 10 minutes, then add them to the pot and simmer for 8 minutes to heat them through. Add a squeeze of lemon juice and the nutmeg, taste, and adjust the seasoning.

Ladle the bisque into bowls and garnish with the stuffed crawfish heads, parsley, and green onions.

NOTE: *Feel free to use crawfish tails from a batch you've boiled yourself in place of the parcooked store-bought ones. Since they've already been seasoned (the store-bought ones have not), taste them and season with salt, black pepper, cayenne, and hot sauce as needed, disregarding the quantities provided. Simmer them in the bisque for just 5 minutes to heat through.*

CRAWFISH TALES

American Indians were the first to taste Louisiana's crawfish, long before European settlers arrived. Much later, marsh dwellers fished crawfish out of swamps and ditches and learned to prepare them. The Houma Indians in Terrebonne Parish have a crawfish as their war emblem and tell a tale of crawfish forming the delta land. The Acadians have their own tale of crawfish following them from the Canadian Maritimes to South Louisiana, the crawfish losing weight along the way and going from lobster size to crawfish size. Both are great myths in the evolution of South Louisiana's cuisine.

Crawfish make themselves known all over the bayou and can be found in almost any water source or puddle. During the season, folks line the tiny bayous and waterways (ditches) on the side of the road, crawfishing with nets. When my parents were growing up, crawfish were free and abundant. Even in my childhood, we never had to pay for crawfish. My aunt and uncle had a pond behind their house, and we all reaped the benefits all season long.

Eating crawfish was once considered a sign of poverty (much like eating lobster was as well). Crawfish have always fed working-class South Louisiana natives, but today it's tough to believe there was a time when only the poor and those "in the know" ate crawfish in New Orleans. It's becoming harder and harder to access and eat crawfish during the season—unless you have money to spare. Crawfish are a hot commodity, and supply and demand are at work during the season.

Over the last seventy-five years, crawfish have gone from 5¢ per pound to $3.00 per pound. During that same period of time, crawfish farms skyrocketed from covering 10,000 acres to 160,000 acres in Louisiana. From the mid-1960s to the present, crawfish aquaculture grew to become the largest freshwater crustacean industry in the United States, and today, Louisiana produces 90 percent of the nation's supply.

While the growth of the commercial industry is impressive, the basics behind crawfish farming remain simple. If you have a pond, a pirogue, and crawfish traps, you can harvest crawfish. Crawfish are tightly woven into our landscape and food system in South Louisiana.

GUMBO

GUMBO IS THE TIE THAT BINDS IN SOUTH

Louisiana. It symbolizes family, a shared table, local ingredients, patience, and the subtleties of culture and tradition. For most South Louisiana families, eating gumbo is a weekly act.

And gumbo is like a religion. The 1885 *Creole Cookery Book*, for instance, called gumbo-making an "occult science." Whether they're award-winning New Orleans chefs or home cooks, people swear by their methods. New Orleans gumbos are never shy with ingredients, featuring chicken, sausage, pork, crab, oysters, shrimp, okra, and more. In rural Louisiana, gumbo made with a dark roux, chicken, and andouille sausage is the mainstay. Down on the bayou, a simple shrimp or chicken gumbo is served almost every Sunday right after Mass, always with sides of rice and potato salad.

With numerous conflicting sources on its origins, gumbo cannot be attributed to one culture. Even the word's etymology doesn't point in any one direction. Gumbo may have derived from an okra-based West African soup, a filé-thickened American Indian dish, a roux-based French soup or bouillabaisse, or all of the above—and more. Gumbo, certainly history in a bowl, intersects different countries' culinary traditions and is emblematic of the nations whose people became the building blocks of Louisiana. The beginnings and ends of this dish are ever evolving.

Gumbo represents what's been learned from our ancestors and our communities. Each person cooks one that expresses the way they view food, the culture with which they identify, and their relationship to the food around them. Gumbo is synonymous with Cajun culture, but it would be erroneous to imply that gumbo is solely a Cajun dish. With a past steeped in so many places, gumbo is a personal dish, and each version has a place in the gumbo continuum. It is a multiethnic group project that constantly changes.

LOST SHRIMP GUMBO

SERVES 6 TO 8

3 tablespoons canola oil

6 pounds (2.7 kg) yellow onions, finely diced

1 cup (110 g) finely diced celery

1 cup (180 g) finely diced green bell pepper

1 bay leaf (see Note, page 46)

1 medium tomato, cored and diced

3 pounds (1.35 kg) small shrimp, peeled and deveined (see page 33)

2 tablespoons kosher salt, plus more as needed

½ teaspoon cracked black pepper, plus more as needed

½ teaspoon cayenne pepper, plus more as needed

2 tablespoons hot sauce, preferably Original Louisiana Hot Sauce, plus more as needed

12½ cups (3 L) water or chicken stock (page 304)

Filé powder (optional)

6 hard-boiled eggs, peeled (optional)

Cooked rice (see page 209), for serving

¼ cup (13 g) finely chopped fresh flat-leaf parsley, for garnish

¼ cup (20 g) finely chopped green onions, for garnish

Potato Salad (page 280), for serving

Pickles (see pages 300–303), for serving

I remember this shrimp gumbo from my childhood. As with most dishes we ate, there was no written recipe, so I sought to re-create it. This gumbo is thin, more like soup, but my grandmother would never have called it a soup. It's a gumbo. Even though it's not a roux-based gumbo, this dish packs a lot of flavor from the tasty small shrimp and the onions. You need to cook the onions until they are dark brown, right before they seem like they might burn, to allow their natural sweetness to come out. You can add crabs or oysters or both. Adding boiled eggs is customary down the bayou to help stretch the meal.

Warm a heavy-bottomed soup pot or Dutch oven over medium heat for 2 minutes, then add the oil and heat for 30 seconds. Add the onions to the pot and stir, stir, stir. This starts the very long process of browning the onions. Cook the onions for 1 hour to 1 hour 30 minutes, depending on how hot your stove runs, watching them very closely and stirring every 2 minutes. If the onions start to stick too much, add a little bit of water or stock to loosen them, then stir to incorporate the browner onions and scrape up any stuck-on bits from the bottom of the pot. Stir, stir, stir. If you're worried about burning, lower the heat. You really don't want to walk away from the pot at any point. This is your time with your onions. All the other steps will be easy. Stir, stir, stir until the onions are deeply caramelized and resemble dark chocolate in color.

Add the celery, bell pepper, and bay leaf and stir. Reduce the heat to its lowest setting, cover, and let the vegetables smother together until very soft, with no bite remaining, about 30 minutes.

Add the tomato and stir to combine. Cover and smother for 30 minutes more, until the tomato has completely broken down.

Put the shrimp in a large bowl and season with 1 tablespoon of the salt, the black pepper, cayenne, and hot sauce. Stir the shrimp into the vegetables, cover, and smother for about 10 minutes.

Add the water and the remaining 1 tablespoon salt and stir to combine. Raise the heat to medium to bring the liquid to a simmer, then reduce the heat so the gumbo is just barely at a simmer and cook for

20 minutes more. Turn off the heat and let the flavors marry for another 20 minutes before serving. Taste and adjust the seasoning. If you like, add a teaspoon of filé to the pot (or put filé on the table for folks to add to their own bowls). You can also add boiled eggs to the gumbo for a bit of extra protein. They were always floated whole in gumbos down the bayou.

Serve the gumbo over rice, garnished with the parsley and green onions, with a side of potato salad and some pickles.

Gumbo, Act I:
Sassafras, Kombo, Filé

IF YOU'RE LOOKING for a "nose-to-tail" kinda tree, look no further than the American sassafras. All of its parts—roots, stems, twigs, leaves, bark, flowers, and fruit—can be used for medicinal or culinary purposes. American Indians have been hip to its resources for centuries.

Sassafras trees grow in the South, and their leaves are dried and pounded to make filé powder, which was used to thicken gumbo during the winter months when okra wasn't available. The Choctaws, one of the many American Indian tribes populating Louisiana, Mississippi, and other Southern states, are responsible for the filé we use in our gumbo today. American Indians shared their knowledge of the sassafras tree, including the thickening qualities of filé and how to procure and use it, with European settlers. The Choctaw word for filé is *kombo*, and some people link the word *gumbo* to *kombo*. American Indians were eating lots of stews and gumbo-like dishes over corn. Some would argue that these were the first gumbos: a mess of ingredients thickened with filé and served over corn.

Down on the bayou, everyone has a little bottle of filé in their freezer, where it stays freshest. Folks still thicken their gumbo with filé at the very end of cooking. It's customary to have the bottle on the table next to the pickled peppers and hot sauce so everyone can add it to their own bowl of gumbo to taste. When I'm in Chauvin, I buy filé in tiny nondescript bottles at the grocery store. It is made by elders of local tribes. The ingredients: 100 percent sassafras leaves, dried and pounded one bayou over in Montegut, Louisiana. I sprinkle it on my gumbo and my potato salad, and we use it to make ice cream, too.

MAXINE'S SHRIMP OKRA GUMBO

SERVES 6 TO 8

3 tablespoons canola oil

1 pound (455 g) yellow onions, finely diced

2 cups (450 g) Smothered Okra (page 265)

1 bay leaf (see Note, page 46)

3 pounds (1.35 kg) small shrimp, peeled and deveined (see page 33)

1 tablespoons plus 2 teaspoons kosher salt, plus more as needed

½ teaspoon cracked black pepper, plus more as needed

⅛ teaspoon cayenne pepper, plus more as needed

2 tablespoons hot sauce, preferably Original Louisiana Hot Sauce, plus more as needed

1 small ripe tomato, cored

Cooked rice (see page 209), for serving

¼ cup (13 g) finely chopped fresh flat-leaf parsley, for garnish

¼ cup (20 g) finely chopped green onions, for garnish

My mom, Maxine, uses only shrimp in her okra gumbo. A purist at heart, she doesn't want to overwhelm the shrimp's flavor with meat. She wants her shrimp—the very best—to stand out. Her gumbo is subtle, modest, and timeless. The perfect shrimp, a few vegetables, a couple of seasonings, and her Magnalite pot bring her gumbo to life. It's so simple yet achingly difficult to mimic its flavor. When I get it just right, I feel in sync with her. This is the ultimate gumbo, the one against which I judge all others.

Don't rush these steps. Gumbo is about developing flavors and letting them marry—it takes time for something this good to come together.

Warm a heavy-bottomed soup pot or Dutch oven over medium heat for 2 minutes, then add the oil and heat for 30 seconds. Add the onions and cook, stirring occasionally, until golden and translucent, about 30 minutes.

Stir the smothered okra into the onions, add the bay leaf, and reduce the heat to its lowest setting. Cover and let smother together, stirring occasionally, for about 10 minutes.

Put the shrimp in a large bowl and season with the salt, black pepper, cayenne, and hot sauce. Let sit at room temperature to marinate while the vegetables cook.

Add the tomato to the vegetables and stir to combine. Cover and let smother until the tomato has completely broken down, about 45 minutes.

Stir the shrimp into the vegetables, cover, and smother for 10 minutes.

Add 3 quarts (3 L) room-temperature water and stir to combine. Raise the heat to medium and bring the liquid to a simmer, then reduce the heat to maintain a simmer and cook for 20 minutes more to let the flavors marry. Taste and adjust the seasoning.

Serve the gumbo over rice, garnished with the parsley and green onions.

Gumbo, Act II:
Okra = Gombo

IN MY RESEARCH into the truths and myths of gumbo and okra, I often turn to food historian Jessica Harris. She has made it her life's work to ensure that the contributions of enslaved Africans to America's culinary traditions do not go unacknowledged.

The origins of okra in Louisiana can be traced along slave routes back to West Africa. Where Bantu is spoken in West Africa, New Guinea, and the present-day Democratic Republic of Congo, okra is referred to as *gombo*, which is also the word for "okra" in French; enslaved Africans from Angola called okra *ngumbo*. The vegetable was brought to the American South by way of the slave trade around 1719, and along with the okra itself, enslaved Africans brought their knowledge of planting, harvesting, and cooking with it.

The gumbo plot thickens: accounts of enslaved Africans in New Orleans mixing cooked okra and rice to make a meal date back to 1764. This was a form of what we would now consider okra gumbo. The Africans used okra and New World ingredients as the base for their gumbo, augmenting it with any less-desirable cuts of meat their owners had discarded.

Without Africans bringing their ingredients and cooking traditions to South Louisiana, the gumbo many of us are accustomed to would likely never have existed. They prepared soups thickened with okra in plantation kitchens. They taught us how to use ingredients from their home country. Their contributions to the gumbo I enjoy and create now are unmistakable.

MOSQUITO SUPPER CLUB'S SHRIMP, OKRA, AND CRAB GUMBO

SERVES 8 TO 10

3 tablespoons canola oil or leaf lard

4 pounds (1.8 kg) yellow onions, finely diced

2 cups (450 g) Smothered Okra (page 265)

3 bay leaves (see Note, page 46)

1 large ripe tomato, cored

16½ cups (4 L) chicken stock (page 304)

4 pounds (1.8 kg) head-on small shrimp, peeled and deveined (see page 33), heads reserved

2½ cups (310 g) finely diced celery

1½ cups (220 g) finely diced green bell peppers

6 small gumbo crabs (1½ pounds/680 g), cleaned (see page 81) and cracked in half

1 tablespoon plus 2 teaspoons kosher salt, plus more as needed

1 tablespoon cracked black pepper, plus more as needed

½ teaspoon cayenne pepper, plus more as needed

2 tablespoons hot sauce, preferably Original Louisiana Hot Sauce, plus more as needed

Cooked rice (see page 209), for serving

¼ cup (13 g) finely chopped fresh flat-leaf parsley, for garnish

¼ cup (20 g) finely chopped green onions, for garnish

I came to this recipe by drawing on what I've learned from cooking my mom's gumbo and the flavors I encountered from eating gumbos all my life. It captures the flavors of the gumbos I love. There's a simplicity in the trio of shrimp, okra, and onions. You can pick out their distinct flavors as three separate entities brought together by liquid. This gumbo builds on this basic combination, but it is richer, bolder, and more complex. Enhancing the base with stock, celery, bell pepper, and a bit more okra builds in more flavor. And it includes crabs, which infuse the gumbo with another layer of bayou essence and are as visually stunning as they are delicious.

Making this gumbo takes time and patience. You'll need about four hours to gradually build layers of flavor into the gumbo. Don't rush this process. Gumbo is always better the next day. So if you're having a dinner party, cook the gumbo the night before. Serve it with Pickled Okra (page 300) and Potato Salad (page 280) alongside.

Warm a large heavy-bottomed soup pot or Dutch oven over medium heat for 3 minutes, then add the oil and heat for 1 minute. Add the onions and cook, stirring occasionally, until golden brown, about 45 minutes.

Add the smothered okra and the bay leaves and stir. Reduce the heat to its lowest setting, cover, and let them smother together for about 20 minutes, until they are soft and have lost their bite. Crush the tomato into the pot using your hands. Cover and smother for 20 minutes more.

Meanwhile, in a large saucepan, combine the stock and shrimp heads and bring to a simmer over medium heat. Reduce the heat to low and simmer while you cook the vegetables, about 1 hour, to infuse the stock with the flavor of the shrimp. Strain the stock, discarding the solids, and return it to the pan. Keep warm until ready to use.

Add the celery and bell peppers to the pot with the other vegetables and stir to combine. Cover and smother until the tomato has completely broken down and the celery and bell peppers are very soft, with no bite remaining, about 20 minutes.

Continued →

Put the crabs in a large bowl and season with 1 tablespoon of the salt, ½ teaspoon of the black pepper, the cayenne, and 1 tablespoon of the hot sauce; let sit for 10 minutes. Add the crabs to the pot and smother with the vegetables, uncovered, for 10 minutes, building a layer of crab essence into the gumbo.

Add the stock to the gumbo and simmer for 1 hour, until the liquid is a deep brown, the color of peanut butter.

Meanwhile, put the shrimp in a large bowl and season with the remaining 2 teaspoons salt, ½ teaspoon black pepper, and 1 tablespoon hot sauce and let marinate.

Add the shrimp to the pot and simmer, uncovered, for 15 to 20 minutes.

Taste the gumbo and adjust the seasoning.

Serve the gumbo over rice, garnished with the parsley and green onions.

CHICKEN AND OKRA GUMBO

SERVES 6 TO 8

3 tablespoons canola oil

3 pounds (1.35 kg) yellow onions, finely diced

1 (5-pound/2.3 kg) good-quality whole chicken (see sidebar, page 178), cut into 8 pieces, skin removed

2½ tablespoons kosher salt, plus more as needed

½ teaspoon cracked black pepper, plus more as needed

½ teaspoon cayenne pepper, plus more as needed

2 tablespoons hot sauce, preferably Original Louisiana Hot Sauce, plus more as needed

2 cups (450 g) Smothered Okra (page 265)

1 bay leaf (see Note, page 46)

1¼ cups (160 g) finely diced green bell peppers

1¼ cups (135 g) finely diced celery

12½ cups (3 L) chicken stock (page 304), plus more as needed

Cooked rice (see page 209), for serving

¼ cup (13 g) finely chopped fresh flat-leaf parsley, for garnish

¼ cup (20 g) finely chopped green onions, for garnish

There are two ways you can approach this gumbo: You can sear skin-on chicken in the pot, then remove the chicken and cook the onions in the fat and debris the chicken left behind, or you can follow the directions below and remove the skin from the chicken to give the gumbo a cleaner taste. Some people think it's sacrilegious to remove the skin—there's a lot of flavor in there. I respect that school of thought, but I think leaving the skin on the chicken makes the gumbo fattier and requires more skimming during simmering. With or without the chicken skin, this gumbo is excellent.

Warm a heavy-bottomed soup pot or Dutch oven over medium heat for about 2 minutes, then add the oil and heat for 30 seconds. Add the onions and cook, stirring often, until golden brown, about 45 minutes.

Meanwhile, put the chicken in a large bowl and season with the salt, black pepper, cayenne, and hot sauce. Set aside to marinate at room temperature while the vegetables cook.

Stir the smothered okra into the onions, add the bay leaf, and reduce the heat to its lowest setting. Cover and let the vegetables smother together for about 20 minutes to let the flavors marry.

Add the bell peppers and celery and stir. Cover and smother together until the bell peppers and celery are very soft, about 20 minutes.

Move all the vegetables to one side of the pot and place the chicken pieces on the bottom of the pot. Rearrange the vegetables so they cover the chicken. Reduce the heat to low and cook, covered, for 30 minutes.

Add the stock and bring to a simmer over medium heat. Reduce the heat to maintain a simmer and cook until the chicken is falling off the bone, about 1 hour 30 minutes.

Turn off the heat and let the gumbo sit, covered, for 1 hour before serving. Taste and adjust the seasoning—I usually add a lot of hot sauce at the end because I like my gumbo to have a vinegary flavor.

Serve the gumbo over rice, garnished with the parsley and green onions.

MAXINE'S CHICKEN GUMBO

SERVES 6 TO 8

3 tablespoons canola oil

3 pounds (1.35 kg) yellow onions, finely diced

1 (5-pound/2.3 kg) good-quality whole chicken (see sidebar, page 178), cut into 8 pieces, skin removed

3 tablespoons kosher salt, plus more as needed

½ teaspoon cracked black pepper, plus more as needed

½ teaspoon cayenne pepper, plus more as needed

2 tablespoons plus 2 teaspoons hot sauce, preferably Original Louisiana Hot Sauce, plus more as needed

½ cup (55 g) finely diced celery

¼ cup (35 g) finely diced green bell pepper

3 bay leaves (see Note, page 46)

12½ cups (3 L) chicken stock (page 304) or water

Cooked rice (see page 209), for serving

¼ cup (13 g) finely chopped fresh flat-leaf parsley, for garnish

¼ cup (20 g) finely chopped green onions, for garnish

Potato Salad (page 280), for serving

Filé powder, for serving

This is the chicken gumbo I grew up with. My mom made it every week. It's still the leftovers I look for in her fridge when I go home to visit. It's a thin gumbo, made without roux, but it's brothy and rich, with simple parsley and green onions cutting the layered flavors of the onions and poultry.

Warm a heavy-bottomed soup pot or Dutch oven over medium heat for 3 minutes, then add the oil and heat for 1 minute. Add the onions and cook, stirring often, until soft and golden brown, about 30 minutes.

Put the chicken in a large bowl and season with the salt, black pepper, cayenne, and hot sauce. Set aside to marinate at room temperature while the vegetables cook.

Add the celery, bell pepper, and bay leaves to the onions and reduce the heat to its lowest setting. Cover and let the vegetables smother together until the celery and bell pepper are very soft, with no bite remaining, about 20 minutes.

Move all the vegetables to one side of the pot and place the chicken pieces on the bottom of the pot. Rearrange the vegetables so they cover the chicken. Raise the heat to medium and brown the chicken for 8 minutes, then flip the chicken onto the other side to cook for another 8 minutes. Reduce the heat to its lowest setting and let everything smother together for 20 minutes.

Add the stock and bring to a simmer over medium heat. Reduce the heat to maintain a simmer and cook until the chicken is falling off the bone, 45 minutes to 1 hour. Keep the heat low so you don't boil off all the liquid; if the gumbo looks dry, just add some more stock.

Turn off the heat and let the gumbo sit, uncovered, for 1 hour before serving. Taste and adjust the seasoning—I usually add a lot of hot sauce at the end because I like my gumbo to have a vinegary flavor.

Serve the gumbo over rice, garnished with the parsley and green onions, with potato salad alongside. Pass the filé at the table for everyone to add as they like.

THE BEST CHICKEN GUMBO

Chicken gumbo is best made with a mean, tired old hen. It's time to take her out of her misery and cook her into a gumbo—that's what the Cajuns used to do. No one cooked with young chickens; those were for producing eggs. The older hens were destined for the pot. The tougher meat on an older bird holds up to a lot of simmering. It takes longer for that tough meat to break down, but when it does, it's perfect. A younger bird cooks quicker, but you have to skirt the line between long cooking and not drying out the meat. That's why Cajun ladies swore by old hens for long-simmered gumbos.

Unfortunately, unless you're raising your own birds, getting your hands on an older hen isn't a reality anymore. Chickens are typically slaughtered when they are six to seven weeks old. Try asking a local farmer for an older hen. If you can't get ahold of one, just buy a good-quality organic bird, raised without antibiotics, that lived a happy chicken life (see page 22 for more on good chickens).

Once you've got the right bird, you can make chicken gumbo any way you like.

The Shades of Roux

The different colors of roux are the result of how long you cook the mixture. Whichever roux you choose, just remember the guiding principle: mix slowly, continuously, and with intention.

A *blond roux* is a quick roux cooked for 10 to 15 minutes and is the color of condensed milk; it can be used for bisque, gumbos, stew, and gratins.

A *medium roux* is brown, ranging anywhere from the color of café au lait to that of peanut butter, and is used for gumbos, stews, and étouffées.

A *dark roux*—cooked for 15 to 30 minutes— moves into the brown shades ranging from milk chocolate to dark chocolate and is used in some gumbos.

Gumbo, Act III:
To Roux or Not to Roux

A ROUX IS a mixture of equal parts flour and fat—cooking oil, bacon grease, leaf lard, duck fat, chicken fat, or butter—stirred together into a paste that can be used to thicken sauces, soups, gumbos, stews, étouffées, and more. If developed properly, roux also adds layers of complex flavor to a dish. Roux has been around for over three hundred years in French cooking and is the basis for many French sauces, though the actual influence of French roux on gumbo is debatable. Understanding roux, its significance in Cajun cooking, and its influence on gumbo throughout South Louisiana is essential.

Yet I can't say dark roux-based gumbo is my favorite kind. It is rich and decadent, and I prefer my gumbo on the lighter and thinner side. If you ask folks in Terrebonne Parish if they make roux for their gumbo, most of them will say no. Gumbos in this part of the state don't use roux as a thickener. Really thick dark-roux gumbos are more common in restaurants than in Cajun homes. I had never had a gumbo dark, rich, and thick from roux until I lived in New Orleans and tried the ones served in restaurants there. You won't find a roux-based gumbo in Cajun homes on the bayou, but roux certainly have their place in classic Louisiana dishes.

Like building a relationship, making a roux is a process that cannot be rushed. It is about developing flavor and waiting patiently for the complexities to show themselves. It's about committing to standing at the stove and gracefully stirring with a wooden spoon, communing with the flour, fat, and heat. Even if a bit splashes up and burns you, you can't quit—just stir more slowly and less aggressively. Stay light on your feet, and know that after you've put in the hard work, your best intentions will be palpable and present in the final dish.

Once the flour and fat are combined, the roux is cooked and stirred until it reaches the desired shade (your recipe will tell you what that color should be). As a rule, the longer you stir, the darker the roux. There are many different shades of roux, and they are used in many different Cajun dishes. They can be made with different fats and cooked to varying degrees of darkness. I like a 30-minute butter-and-flour roux for étouffées and a 30-minute oil-and-flour roux for stews. I sometimes

make a 30-minute leaf lard–and–flour roux to thicken crab stew. One of my favorite roux is duck fat and flour for a duck gumbo.

I have seen misguided recipes for roux. A well-respected newspaper once published a recipe for making roux in a microwave. To me, that's like speed dating. My advice: Don't do either.

Restaurants sometimes start their roux on the stovetop and finish it in the oven. To do so, start the roux in a cast-iron skillet, cook it to the color of café au lait, then place it in a preheated 350°F (180°C) oven and cook, stirring every 10 minutes, until it has darkened to the desired color. This method works, but there's no romance to it—romance is slowing down and stirring with a wooden spoon, allowing the roux to happen.

DUCK GUMBO

SERVES 6 TO 8

1 (5-pound/2.3 kg) whole duck, cut into 8 pieces, skin removed and reserved

1 tablespoon kosher salt, plus more as needed

1 teaspoon cracked black pepper, plus more as needed

1 teaspoon cayenne pepper, plus more as needed

2 tablespoons hot sauce, preferably Original Louisiana Hot Sauce, plus more as needed

Canola oil, if needed

1½ cups (190 g) all-purpose flour

3½ pounds (1.6 kg) yellow onions, finely diced

½ cup (55 g) finely diced celery

¼ cup (35 g) finely diced green bell pepper

6 garlic cloves, chopped

3 bay leaves (see Note, page 46)

16½ cups (4 L) duck stock (see page 305) or chicken stock (page 304), warmed

Cooked rice (see page 209), for serving

¼ cup (13 g) finely chopped fresh flat-leaf parsley, for garnish

¼ cup (20 g) finely chopped green onions, for garnish

Pickles (see pages 300–303), for serving

Potato Salad (page 280), for serving

If I'm celebrating a special occasion, I pick up a duck to make this gumbo. Be sure to start with a sustainably raised duck. They're not easy animals to raise, so finding a good source can be tricky. Wild ducks are sustainable, of course. Their diet makes their meat taste clean and earthy, as if they've already been seasoned and need just a little salt. During the holidays, my father always has wild ducks for me to cook, but organic free-range ducks are available at butchers and online. The farm-raised variety is meaty and makes for a delicious gumbo.

Put the duck in a large bowl and season with the salt, black pepper, cayenne, and hot sauce. Set aside to marinate at room temperature.

Put the duck skin in a heavy-bottomed pot and cook over medium-low heat, turning occasionally, until all the fat is rendered. Don't let the fat burn; if it looks like it's getting too hot, reduce the heat to low. Strain the fat through a sieve into a liquid measuring cup and discard the solids. You should have 1 cup (240 ml) fat; if you don't have enough rendered fat, go ahead and add some oil.

Return the fat to the pot and set it over medium heat. Add the flour and cook, stirring continuously with a wooden spoon, until the roux is the color of milk chocolate, about 45 minutes.

Add the onions and stir well. (Be careful to avoid splattering the roux when adding the onions—this is when folks sometimes burn themselves.) Cook, stirring occasionally, until the onions are golden brown, about 45 minutes.

Add the celery, bell pepper, garlic, and bay leaves, stir well, and reduce the heat to its lowest setting. Cover and let the vegetables smother until very soft, without any bite remaining, about 20 minutes.

Push the vegetables to the side of the pot and place the duck pieces in the pot. Raise the heat to medium and brown the duck for about 8 minutes per side. Be careful not to bring the heat up too high and burn the vegetables.

Add 1 cup (240 ml) of the stock to deglaze the bottom and scrape up any bits stuck to the bottom of the pot. Reduce the heat to low, cover, and smother until the duck starts releasing liquid, about 20 minutes.

Add the remaining 15½ cups (3.7 L) stock and bring to a simmer over medium heat. Reduce the heat to maintain a simmer and cook until the duck is falling off the bone, about 1 hour 30 minutes. Taste and adjust the seasoning.

Serve the gumbo over rice, garnished with the parsley and green onions, with pickles and potato salad on the side.

NOTE: *Instead of rendering it yourself, you can buy duck fat from a butcher shop or online.*

HOW TO USE A ROUX

There are different schools of thought when it comes to cooking with a roux. Some folks make a roux, reserve it, and then whisk it into the gumbo as a final step. Other folks start by making a roux and then forge ahead with their gumbo in the same pot. You can do either. I've done it both ways with good results, so pick the method you prefer.

GUMBO Z'HERBES

SERVES 6 TO 8

1 pound (455 g) salt pork, homemade (see page 239) or store-bought, diced

Canola oil or leaf lard, if needed

1½ cups (190 g) all-purpose flour

6 pounds (2.7 kg) yellow onions, finely diced

½ pound (225 g) collard greens

½ pound (225 g) turnip greens

½ pound (225 g) kale

½ pound (225 g) Swiss chard

8 garlic cloves, finely chopped

3 bay leaves (see Note, page 46)

1 cup (180 g) finely diced green bell pepper

1 cup (110 g) finely diced celery

16½ cups (4 L) chicken stock (page 304)

1 (1½-pound/680 g) pork bone or ham hock

2½ tablespoons kosher salt, plus more as needed

1 teaspoon cracked black pepper, plus more as needed

½ teaspoon cayenne pepper, plus more as needed

2 tablespoons hot sauce, preferably Original Louisiana Hot Sauce, plus more as needed

Cooked rice (see page 209), for serving

¼ cup (13 g) finely chopped fresh flat-leaf parsley, for garnish

¼ cup (20 g) finely chopped green onions, for garnish

Pre–Hurricane Katrina, I was a young woman who wanted to cook. During a benefit in the French Quarter at Muriel's (a restaurant that overlooks Jackson Square, the Cabildo, and St. Louis Cathedral), I had the honor of being in the kitchen with the late, great Leah Chase as she served her famous gumbo z'herbes, a pinnacle moment for me.

Gumbo z'herbes, also known as green gumbo or herb gumbo, is an earthy gumbo packed with fresh greens straight from the garden. In New Orleans, folks would get their greens for the gumbo from the French Market. Traditionally, it was a vegetarian dish because many Catholic folks, my grandmother included, abstained from eating meat on Friday—especially on Good Friday, a day when gumbo z'herbes is historically served. (But this being South Louisiana, the dish isn't entirely vegetarian; the gumbo is simmered with a ham bone.)

I never ate green gumbo growing up on the bayou, but I make it often now, because I can never get enough greens. According to folklore, for every green you add to the pot, you will make a new friend in the coming year. Use whatever greens you can find at your local market; there are no rules about how many or few varieties you add. You can use all the same type or mix radish, turnip, or mustard greens, spinach, or anything else. Adding thyme or other fresh herbs never hurts, either. Regardless of what you put in, the gumbo will be beautiful. As a bonus, if you keep this gumbo in your fridge so it's ready to eat throughout the week, you'll feel pretty good, too.

Warm a heavy-bottomed 4-gallon (15 L) soup pot over medium heat for 2 minutes. Add the salt pork and cook, turning as needed to brown it on all sides, about 12 minutes. Using a slotted spoon, transfer the pork to a plate and set aside. You should have about 1 cup (120 ml) rendered pork fat left in the pot—if you're under, add a little oil or leaf lard. You want the fat to be about ¼ inch deep.

Add the flour to the pot and cook, stirring continuously with a wooden spoon, until the roux is the color of café au lait, about 30 minutes.

Add the onions and stir to combine. Cook, stirring often to avoid sticking, until the onions are caramelized, about 45 minutes.

While the onions are cooking, wash and dry the collard greens, turnip greens, kale, and chard, then separate the leaves from the stems. Finely chop all the stems and cut all the leaves into strips

about 1 inch (2.5 cm) wide and 4 to 6 inches (10 to 15 cm) long. Set aside the stems and leaves separately.

Add the garlic and bay leaves to the onions and stir to combine. Cook until the garlic is fragrant and softened, about 5 minutes. Add the bell pepper, celery, and the stems of the greens and stir well. Reduce the heat to its lowest setting, cover, and let the vegetables smother together until very soft, with no bite remaining, about 45 minutes.

Add the stock and pork bone, return the salt pork to the pot, and season with the salt, black pepper, cayenne, and hot sauce. Bring to a simmer over medium heat, then reduce the heat to maintain a simmer and cook for about 1 hour 30 minutes to let the flavors marry.

Taste and adjust the seasoning. Turn off the heat and stir in the leaves from the greens. Let sit for 15 minutes before serving.

Serve the gumbo over rice, garnished with the parsley and green onions.

CAJUNS AND CREOLES

We have an ongoing debate about what constitutes Cajun cuisine, what delimits Creole cuisine, and how they overlap. But debating this is like asking folks to name the color of the sea: on first glance, the waters look blue, but on closer inspection, a whole spectrum of colors reveals itself. We need to recognize all the colors in the continuum of South Louisiana's cuisine, and acknowledge that the shades are more similar than commonly believed.

What is Cajun food? What is Creole food? And what are the differences? I get asked these questions regularly at Mosquito Supper Club. My answer is vague, because it's a long story with many explanations. Cajun cuisine and Creole cuisine are real and distinct, even though the lines between them can be blurred.

Let's think of this as a chain—a food chain, if you will. American Indians aided the original European settlers who came to North America; without that guidance, the settlers would not have survived. American Indians thus form the first link in our food chain. The intermingling of the first Spanish and French settlers with original inhabitants began the next links. The horrors of slavery displaced enslaved Africans all over the South. They added the most important link. Eventually, Acadians made their way from Canada's Maritime Provinces to the bayous and

marshes of West Louisiana, adding another link and strengthening the food chain. At the same time, other immigrant groups converged on South Louisiana: Portuguese, German, Irish, Isleño, Italian, Filipino, Croatian, Chinese, Sicilian, Caribbean—the links in the chain grew exponentially, the chain strengthened, and one of the most important regional cuisines in North America was born. This is Cajun, but this is Creole, too.

The word *creole* comes from the Spanish *criollo* (the Latin origin is "to create") and was most commonly used to describe a person of French or Spanish descent who was born in the New World. People born in Spain or France were Spanish or French; those born in Louisiana to French or Spanish parents were Creole.

"Creole" has also referred to a way of life—customs, religion, language, and traditions—brought by the French to South Louisiana. It has also been used to refer to geographical locations where different people settled in New Orleans—"the Creole part of town," for example. The word has referred to both high society and the poorest neighborhoods. It has simultaneously defined excellence and been riddled with negative connotations.

Cajun is a variant of "Acadian," meaning someone from Acadia, a region in the Canadian Maritime Provinces. (The name

"Acadia" itself may be a derivation of Arcadia, a region in ancient Greece often characterized as peaceful and pastoral.) Control of Acadia was contested by the British and the French throughout the fifteenth and sixteenth centuries, and in 1755, many French inhabitants of the region were exiled by the British. Some of these exiles made their way to South Louisiana, where they settled along the prairies, marshes, and bayou. Someone with ties to these original French settlers would be considered Cajun.

One hundred years ago on the bayou, "Creole" distinguished things as high quality. "Cajun" was used to describe people and things related to the original descendants of Acadia. Both words took on new meanings and are still evolving, for better or worse. I once read a comment thread online (which I definitely should have avoided) that lamented the existence of Cajun food, calling Cajuns "impostors," saying that they borrowed from more prominent groups and that the "Cajun" label was a marketing ploy popularized in the 1960s and '70s: Cajun seasoning, Cajun chicken sandwich, Cajun wings, and so on. The commercialization and Americanization of "Cajun" is undeniable, but if my French grandmother wasn't cooking Cajun food, then what was she cooking? In New Orleans, when the "Cajun encounter" tour bus passes me by, I always wave to the folks on board—I may be the most authentic Cajun encounter they'll have all day. (It certainly won't be when they feed marshmallows to alligators.)

I grew up Cajun, but I've come to know Creole from twenty-plus years of living in New Orleans, eating and studying Creole foods, and collecting and reading Creole cookbooks. I know Creole from the restaurants and architecture that surround me. I understand the Creole architecture that was adopted in New Orleans and is suited to our humid conditions. I know the difference between a Creole *cala* and a beignet. I know that growing up Cajun, I never ate trout meunière or trout amandine. I also never saw a mushroom except during family outings to the fanciest restaurant in Houma, Louisiana—the Pizza Hut. But in Creole restaurants, mushrooms are commonplace, and fish are smothered in mushroom-rich shrimp Diane sauce. I never ate oysters Rockefeller, eggs Sardou, or hollandaise sauce—all classic French preparations—in my mom's kitchen. My French-speaking family did not grow up with this cuisine. There were no rich sauces in the kitchens of my childhood; the foods served were cleaner and not accompanied by emulsified butter sauces. In higher-end Creole restaurants, however, these classic French dishes share a menu with the Creole food I have come to love in New Orleans. The Creole food I feel connected to is the cuisine found in New Orleans's oldest neighborhoods. That Creole food is the history book of New Orleans. Disney did a fun job of animating this in *The Princess and the Frog*, which was inspired by Leah Chase (see page 184).

The idea that Creole is fancy or aristocratic, even highbrow, and Cajun is

country or peasant never sits well with me. Creole food is the food of New Orleans as a city, but its roots are far removed from the place that made it famous. Cajun is rustic, yes, but the Creole food I eat on the streets of Tremé or at a church benefit is just as rustic. Cajun food is peasant food, but at one time, the cooks in Creole plantation kitchens were enslaved Africans. The two cuisines developed across South Louisiana based on the ingredients that women, cooks, chefs, and enslaved Africans could obtain and

the knowledge they held and passed down from generation to generation. Creole food developed in and around the city of New Orleans, where cooks had access to many more ingredients than Cajuns did on the bayou. Cajuns weren't entirely cut off from the city, but they made do with a lot less. As writer and historian Lolis Eric Elie says, we are hybrids of each other because of cultural sharing. Some of those ingredients came together to create Louisiana's most famous dish: gumbo.

POULTRY, MEAT, AND RICE

ONE OF THE DIFFERENCES BETWEEN GROWING

up Cajun on the bayou and growing up in the northern parishes (or "Cajun prairie country") was the availability of seafood and meat. Parishes that weren't located on the bayou weren't immersed in the seafood industry, and eating seafood wasn't an everyday occurrence.

In Cajun prairie country, meat markets, known as *boucheries* (French for "butcher shops"), were more common than shrimp docks and oyster docks. Jambalayas were chicken- and sausage-based, not seafood-based, and the use of pork products and dishes such as rice and gravy (see page 203) were common on tables. Cajun prairie country is known for its sausages: smoked andouille, smoked green onion sausage, and boudin, to name a few.

My great-grandparents raised cows, but not for slaughter; the cows were primarily used for their milk. The family never consumed meat unless it was for special occasions, a practice that mirrored life in Acadia. When my grandfather was able to sell a load of oysters and make a little money, he would bring home a piece of beef from the local butcher so his wife could cook it for the family. She would cut the meat into small pieces and cook it in a slow stovetop braise for a couple of hours, until it was just starting to fall apart. The meat was served with gravy over rice. Even when meat became more readily available, my grandmother, a devout Catholic, never ate meat on Fridays, and rarely cooked it otherwise. In the Cajun kitchen I grew up in, meat was usually beef and poultry, and it was always eaten with or stretched with rice. The only pork we ate was salt pork.

In other parishes across the state, boucheries were prevalent. At a boucherie, animals are slaughtered and readied for sale—and for Cajuns, a day of boucherie is an art form and family affair. This mirrors Acadian life. Every part of the pig is preserved, cooked, or turned into sausages; cracklins are fried fresh; and festivals in Cajun prairie country celebrate with a *cochon de lait*, a suckling pig roasted on a spit over an open fire.

A dish made in a kitchen in the coastal parishes may be distinctly different from one by the same name made in prairie Cajun country, and all across Acadiana, there are variations on our language, lives, and preferred ingredients. Yet for all our differences, when you're Cajun, there is an overarching feeling of belonging to something bigger.

SMOTHERED CHICKEN

SERVES 6 TO 8

1 (5-pound/2.3 kg) good-quality whole chicken (see sidebar, page 178), cut into 8 pieces (see Note) and skin removed

1 tablespoon kosher salt, plus more as needed

1 teaspoon cracked black pepper, plus more as needed

1 teaspoon cayenne pepper, plus more as needed

2 tablespoons hot sauce, preferably Original Louisiana Hot Sauce, plus more as needed

¼ cup (60 ml) canola oil

3 pounds (1.35 kg) yellow onions, finely diced

1 tablespoon water or chicken stock (page 304), plus more as needed

1¼ cups (135 g) finely diced celery

½ cup (70 g) finely diced green bell pepper

Cooked rice (see page 209), for serving

¼ cup (13 g) finely chopped fresh flat-leaf parsley, for garnish

¼ cup (20 g) finely chopped green onions, for garnish

Smothered—or choked—chicken is made using the age-old technique of slow cooking. The latter name comes from the actual act of wringing a bird's neck and the former from smothering the bird slowly in a heavy-bottomed pot with onions, celery, and bell pepper. You can add garlic, if you like, or if you want heat, add fresh or dried hot peppers. Add fresh or dried savory, marjoram, thyme, or any herbs you like to enhance the flavor, or try it with rosemary and potatoes. Throw in one or two tomatoes. The options are endless. Have patience with this meal—it will take nearly two hours to make, but it's worth the wait.

Put the chicken in a large bowl and season with the salt, black pepper, cayenne, and hot sauce. Set aside to marinate at room temperature for 15 minutes.

Warm a heavy-bottomed 4-gallon (15 L) Dutch oven over medium heat for 2 minutes, then add the oil and heat for 30 seconds. Add the chicken and cook until browned on both sides, about 5 minutes on each side. Add the onions and the water and stir vigorously to scrape up any browned bits from the bottom of the pot.

Reduce the heat to its lowest setting, cover the pot, and smother the chicken for 20 minutes. Add the celery and bell pepper and stir to combine. Cover and smother together until the chicken is falling off the bone, 1 hour 40 minutes, giving the pot a quick stir every 20 minutes. If it looks dry, add a bit of stock or water. (Usually the chicken and vegetables will release enough liquid that you don't need to add any, but sometimes they need a little help. Adding a cup or two of stock won't hurt anything.)

Taste the finished product and season with salt and black pepper, if needed. If you'd like more heat, add a touch more cayenne or hot sauce.

Serve the chicken over rice, garnished with the parsley and green onions.

NOTE: *When you break down the chicken, save any offal for another meal and save the backbone to use for stock—just pack them in bags, label, and store them in your freezer for up to 3 months.*

STUFFED BELL PEPPERS

SERVES 12

12 bell peppers (about
5 ounces/140 g each)

3 pounds (1.35 kg) ground
pork

1 pound (455 g) mixed
chicken and duck offal
(livers, gizzards, and hearts),
ground

1 tablespoon plus 1 teaspoon
kosher salt, plus more as
needed

1 teaspoon freshly ground
black pepper, plus more as
needed

⅛ teaspoon cayenne pepper

1 tablespoon hot sauce,
preferably Original
Louisiana Hot Sauce

2 tablespoons canola oil

2 pounds (910 g) yellow
onions, finely diced

1 cup (110 g) finely diced
celery

2 garlic cloves, finely diced

1 tomato, diced

5 cups (975 g) cooked rice
(see page 209)

8 cups (540 g) cubed
country bread (cubes a little
larger than 1 inch/2.5 cm)

2 tablespoons unsalted
butter, melted

Bell peppers show up in almost every Cajun recipe. They're delicious raw or cooked, and they really shine when stuffed with pork, offal, and rice.

Cut off the tops of the bell peppers and scoop out the seeds and membranes. Discard the stems, then dice the tops and set aside.

Put the pork and offal in a large bowl and season with the salt, black pepper, cayenne, and hot sauce. Use your hands to incorporate the ingredients.

Warm a heavy-bottomed pot over medium heat for 3 minutes, then coat the bottom with the oil. Add the meat mixture and cook, stirring, until browned and just barely cooked through, about 8 minutes. Using a slotted spoon, transfer the meat mixture to a clean large bowl or a baking sheet. Skim off any excess fat.

Return the pot to medium heat. Add the onions and cook, stirring often, until translucent, 15 to 20 minutes. Add the celery, diced bell pepper tops, and garlic and cook until the vegetables are soft, about 15 minutes.

Preheat the oven to 350°F (180°C).

Add the tomato to the pot with the vegetables, reduce the heat to low, and cook for 10 minutes, stirring occasionally. Season with salt and black pepper. Turn off the heat, add the rice and the meat mixture, and stir to combine. Let sit for about 15 minutes.

Meanwhile, bring a large pot of water to a rolling boil. Fill a large bowl with ice and water. Carefully add the bell peppers to the boiling water and blanch for 4 minutes, then transfer to the bowl of ice water. Line a baking sheet with a clean dish towel, then remove the peppers from the ice water and set them upside down on the towel to drain.

Dry the bell peppers with a dish towel and stand them upright in a large casserole dish. Stuff them with the filling, dividing it evenly. Top with the cubed bread and melted butter. Bake for 30 minutes, uncovered, until the bread cubes are golden.

Serve warm with a side salad.

BRAISED DUCK LEGS

4 pounds (1.8 kg) skin-on duck legs (6 to 8 legs)

1 teaspoon kosher salt, plus more as needed

½ teaspoon freshly ground black pepper, plus more as needed

⅛ teaspoon cayenne pepper, plus more as needed

1 tablespoon canola oil

4 cups (1 L) chicken stock (page 304), plus more as needed

2 tablespoons cane syrup, preferably Steen's (see Resources, page 359), or molasses

2 tablespoons cane vinegar, preferably Steen's (see Resources, page 359), or apple cider vinegar

2 pounds (910 g) yellow onions, coarsely chopped

1 celery stalk, coarsely chopped

1 bay leaf (see Note, page 46)

Rice Dressing (page 208) or a green salad, for serving

Braised duck legs are the perfect dish to make during the late fall and winter months. For those on the bayou, that's when the rice has been harvested and the fields plowed over, and the frenzy of duck hunting season begins. The cooler air in Louisiana also means we can turn on our ovens for the long braising time this dish requires. This is a simple dish, and convenient, too, because you can make it ahead of time and it is easy to reheat.

Preheat the oven to 300°F (150°C).

Remove the duck legs from the fridge and set them on your counter for about 30 minutes to come to room temperature. Season the duck legs with the salt, black pepper, and cayenne.

Warm a heavy-bottomed flameproof roasting pan over medium heat. Add the oil and heat until it shimmers, then add the duck legs and sear until golden on both sides, about 4 minutes per side.

Pour 2 cups (480 ml) of the stock into the pan and stir, scraping up all the good bits from the bottom of the pan. Stir in the cane syrup and vinegar until combined, then add the remaining 2 cups (480 ml) stock; it should come halfway up the duck legs—if it doesn't, add more stock or water as needed.

Place the onions, celery, and bay leaf around the duck legs. Transfer the pan to the oven and braise until the meat is tender and easily pulled apart with a fork, about 2 hours. Every 20 minutes, dip a pastry brush into the liquid in the pan and brush the tops of the duck legs.

Remove the pan from the oven and transfer the duck legs to a platter. Strain the braising liquid into a small saucepan, discarding the solids. Skim the fat off the braising liquid, then cook over medium-high heat until thickened, about 10 minutes. Taste and adjust the seasoning.

Serve the duck legs over the rice dressing or with a delicious salad.

NOTE: *If you are using braised duck legs for another recipe, allow the legs to cool, then pick the meat off and refrigerate. Refrigerate the stock separately, and save the bones for stock at a later time. You can freeze them in a ziplock bag.*

DUCK JAMBALAYA

SERVES 8

½ cup (105 g) duck fat (see Note)

3 pounds (1.35 g) yellow onions, finely diced

⅓ cup (40 g) finely diced celery

½ cup (70 g) finely diced green bell pepper

1 bay leaf (see Note, page 46)

2½ pounds (1.2 kg) cooked duck meat (from Braised Duck Legs, page 199)

1 tablespoon kosher salt

¼ teaspoon freshly ground black pepper

¼ teaspoon cayenne pepper

2 tablespoons hot sauce, preferably Original Louisiana Hot Sauce

4 cups (740 g) medium-grain white rice

5 cups (1.3 L) duck stock (see page 305), plus more as needed

¼ cup (13 g) finely chopped fresh flat-leaf parsley, for garnish

¼ cup (20 g) finely chopped green onions, for garnish

To update my favorite childhood jambalaya, I switched the protein from shrimp to duck. The dish is prepared in the same straightforward, simple way, but the rich duck meat paired with stock, caramelized onions, and smothered vegetables makes a heartier entrée.

Some folks say duck meat is gamey, but I don't buy it. To me, duck meat is similar in flavor to the tastier dark meat of a chicken. Duck is fattier than chicken, so it cooks like a well-marbled steak, the fat continuously basting the meat as it renders so it doesn't dry out. And duck can handle the long cooking time this dish requires without losing its taste or texture. Buy your duck from a reputable source that raises the animal humanely.

Top duck jambalaya with sauerkraut or kimchi, or eat it with a crisp summer salad. It's a great dish to bring to a potluck, too—your friends will thank you.

Warm a heavy-bottomed 8-quart (8 L) Dutch oven over medium heat for 2 minutes, then add the duck fat. When it has melted, add the onions to the pot and stir, stir, stir. This starts the very long process of browning the onions. Cook the onions for about 1 hour, watching them very closely and stirring every 2 minutes. If the onions start to stick too much, add a little bit of water or stock to loosen them, then stir to incorporate the browner onions and scrape up any stuck-on bits from the bottom of the pot. Stir, stir, stir until the onions are deeply caramelized.

Add the celery, bell pepper, and bay leaf to the pot and stir. Cover and cook over low heat for 15 minutes, stirring every 5 minutes.

Meanwhile, put the duck in a large bowl and season with the salt, black pepper, cayenne, and hot sauce. Set aside to marinate at room temperature for 5 minutes.

Add the rice to the pot with the vegetables and stir to combine. Raise the heat to medium and cook, letting the flavors mingle and marry, for 5 minutes. Add the duck meat and stir to incorporate.

Add the stock and bring to a boil, then reduce the heat to low and simmer until the liquid has almost completely evaporated or looks like little puddles of water, about 8 minutes. When it's at the point of

puddling—this is a judgment call based on temperature, pot size, and your stove—put the lid on the pot and set the heat to its lowest setting. From here, the cooking time is going to be 45 minutes total, and you can't remove the lid the entire time. This is a tough, long 45 minutes. But trust yourself. You'll want to peek, but don't.

Set a timer for 20 minutes. When it goes off, turn off the heat and let the jambalaya sit, covered, for 25 minutes before you lift the lid. (If you live with a lot of people, you might want to make a note and place it near the stove: "Please do not lift the lid off the pot." This lets everyone know you did not stir onions for over an hour just to have someone uncover the pot and ruin your dish.)

After 45 minutes, uncover the pot and stir the jambalaya. There may be a little burnt rice on the bottom—this is called the "grat" or "gratin." It's some folks' favorite part of the jambalaya.

Serve the jambalaya garnished with the parsley and green onions.

NOTE: *You can buy duck fat from a butcher shop or online, or you can render your own by cooking it at a low temperature until it melts into liquid fat; then you can reserve it in the refrigerator for later use.*

BEEF RICE AND GRAVY

SERVES 8

3 pounds (1.35 kg) beef shoulder

1½ tablespoons kosher salt, plus more as needed

1 tablespoon freshly ground black pepper, plus more as needed

Pinch of cayenne pepper, plus more as needed

2 tablespoons canola oil

8 cups (2 L) beef stock

1 tablespoon cane vinegar, preferably Steen's (see Resources, page 359), or apple cider vinegar or sherry vinegar

1 teaspoon cane syrup, preferably Steen's (see Resources, page 359), or molasses

1 pound (455 g) yellow onions, finely diced

½ cup (55 g) finely diced celery

½ cup (70 g) finely diced green bell pepper

1 bay leaf (see Note, page 46)

Cooked rice (see page 209), for serving

Braising beef makes a delicious dish rich with gravy to serve over rice. In South Louisiana, we call this dish "en daube." In prairie Cajun country, the dish is called rice and gravy, and refers to any slow-cooked protein-rich gravy served over rice. It can be made with pork, beef, chicken, or any other meat or poultry. Serve it with green beans, lima beans, or peas.

Remove the beef shoulder from the fridge and set it on your counter for 30 to 45 minutes to come to room temperature (the timing will depend on the climate you're in). Season the beef with the salt, black pepper, and cayenne.

Warm a large heavy-bottomed pot over high heat for 4 minutes, then add the oil and heat for another 30 seconds. Add the beef and sear until dark golden brown on all sides, 5 to 7 minutes per side. Add 1 cup (240 ml) of the stock to the pot and use tongs to lift the beef (no need to remove it completely) so you can scrape up any bits stuck to the bottom of the pan.

Add the remaining stock, the vinegar, cane syrup, onions, celery, bell pepper, and bay leaf and bring the liquid to a simmer. Reduce the heat to maintain a simmer, cover, and cook for 3 to 4 hours, until the beef can be easily pulled apart with a fork.

Transfer the beef to a platter. Strain the braising liquid, discarding the solids, and return it to the pot. Cook the braising liquid over medium-high heat until thickened to the consistency of gravy (see Note), about 20 minutes. Taste and adjust the seasoning—add cayenne if you want a little heat. Pull the beef apart with forks.

Serve the shredded beef over rice, topped with the gravy.

NOTE: *If you need to thicken the gravy even further, you can add a cornstarch or flour slurry: Ladle about ½ cup (120 ml) of the cooking liquid into a small bowl and add ¼ cup (30 g) cornstarch or all-purpose flour. Whisk until you have a thick, smooth paste. Pour the paste into the pot with the rest of the liquid and whisk until combined, then cook until the gravy has thickened and reduced to the consistency you like.*

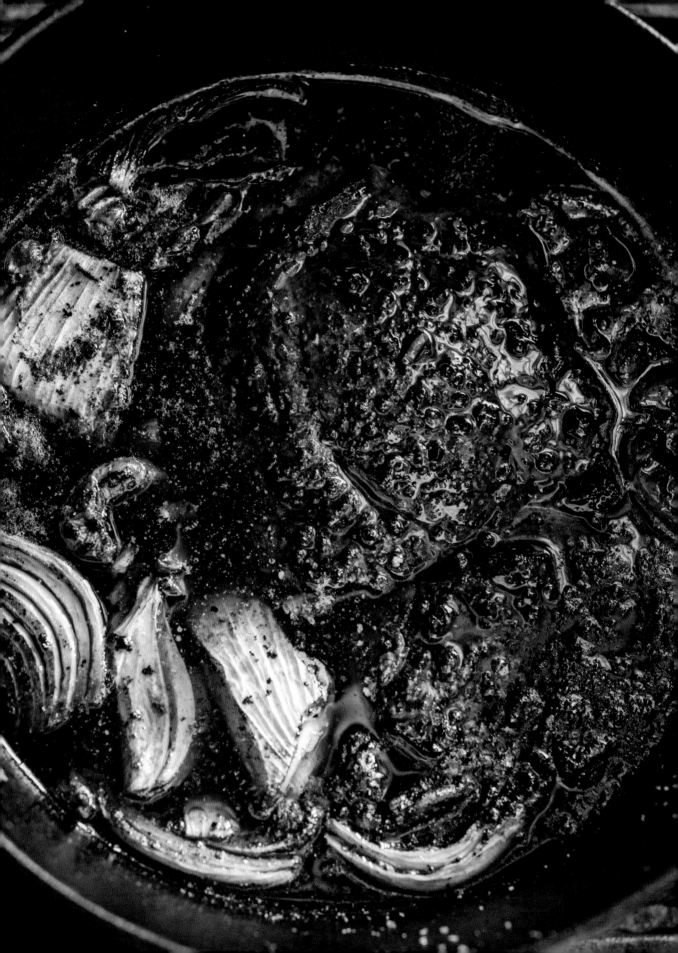

Rice and Crawfish

THE FARMING AND distributing of crawfish started around the 1970s with the genius move to farm crawfish and rice together. Even with local rice mill co-ops, it became difficult to make a living with a small rice farm. A farmer who could once support a family on a couple hundred acres now needed a couple *thousand* acres to turn a profit. Cajuns are known for their ingenuity, and it didn't take long for farmers to realize that they could use their fields to cultivate rice and farm crawfish harmoniously together.

Crawfish live in the rice fields, burrowing deep down into the mud and coming out of their hiding places in the fall when fields are flooded. Farmers could add a bit of seed crawfish—small young crawfish, 1 to 2 inches (2.5 to 5 cm)—and end up with a sizable harvest. Farmers took this natural rhythm and created a new culture.

It goes like this: Rice is planted in early March and April in about 2 inches (5 cm) of water. By early June, beautiful lush green rice fields blanket South Louisiana, and the rice is tall enough to keep the couple inches of water in which it's growing cool. The cool water is an optimal temperature for seed crawfish. Seed crawfish are brought from the Atchafalaya Basin and other sources and introduced into the rice fields. As the summer heat rises, the crawfish seek cooler temperatures and burrow into the mud. By late July and early August, the golden rice fields are ready for harvesting. The fields have dried out and hardened just enough to use a combine to harvest the rice. After the rice is harvested, the parts of the plant that remain will be food for crawfish in the fall. In late September, the rice fields are flooded and the crawfish can emerge from their underground hiding spots. The female crawfish can produce four hundred to nine hundred offspring multiple times in a season, with those offspring reaching market size after only ninety days.

Crawfish season can start as early as November and last until July, but most locals know that crawfish are best from February to April.

RICE DRESSING

SERVES 6 TO 8

½ pound (225 g) ground pork

½ pound (225 g) ground beef

¼ pound (110 g) duck or chicken gizzards and liver (see Note, page 195), ground

2 teaspoons kosher salt, plus more as needed

½ teaspoon freshly ground black pepper, plus more as needed

⅛ teaspoon cayenne pepper, plus more as needed

1 tablespoon hot sauce, preferably Original Louisiana Hot Sauce, plus more as needed

2 tablespoons canola oil

2 pounds (910 g) yellow onions, finely diced

½ cup (70 g) finely diced green bell pepper

½ cup (55 g) finely diced celery

¼ cup (20 g) minced garlic

½ cup (26 g) finely chopped fresh flat-leaf parsley

½ cup (40 g) finely chopped green onions

2 cups (390 g) cooked rice (see opposite)

Rice dressing is what the rest of the world calls "dirty rice" (thanks, Popeyes). Down on the bayou, we serve rice dressing with duck, chicken, roast beef, or turkey. It can be eaten alone or with delicious sides like sweet peas and green beans. This is an offal-heavy dressing and is always on the table for Thanksgiving and Christmas. You can make this recipe ahead of time and store it in the refrigerator for up to a week. In fact, it always tastes better the next day, after the flavors have had time to marry.

Put the pork, beef, gizzards, and liver in a large bowl. Season with the salt, black pepper, cayenne, and hot sauce. Using your hands, mix the ingredients until evenly combined.

Warm a heavy-bottomed pot over medium-high heat for 2 minutes, add the oil, and warm for 30 seconds. Add the meat mixture and cook, breaking up the meat with a wooden spoon as it cooks, until browned and crumbled, about 8 minutes. Using a slotted spoon, transfer the meat mixture to a clean large bowl. Reserve 1 tablespoon of the fat from the pot and drain the rest.

Return the pot to medium heat and add the reserved 1 tablespoon fat. Add the onions and cook, stirring occasionally, until golden, about 15 minutes. Add the bell pepper, celery, and garlic and cook for about 15 minutes, until the bell pepper and celery are soft, stirring every 5 minutes to make sure the vegetables aren't sticking.

Return the meat mixture to the pot, stir to combine, and cook for 10 minutes. Remove from the heat and stir in the parsley, green onions, and rice. Taste and adjust the seasoning.

Serve immediately, or let the dressing cool, then store it in an airtight container in the fridge to enjoy the next day—it will taste even better. Rice dressing keeps for a week in the refrigerator. Reheat before serving.

BOILED RICE

**MAKES ABOUT 6 CUPS
(1.2 KG)**

1 tablespoon kosher salt

**2 cups (400 g) medium-
grain white rice**

The rice cooker reigns supreme for some in South Louisiana. I've watched my aunts go through every brand and proclaim which cooker is the best, casting out all others. The Hitachi Chime-o-Matic rice cooker was long a mainstay in Cajun homes. Rumor has it that Japanese businessmen came to Louisiana knowing we eat rice with the frequency of Asians and marketed the rice cooker directly to us. But for my grandmother and my mom and me, our preferred method is to boil rice. Boiled rice stays fluffy and doesn't dry out, even a few days after cooking. If you're concerned about this method, have no fear—it's just like cooking pasta, and you can taste the rice along the way so you'll know when it's ready. Make extra, because you can always find a use for leftover rice.

In a large pot, combine 6 quarts (6 L) water and the salt and bring to a rolling boil over high heat. Add the rice and cook for 12 minutes. Strain the rice through a fine-mesh sieve, then spread it out on a baking sheet to cool for a few minutes before serving. Leftover rice can be stored in an airtight container in the refrigerator for up to 2 days.

LOUISIANA RICE

In Louisiana, the devotion to rice is extreme; we eat rice with almost everything. We use rice to stuff our peppers and add it to our boudin. Gumbo is served with rice; beans come with rice, and so does gravy. I remember once being told we ate rice because we were poor. Rice held the poverty stigma for some time, but it has shaken that identity. It helps that folks are starting to understand that peasant food is gourmet food. The whole farm-to-table movement is built on what is available seasonally, and in Louisiana our culinary roots were developed on that same sentiment.

Rice is not native to Louisiana or America; it was brought to America by enslaved Africans. Women hid rice seeds in their hair and used their expertise in growing it. The rice industry started in the Carolinas and swept through the South, eventually making its way to Louisiana. Like the sugar industry, the rice industry was built on the hard labor of enslaved Africans, under lethal conditions. Rice was not an important crop in Louisiana until after the Civil War, when it was grown on desolate sugar and cotton plantations. Like sugar, rice flourished because of Africans' expertise in growing it.

In South Louisiana's delta soil, rice grew prolifically. The soil held water like a sponge but was solid enough that farmers could maneuver equipment on it. Machinery, railroads, and mills revolutionized the rice industry, though not necessarily for the better. Big rice mills were located in New Orleans on North Peters Street or Rice Row. These mills relied on rice from the areas outside of New Orleans and easily moved rice via the railroad and the Port of Orleans. Eventually, rice growers wanted more control of their product and formed co-ops. Local producers gaining control of their product has been imperative to rice farmers' survival. The Falcon Mill in Crowley, Louisiana, remains the oldest family-run mill in the country, and Conrad Rice Mill in Bayou Teche is the oldest rice mill in America.

Today, with just under one thousand rice farms, Louisiana is the third-largest producer of rice in the United States, behind California and Arkansas. Our producers grow more than twenty different varieties of rice, and Louisiana supplies rice to the nation and exports rice, brown and white, around the world. Some rice is grown specifically for crawfish fields. We're also responsible for most of the rice in Kellogg's famed Rice Krispies cereal.

FISH

IN CHAUVIN, WE EAT REDFISH THAT IS REELED IN

by my dad, taken home, and immediately gutted. My uncle Gordon grills it on a pit with the skin and scales on (we call this "redfish on the half shell"). We'll eat it for dinner, and I'll have it for breakfast in the morning, too. Redfish is one of the best things I've ever had the privilege of eating. It's a bayou-to-fork moment that illustrates the old adage "Teach a man to fish . . ." (you know how it goes), which is magnified in life on the bayou.

My dad says he learned to fish when he was one year old on the bayou with his father. It's the same for most kids growing up in a fishing village. For us, fishing is a day-to-day activity for fun and to stock our larders. Fishing gives you a moment of peace, some solitude, and it puts dinner on the table.

There is something so wholesome, sustainable, and universal about fishing. Catching fish one by one with a rod and reel feels different from procuring other seafood in South Louisiana. There's the weight of a fighting fish, pitting yourself against the pull of nature, and then the win. Every time we reverently toss a fish into the ice chest, we appreciate its sacrifice. And when a fish is too small to keep, per permits and regulations set forth by our state, we carefully wiggle out the hook and toss the fish overboard before it dies.

Redfish and trout are especially celebrated in our region. These fish are for home use only, and selling them to restaurants is banned. So the only way to try Louisiana redfish or trout is to catch one yourself or have it in someone's home kitchen. Redfish is versatile, holds up on a grill, and can be smothered for some time in a thick stew known as a courtbouillon. It's delicate enough to be prepared raw and is mouthwatering when pan-sautéed; the flesh is buttery and rich. On the bayou, we like to fry our fish and serve it with green beans, red beans, white beans—any kind of bean. In the summer, we eat fish with a salad of cucumbers and tomatoes (see page 281) on the side; the rest of the year, we serve fish with lots of pickles and beans. We might smother or dredge fish for frying, but a good piece of fish simply needs salt and pepper and at most a squeeze of lemon to finish it off. Don't underestimate the taste of a beautiful poached fish in a rich fish broth for a simple meal any night of the week.

So you can enjoy fresh fish where you live, find a great fishmonger. Ask for line-caught domestic fish. Don't buy farmed fish, and certainly stay away from fish that's been shipped from somewhere else in the world. Look for the fish that swims closest to your home and is sustainable and not overfished. Or, if you live near the water, get a line and pole, and a fishing license, and forge ahead with your own fishing adventures.

Note: Fish is best cooked after it has been allowed to come to room temperature. I know doing this worries some people, but any protein needs a few minutes to acclimate to room temperature.

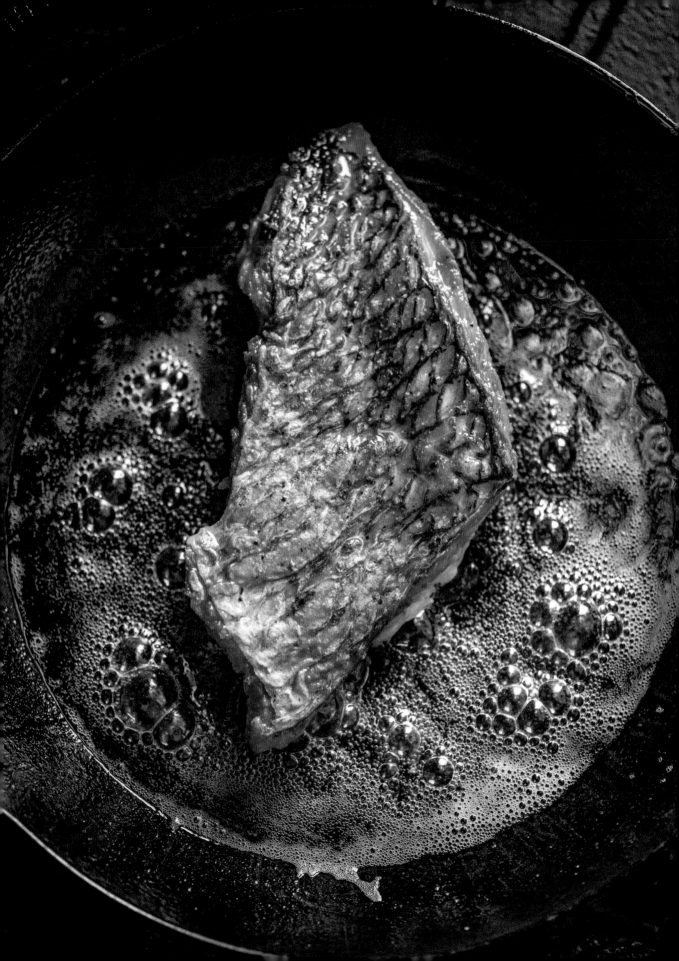

CRISP-SKINNED PANFRIED REDFISH

SERVES 2

1 pound (455 g) skin-on redfish fillets or any kind of white-fleshed fish fillets

⅛ teaspoon kosher salt, plus more as needed

Pinch of cracked black pepper or a couple turns of the pepper mill, plus more as needed

3 tablespoons canola oil

2 tablespoons unsalted butter

Lemon wedges, for serving

I'm not reinventing the wheel here. I just want to remind you of the beauty of panfried fish, especially one you've pulled right out of the water. There is nothing quite like it. A skin-on fish will be perfectly cooked if you follow the 80/20 rule: cook it 80 percent of the allotted time on the skin side and 20 percent on the flesh side.

Put the fish flesh-side down on paper towels or a clean dish towel. Season the skin side with the salt and pepper (this dries the skin out a bit so it gets crispier when you fry it). Let the fish sit until it comes to room temperature, 5 to 10 minutes.

Warm a cast-iron or other heavy-bottomed skillet over high heat. When your pan is just about to start to smoke, add the oil. Careful now—the oil is hot, but don't fear the heat. Turn the heat down just slightly to medium-high. Put the tip end of one fillet skin-side down in the hot oil on the side of the pan closest to you and lay it carefully toward the back of the stove, away from your body. Repeat with the other fillet. Use a fish spatula (see Note) to lightly press down on the fish to make sure it is making good contact with the pan. At this point, you can season the flesh side of the fish with a little more salt and pepper. Cook the fish until you achieve a cracker-like crust on the skin side, about 6 minutes. Tap it with your finger to check it. The edges should be crispy. Watch your heat level: you don't want your oil smoking, so turn it down slightly if you think the pan is getting too hot.

Gently flip the fish, add the butter to the pan, and cook on the flesh side until cooked through, 3 to 4 minutes. Tilt the pan toward you slightly so the butter pools at the bottom and use a spoon to ladle the butter over the fish. Baste the fish for 1 to 2 minutes. To determine if the fish is cooked all the way through, insert a paring knife into the flesh side. You should be able to slide it quickly in and out without any resistance.

Transfer the fish to a paper towel or a rack set over a pan and allow the excess oil to drain away. Serve with lemon wedges alongside.

NOTE: *A fish spatula is a slotted flat metal spatula, usually slightly offset from the handle. Having one makes it easy to flip delicate pieces of fish without breaking up the meat.*

TROUT MEUNIÈRE

SERVES 2

1 pound (455 g) skin-on trout fillets

1 teaspoon kosher salt, plus more as needed

2 egg yolks

1 cup (240 ml) buttermilk

1 tablespoon hot sauce, preferably Original Louisiana Hot Sauce

1 cup (125 g) all-purpose flour

½ teaspoon freshly ground black pepper

Pinch of cayenne pepper

½ cup (120 ml) clarified butter (see Note, page 89)

Cooked rice (see page 209), for serving

1 tablespoon finely chopped fresh flat-leaf parsley, for garnish

1 tablespoon finely chopped green onion, for garnish

Lemon wedges, for serving

Fresh corn, for serving (optional)

Cucumber and Tomato Salad (page 281), for serving (optional)

Meunière **translates to "miller's wife."** And in this tale, the miller's wife cooks everything with a little flour. In New Orleans, this dish is on the menu of many of the legendary restaurants. It's topped with almonds, smothered crawfish, lemons, pecans, or shrimp.

For this simple approach to meunière, dip the fish in an egg wash and coat it evenly with seasoned flour before frying. Fry the trout in clarified butter: regular butter has a smoke point of 350°F (180°C); clarified butter has a much higher smoke point. You want to panfry the fish at 375° to 400°F (190° to 200°C). If you can't find clarified butter, you can use a combination of canola oil and butter. The oil will help bring the butter smoke point up. Or you can make your own clarified butter.

Put the fish flesh-side down on paper towels or a clean dish towel. Season the skin side lightly with salt (this dries the skin out a bit so it gets crispier when you fry it). Let the fish sit until it comes to room temperature, 5 to 10 minutes.

In a wide, shallow bowl, whisk together the egg yolks, buttermilk, and hot sauce.

In another wide, shallow bowl, combine the flour, salt, black pepper, and cayenne.

Warm a large heavy-bottomed sauté pan or skillet over medium-high heat for 3 minutes, then add the butter. As soon as the butter has melted, dredge the trout fillets in the buttermilk-egg mixture, then in the flour, and place them skin-side down in the sizzling butter. Cook for 3 minutes, until the edges are crispy, then use a fish spatula to flip the fillets. Cook on the second side, using a soupspoon to baste the top of the fish with the melted butter, for 2 minutes. (If your trout is unusually thick, you may need to cook it a bit longer. If you can insert a paring knife into the flesh and easily pierce the fish, then the flesh is cooked.) Transfer the fish to paper towels or a rack and allow the excess butter to drain.

Serve the fish over rice, garnished with the parsley and green onion, with lemon wedges alongside. You could also eat it with a side of fresh corn and a cucumber and tomato salad.

HOW TO CLEAN A FISH

It's satisfying to catch and clean your own fish. To clean a fish, gently run a sharp knife or a spoon from the tail end to the head, angling the knife slightly to get under and flake off the scales. Rinse your knife and gently wipe the fish with dry towels or paper towels. After the scales have been removed, you can gut the fish: Lay the fish flat on a cutting board with the head facing right. Using a sharp knife, insert the knife into the left side of the fish directly in front of the back (swimming) fins. Run the knife all the way from the left to the right, stopping right before the mouth, keeping your knife flat and parallel to the cutting board. Use your fingers to reach into the cavity of the fish and pull out the guts (this is easy to do, and you'll know what the guts are when you see them). Wipe the fish down again with clean dry towels. Now your fish is ready to fry.

REDFISH COURTBOUILLON

SERVES 6 TO 8

6 tablespoons (¾ stick/85 g) unsalted butter

¼ cup plus 2 tablespoons (50 g) all-purpose flour

2 pounds (910 g) yellow onions, finely diced

¼ cup (30 g) finely diced celery

¼ cup (35 g) finely diced green bell pepper

2½ pounds (1.2 kg) ripe tomatoes, cored

4 garlic cloves, finely diced

3 bay leaves (see Note, page 46)

2 teaspoons kosher salt, plus more as needed

½ teaspoon freshly ground black pepper, plus more as needed

4 cups (1 L) fish stock (page 228)

2 pounds (910 g) redfish, black drum, or any white fish, cut into large cubes, skinless or skin on

⅛ teaspoon cayenne pepper, plus more as needed

1 teaspoon hot sauce, preferably Original Louisiana Hot Sauce, plus more as needed

Cooked rice (see page 209), for serving

¼ cup (13 g) finely chopped fresh flat-leaf parsley, for garnish

¼ cup (20 g) finely chopped green onions, for garnish

In Louisiana, the term *courtbouillon* is used to describe a fish dish smothered in tomatoes. It is made using almost the same method as an étouffée and can be made with or without a roux. It can be served as a thick stew of tomatoes or a slightly thinner version. You can use any fish, but in my parts we use only redfish, and some of my aunts will eat it only with redfish caught from a certain bayou. It's superstition, maybe, but it's part of the old ways. When my dad brings in the "right" redfish, my aunt Earline, who carries a torch for courtbouillon, cooks up this recipe.

Warm a heavy-bottomed pot over medium heat for 3 minutes, then add the butter. When it has melted, add the flour and cook, stirring continuously with a wooden spoon, until the roux is the color of condensed milk, about 15 minutes.

Add the onions and stir them into the roux. (Be careful to avoid splattering the roux when adding the onions—this is when folks sometimes burn themselves.) Cook, stirring occasionally, until the onions are translucent, about 15 minutes. Add the celery and bell pepper and stir to combine. Reduce the heat to medium-low, cover, and let the vegetables smother together until tender, about 15 minutes.

Add the tomatoes, garlic, bay leaves, salt, and black pepper and stir. Reduce the heat to its lowest setting, cover, and smother, lifting the lid occasionally to stir, until the tomatoes have broken down, about 2 hours.

Add the stock and stir. Raise the heat to medium to bring the stock to a simmer, then reduce the heat to maintain a simmer and cook, uncovered, for 20 minutes.

Season the fish with the cayenne, the hot sauce, and salt and black pepper and add it to the sauce. Raise the heat to medium to bring the sauce to a simmer (don't let it come to a rolling boil), then reduce the heat to maintain a simmer and cook for 10 minutes. Taste and adjust the seasoning.

Serve the fish courtbouillon over rice, garnished with the parsley and green onions.

The Time for Reclamation

AUTHOR NORMAN MACLEAN etched out fishing, brotherhood, and friendship deeply and passionately in *A River Runs Through It*. The characters in the book are brothers, and fishing is their pastime and the tie that binds them. The underlying theme is one brother trying to help the other. While there is really nothing he can do—his brother's pain is apparent and deep—they must search the darkness together in order to find the light.

Louisiana is that brother in need of help. My generation in South Louisiana can easily see the darkness; the evidence is in front of us. For our parents and grandparents, who were caught up in trying to survive, the chaos outpaced them. The state has astounding natural resources: oil, furs, hides, shrimp, crabs, crawfish, oysters, squid, snails, alligators, a multitude of fresh- and saltwater fish, ducks, rabbits, frogs, turtles, coons, deer, squirrels, sugarcane, rice, delta soil likened to gold, and even salt domes from an ancient sea. We have family, camaraderie, and community. We are part land and part sea, tethered by marsh. A marsh in constant flux, first filled with American Indians and then with hardworking explorers, hunters, trappers, and fishermen who settled in these forgotten, castaway places—people who found home and sustenance in a place no one else cared about, until that place seemed profitable. The marsh and swamp fell prey to gentrification and exploitation.

It's a hardscrabble life in the swamp; we tried to keep up by selling our Spanish moss in cypress boxes to Henry Ford (to stuff into the seats of the first Model Ts). We have sold eggshells from our bird population to glue and photo film manufacturers and plumes and feathers to adorn hats to haute fashion houses, along with nutria and muskrat furs, and we've moved thousands of wild ducks, a cornucopia of seafood, alligator hides, catfish, and terrapins to New Orleans markets and beyond.

Thousands of people of many different nationalities formed a human quilt, living off the land and water, making use of every available resource to piece together a patchwork of livelihoods that turned into our culture and traditions, and the seasons and rhythms that make a community. The endless supply of crabs in our iceboxes during the summer; the first catch of shrimp pulled in on a Lafitte skiff, full moon blaring, signaling the start of the spring season; the burning of cane; the culling of oysters, sweet sugar and salty brines on our palates—these rhythms are what define us.

After years of exploitation of all of our resources, we're in a time now where we are trying to reclaim these rhythms, to regain some normalcy and balance. My father traded a life as a fisherman, as a steward of the land and water, for work in the oil industry. He did it to feed and clothe his children. Now that he's retired, he can finally return to a life on the water. I call him the fish whisperer. We can talk endlessly of baits and hooks, lines and "crappy lines," fishing spots, and fishing mishaps. It is in his blood to fish these waters. When we fish in Lake Boudreaux, it's normal to tie up our boat to oil industry debris, ghostly litter left behind. My dad points out the names of bayous that no longer exist, spots that used to be land, and the places where all the cypress forests once were. He teaches me how to fish, and I am enamored of his expertise. He tells me stories of oyster fishing and shrimping. We reminisce and remember, and we still find peace and solace in what remains.

What should we remember? What are we meant to pass down? A stitching pattern for a fishing net? A technique for smothering okra? The way the moon moves sea life and the best fishing spots? Will there be resources left to apply this knowledge? And people to carry on the traditions?

I grew up not even knowing the word *Cajun* yet living a "Cajun" life. In South Louisiana today, Cajuns are standing guard at our stoves, resilient to the changing landscape; we are the bridge from the past to the present, holding the land and sea together. We're a history book unfolding, and the unfortunate test subjects. We aren't just a quick whirl around the Cajun dance floor, a photo snapped by a photographer, a bowl of rice and gravy; we are not that blithe experience. We are the experience of centuries of blood, sweat, and tears that came before, centuries of hardworking people from a hardscrabble marsh. We are Cajuns still searching for the light.

FRIED CATFISH FOR ELLEN

SERVES 4

Peanut oil, for frying

4 egg yolks

1 teaspoon hot sauce, preferably Original Louisiana Hot Sauce

1 teaspoon yellow mustard

2 cups (360 g) cornmeal, preferably freshly milled

1 cup (130 g) cornstarch, preferably organic

1 tablespoon kosher salt, plus more as needed

1 teaspoon freshly ground black pepper, plus more as needed

¼ teaspoon cayenne pepper

1 pound (455 g) skinless catfish fillets

Lemon wedges, for serving

My friend Ellen loves catfish; it reminds her of her youth. Catfish is abundant in Louisiana. Folks catch and cook it every day. Catfish are basically free in South Louisiana because if you know how to fish, you won't ever go hungry—there are always catfish. They're a perfect accompaniment to red beans or white beans—or any beans, for that matter. At the fish market, be sure you're buying high-quality domestic catfish from a reputable source. You can apply this method to frying any fish.

Fill a large heavy-bottomed pot with 4 inches (10 cm) of peanut oil and heat the oil over medium-high heat to 375°F (190°C). (Alternatively, use a tabletop fryer; see page 25.)

In a shallow bowl, whisk together the egg yolks, hot sauce, and mustard. In a separate shallow bowl, combine the cornmeal, cornstarch, salt, black pepper, and cayenne.

Season the fish lightly with salt and black pepper. Dip each slice in the egg mixture, letting any excess drip off, then dredge in the cornmeal mixture, coating the fish completely. Working in small batches, add the fish to the hot oil and fry until golden brown, 3 to 4 minutes. Using tongs, transfer the fried fish to paper towels or brown paper bags to absorb excess oil.

Serve the catfish with lots of lemon wedges for squeezing over the top.

FISH STOCK

MAKES 8 QUARTS (8 L)

2½ pounds (1.2 kg) onions, coarsely chopped

2 cups (210 g) coarsely chopped celery

1 pound (455 g) green bell peppers, coarsely chopped

1 tablespoon whole black peppercorns

½ ounce (14 g) parsley stems

4 green onions

3 bay leaves (see Note, page 46)

3 pounds (1.35 kg) fish heads and bones, cleaned (see Note)

Kosher salt

One of my favorite gumbos in Cocodrie is made from a powerful stock of fish heads and bones; the stock is simmered all day and is a base for an incredible seafood gumbo. This stock can be used to make so many tasty foods, from a simple clear soup with fish and potatoes, to gumbos and Cajun courtbouillons, to lightly poached fish. When I'm not feeling well, I warm up fish stock, add a bit of salt and cayenne, and drink it for breakfast. I make this stock with redfish or trout, but you can use any fish you have, including cod, sea bass, or halibut. Some say that trout is too fatty for stock and that some kinds of fish won't work as well as others. The truth is, each fish will lend a different flavor profile to the stock. Experiment and see what you like.

In a large stockpot, combine the onions, celery, bell peppers, peppercorns, parsley, green onions, bay leaves, and 8 quarts (8 L) water and bring to a boil over medium-high heat. Reduce the heat to maintain a simmer and cook for 2 hours.

Add the fish heads and bones and return the stock to a simmer. Cook for 45 minutes.

Ladle a bit of the stock into a cup, add a pinch of salt, and taste it: if it's flavorful, it's ready; if not, simmer for 15 minutes longer and taste again, until the flavor is to your liking. Strain the stock through a strainer lined with cheesecloth. Discard the solids.

Use immediately, or let cool, then transfer to airtight containers and store in the refrigerator for up to a week and in the freezer for up to a year.

NOTE: *If you don't have access to fish bones, ask your fishmonger to butcher a whole fish for you and reserve the head and carcass.*

POACHED FISH OVER RICE

SERVES 2

4 cups (1 L) fish stock (page 228)

2 teaspoons kosher salt

2 pinches of cayenne pepper

1 bay leaf (see Note, page 46)

1 ounce (28 g) parsley stems, plus finely chopped parsley for garnish

2 green onions, finely chopped, white and green parts separated

1 pound (455 g) skinless redfish fillets or other white-fleshed fish fillets

½ teaspoon cracked black pepper

1 tablespoon unsalted butter

Cooked rice (see page 209), for serving

Hot sauce, preferably Original Louisiana Hot Sauce, for serving

Poached foods have a bad reputation, but if it's done correctly, poached fish is flaky and tender and not overcooked, plus it's an easy and healthful meal. Poaching needs to happen at 140°F (60°C). This is when an instant-read thermometer is handy, or you have to watch the liquid closely. You don't want it boiling or simmering; you want it to barely shake. This is the optimal temperature to poach fish so it doesn't become a rubbery mess.

I like simple recipes that you can easily build on, and this is one of them. If you have a great stock already made, then you can have this dinner on the table in less than 20 minutes. Add some vegetables, such as potatoes, turnips, or greens, to the stock for a complete meal.

In a large saucepan or fish poacher (see Note), bring the stock to a simmer over medium-low heat until an instant-read thermometer registers 140°F (60°C). If you don't have a thermometer, bring the stock up to a simmer and then turn down the heat so the liquid is shaking and steaming; there will be a couple of bubbles here and there but not a constant parade of bubbling. Add 1 teaspoon of the salt, a pinch of the cayenne, the bay leaf, parsley stems, and green onion whites.

Cut the fish fillets into long pieces that will fit in the pan and season them with the remaining 1 teaspoon salt, the black pepper, and the remaining pinch of cayenne.

Add the butter to the stock, then add the fish. Poach the fish until a paring knife easily pierces through it, 8 to 10 minutes, depending on the thickness of the fillets. Use a slotted spoon to transfer the fish to two bowls and ladle the broth on top.

Serve with rice, garnished with the parsley and green onion greens, and offer a bottle of hot sauce at the table.

NOTE: *I invested in an old-school fish poacher. It is rectangular and made of copper, with a pan insert to carefully raise and lower the fish.*

GO FISH

In Louisiana, fishing has always been accessible as a means of sustaining ourselves and our families, and at no time in recorded history did humans not eat fish. On the bayou, our diet always included fish—redfish, flounder, perch, garfish, trout, bass, sac-a-lait, black drum, porgies, croakers, black mullet, and catfish, to name some of the fish swimming in our barrier waters.

My dad remembers fishing for flounder on a long-gone Whiskey Island with his friends as a teenager. Flounder, a flatfish, likes to lie on the sandy bottom in shallow water and eat crustaceans and oysters. My dad and his friends would shine a lantern in the water to spot them, then scoop the flounder out of the shallow sand beds with a shovel—it was that easy.

When my siblings and I were kids, we would dump a bucket of soapy water onto the garden and wait till the worms swam up. We'd grab them and head to the bayou to catch perch, then take the perch home and make our own aquariums in our rooms. Perch were easy to reel in, sheepshead a little harder. They pull back and forth erratically, tossing their oblong bodies around.

Catching and eating catfish is a religion in Louisiana. Up and down the bayou, you can watch men sitting on buckets watching their fishing lines, with bells rigged up to signal a bite. Catfish is used in courtbouillons, in po'boys, and in smoked catfish dips, and is fried for plate lunches.

Down on the bayou, redfish and trout are prized. But in the 1980s, the redfish that was always on my family's table was pushed into near extinction. Some say it was because of the popularization and commercialization of "blackened redfish" by chef Paul Prudhomme; others say wealthy sportfishermen were overfishing our waters. The trout population was similarly low. The Louisiana Department of Wildlife and Fisheries started mandating limits on the number of fish that could be caught on a daily basis recreationally (or, as we would say, for dinner) as a measure of sustainability. Gill nets were banned in this same period, then commercial fishermen were prohibited from fishing for certain species—which made many born-and-bred bayou fishermen who relied on selling both species less than happy. These bans also mean restaurants can't buy Louisiana trout or redfish.

In Cocodrie, only a couple of commercial fishermen are grandfathered in to catch trout and redfish. (The rest can still bring in offshore fish and inland black drum, sheepshead, catfish, flounder, etc.) As residents of the bayou and lakes, we are allowed by the state to catch five redfish or black drum or twenty-five trout a day. We take them home, clean them, and stock our larders with these fish to sustain us.

SALT PORK AND BEANS

WORKING FAMILIES CAN GET A MEAL GOING

on the stove quickly with a heavy-bottomed pot and three ingredients: salt pork, onions, and beans. The recipes in this chapter are simple and require little effort. They were developed by busy women running their households and supporting busy men running seafood boats, but they make an easy lunch or dinner for anyone, no matter where you live.

My great-grandmother Laurencia bought groceries off a little bus that would pass through Cocodrie, her hometown. There was no store in town in those early days. She bartered her chickens and their eggs for dried beans, rice, flour, cornmeal, and other dry goods. Everything came in sacks, and when those sacks were empty, they were cleaned and fashioned into clothing.

In those days, everyone up and down the bayou had a garden, situated near the water for easy irrigation. Gardening wasn't a hobby; it was a necessity. But that meant my great-grandmother raised her family on both fresh and dried peas. And they remain a staple of our meals today.

On the bayou, beans are served as a main dish or a side and with almost every protein, but mostly seafood. My mother swears by Camellia Brand beans (see Resources, page 359), a local brand that's been sold in Louisiana ever since Caribbean folks started asking for it in New Orleans's French Market. Go on your own search for local, heirloom organic beans. Find their origins and take a peek into history. Make a plan for the year to try a different bean every month. Take notes and find your favorites. Every bean is an excellent source of protein, and when slowly cooked, they become creamy, silky, and delicious.

On the bayou, we cook beans with salt pork, and we use salt pork to flavor soups, vegetables, and stews as well. You can make salt pork at home, or talk to your local butcher to find a version made from a humanely raised animal. Some markets carry Wellshire, and it's a great store-bought alternative and not too salty; you might need to ask your grocer to stock it.

Almost any part of the pig can be salted, and salting can be employed to preserve most foods. Salting for preservation and fermentation is magic. Salt is a mineral compound and one of the oldest known seasonings for food. The act of salting food has been recorded farther back than we can keep track. People have been paid in salt, nourished by salt, and healed by salt. Add salt to your water if you feel dehydrated and it will help your body absorb water. Gargle with salt when your throat is feeling raw. And be sure to throw some over your shoulder if you spill any.

SALT PORK

**MAKES 3 POUNDS
(1.35 KG)**

3 pounds (1.35 kg) skin-on
pork belly or pork shoulder

1½ cups (370 g) sea salt or
kosher salt

1 bay leaf (see Note, page 46)

If you're looking for a sustainable salt pork that is not the product of a factory farm, you're going to have a tough time. But you can make salt pork yourself. When Acadians were homesteading in the Canadian Maritimes—a time when refrigeration was a distant speck on the horizon—pork was salted out of necessity. They would make a brine with salt and water and place an egg in the brine to test its salinity: if it floated, the brine was sufficiently salted. The pork was layered with salt in ceramic crocks, then covered with the brine and left outside to cure for the winter. The salt preserved the pork so it could be stored for long periods without spoiling.

You can easily salt-cure pork in the refrigerator. Start by asking your local butcher to get you a piece of clean, humanely raised pork belly. You can salt a whole slab of belly, cut it into pieces, and freeze them to use throughout the year, or just start with a couple of pounds. You can also use pork shoulder and some of the other cuts of the pig that usually require a longer cook time; they'll hold up to the salting process and, later, to long cook times.

You'll need a casserole dish that fits the pork and is deep enough that you can completely cover the pork with salt.

Wash and dry the pork and cut it into pieces that will fit into your casserole dish. Working over the dish, rub the pork liberally on all sides with salt. You want to really press the salt into the pork. Place the pieces in the casserole dish and cover with the remaining salt; add the bay leaf. Wrap the casserole dish with plastic wrap, label it, and date it. Refrigerate the pork for 2 days.

Unwrap the pork and pour off any liquid. Use the salt on the bottom of the dish to give the pork another good rub. Rewrap the dish and refrigerate for 2 days more.

The salt pork should now be ready. You can use it immediately, or cut it into 8-ounce (225 g) chunks, wrap them in plastic wrap or butcher paper and put them in a ziplock freezer bag, and freeze for up to 1 year. Be sure to label each piece with "salt pork" and the date.

Women
Who Cook

I COME FROM a long line of women who cook. My grandmother cooked the same food her mother did, but she didn't learn to cook directly from her mother, and my mom didn't learn directly from her mother. It was the same for me.

We learn to cook Cajun food by osmosis. We don't stand side by side prepping ingredients or stirring pots together, one generation with another, but we wake to the clanking of spoons on the edges of cast-iron pans and Magnalite pots. We wake to the smells of smothered okra and sweating onions. We eat breakfast while supper is being prepared on a crowded stove in a spotless kitchen. The aromas, sights, and sounds of cooking are omnipresent. We unconsciously know how to speak the language. Words are ingredients, and recipes are poems.

I feel Cajun food down in my soul. Its layers brim in my being, in my marrow. When I try to re-create my mom's dishes, I know when I've cracked the code. I walk the flavor back with muscle memory on my tongue. And my mom walks me through the ingredients and the process step-by-step on her flip phone (she won't upgrade!). The recipes are always inside me.

In my family, recipes are verbally passed on with rough guidelines: a silver serving spoon of this, an onion the size of a softball, half a bell pepper. Tads and touches, yes, but never a weight or a measurement. Our Cajun menus are carried on as each generation mirrors the flavors they grew up with.

My mom and her sisters, my grandmother, and the women who came before them represent so much of what Cajun is to me, what Cajun is on the bayou, and what Cajun is in South Louisiana. They are a touchstone for Cajun women, kitchens, and identity. Although they would never call themselves "Cajun"—just simple ladies who come from a humble upbringing. Daughters of fishermen, who grew up down the bayou and lived a luxurious peasant life. They are the queens of their kitchens, the kitchens I grew up in. These women shaped me, and their food is the flavor I'm always chasing.

SMOTHERED CABBAGE

SERVES 4 TO 6

1 tablespoon canola oil

6 ounces (170 g) salt pork, homemade (see page 239) or store-bought, cut into ½-inch (1.5 cm) cubes

1 (2- to 3-pound/910 g to 1.35 kg) green cabbage

Kosher salt (optional)

Cayenne pepper or hot sauce, preferably Original Louisiana Hot Sauce (optional)

Cooked rice (see page 209), for serving

Like many other vegetables, with the addition of a bit of salt pork, a simple head of cabbage becomes a tasty meal. Come January, Louisianans eat a lot of cabbage, and we always make it on New Year's Day. When I was in the third grade at Upper Little Caillou Elementary School, my teacher gave us a form asking us to name our favorite things. One question asked for our favorite food. I answered "cabbage." My teacher must've expected an answer like pizza or hamburgers, so she questioned my choice. I let her know that there were no pizzas or hamburgers at our house and that I loved the vegetable.

Cabbage is easy to smother and doesn't require a lot of attention. You can use green cabbage from the grocery store, but also look for cabbage during the winter at your farmers' market. Buy a cabbage that is a little bit bigger than a cantaloupe but not as big as a basketball. Eat smothered cabbage over rice if you want to stretch the dish.

Warm a heavy-bottomed 6-quart (6 L) pot over medium heat for about 2 minutes, then add the oil and heat for 30 seconds. Add the salt pork and cook until it's brown and a little crispy on all sides, 8 to 15 minutes. Leave it firmly planted in the pot on the first side until this happens, then carefully use tongs to flip the pieces to brown the other sides.

While the salt pork is browning, rinse and dry the cabbage, then coarsely chop it into large pieces—bigger than a large marshmallow, smaller than a deck of cards.

When the salt pork is browned, add the cabbage to the pot and stir to combine. (I'm partial to stirring with a wooden spoon.) Cover the pot, reduce the heat to its lowest setting, and let the cabbage smother for about 2 hours, carefully lifting the lid and giving it a stir every 20 minutes. When you lift the lid, there should be some steam—this means you're properly smothering. If the cabbage looks dry in the pot, add water 1 tablespoon at a time as needed. Smothering is a low, slow process. Trust it.

Taste the cabbage. Because all salt pork is different, I can't tell you if you'll need to add salt. Some salt pork is really salty; other salt pork, not so much. If you'd like some heat, add a little cayenne or hot sauce.

Serve the cabbage over rice.

POTATO SOUP WITH SALT PORK AND GREEN ONIONS

SERVES 6 TO 8

2¾ pounds (1.2 kg) red potatoes (about 22), scrubbed

1 tablespoon canola oil

½ pound (225 g) salt pork, homemade (see page 239) or store-bought, cut into ½-inch (1.5 cm) cubes

1 teaspoon cracked black pepper, plus more as needed

2 teaspoons kosher salt, plus more as needed

¼ cup (13 g) finely chopped fresh flat-leaf parsley, for garnish

¼ cup (20 g) finely chopped green onions, for garnish

My mom swears by potato soup as a "fixer-upper" when you're sick. It was her go-to meal at the beginning of many pregnancies, when the thought of most food sends your body into vertigo. Potato soup is simple, filling, and nourishing, all at the same time, and with so few ingredients, it's easy to put together. I imagine this was a meal Acadians would have cooked.

The fresh, crisp parsley and green onions are a perfect complement to the salt pork. Use the whole green onion—there's no need to discard the whites or the green parts. Everything is edible, flavorful, and delicious.

Peel the potatoes and cut them into large chunks, placing them in a large bowl of cold water as you go (this keeps the potatoes crisp and prevents them from oxidizing). If your potatoes are on the smaller side, you can leave them whole. Drain and rinse the potatoes a couple of times to release some of their starch.

Warm a heavy-bottomed 8-quart (8 L) soup pot over medium heat for 3 minutes, then add the oil and heat for 1 minute. Add the salt pork and cook, turning as needed to brown it on all sides, about 12 minutes.

Drain the potatoes and add them to the pot. Give them a good stir so they are coated with the rendered fat from the pork, then season with the pepper. Reduce the heat to medium-low and cook for 5 minutes.

Add 3 quarts (3 L) water and raise the heat to medium-high to bring the water to a boil. Cook until the potatoes are tender, not too soft but not too al dente, about 10 minutes. Taste the soup and add salt as needed. The soup will be very brothy and clear.

Ladle the soup into bowls and garnish with the parsley and green onions. Top with more pepper and serve.

SMOTHERED GREEN BEANS
WITH RED POTATOES

SERVES 4 TO 6

2 tablespoons canola oil

½ pound (225 g) salt pork, homemade (see page 239) or store-bought, diced

2 pounds (910 g) yellow onions, finely diced

2 pounds (910 g) green beans, trimmed

1 teaspoon kosher salt

½ pound (225 g) small red potatoes (about 4), scrubbed

¼ teaspoon cracked black pepper

⅛ teaspoon cayenne pepper

Summertime in Louisiana means getting the family together under the gazebo and snapping green beans to put away for the year. We pickle a couple of jars and freeze the rest. There is always a slight anxiety—especially when it rains nonstop in the subtropical South—that we might not get enough beans or that it might not be a good year. But without fail, year after year, green beans—whether dwarf or pole beans or any of the hundreds of other varieties—sprout fast and are shockingly easy to grow. A couple of plants will yield a lot of beans.

Whatever you don't freeze, pickle, or salt can be turned into this one-pot four-main-ingredient meal. If you don't have fresh green beans, canned or frozen ones will work just fine, and any potato will do. You can add garlic, red pepper flakes, or herbs, but I love the simplicity of the dish as it is. Green beans pair well with a roasted chicken.

Warm a heavy-bottomed 8-quart (8 L) Dutch oven over medium heat for 2 minutes, then add the oil and heat for 30 seconds. Add the salt pork and cook, turning as needed to brown it on all sides, about 12 minutes. Drain the excess fat from the pot, leaving behind about 1 tablespoon.

Return the pot to medium heat, add the onions to the salt pork and fat, and cook, stirring often, until soft and translucent, about 15 minutes.

Add the green beans and ½ teaspoon of the salt and stir to combine. Reduce the heat to its lowest setting, cover, and let smother until the beans are soft and have lost their structure, about 30 minutes.

Add the potatoes and stir well. Cover and smother until the potatoes are cooked through, about 30 minutes.

Season with the black pepper and cayenne. Taste and season with the remaining ½ teaspoon salt, if necessary, then serve.

LIL' PEAS AND SMALL RED POTATOES

SERVES 4 TO 6

1 tablespoon canola oil

1 pound (455 g) yellow onions, finely diced

1 pound (455 g) shucked fresh or thawed frozen little green peas, or 2 (15-ounce) cans green peas, drained and rinsed

½ pound (225 g) small red potatoes (about 4), scrubbed

1 teaspoon kosher salt, plus more as needed

¼ teaspoon cracked black pepper

¼ teaspoon cayenne pepper

2 tablespoons unsalted butter

Fresh green peas pack so much flavor. But it takes a lot of shucking to get to a pound of fresh peas (and it's hard not to eat them all while you're shucking them). If you have the patience (or help) to shuck a whole bunch, then this dish will be elevated to great heights. If not, just use frozen or canned peas. If you use canned, look for an organic brand that is non-GMO and has no added sugar.

Warm a heavy-bottomed 8-quart (8 L) pot over medium heat for 2 minutes, then add the oil and heat for 30 seconds.

Add the onions and stir. Cook, stirring often, until the onions are soft and translucent, about 15 minutes.

Add the peas, potatoes, and salt and stir to combine. Reduce the heat to low, cover, and let the vegetables smother together until the peas are soft and the potatoes are tender, about 20 minutes, stirring every 5 minutes.

Season with the black pepper and cayenne. Taste and season with more salt, if you'd like. Add the butter and stir to melt and incorporate it. Serve.

MONDAY'S RED BEANS

SERVES 6 TO 8

1 pound (455 g) dried red beans, picked over for pebbles

2 tablespoons canola oil

½ pound (225 g) salt pork, homemade (see page 239) or store-bought, diced small

1 (1½-pound/680 g) pork shank

2 pounds (910 g) yellow onions, finely diced

6 garlic cloves, finely chopped

3 bay leaves (see Note, page 46)

1 teaspoon kosher salt, plus more as needed

1 teaspoon cracked black pepper, plus more as needed

1 teaspoon cayenne pepper, plus more as needed

1 tablespoon hot sauce, preferably Original Louisiana Hot Sauce, plus more as needed

Cooked rice (see page 209), for serving

¼ cup (13 g) finely chopped fresh flat-leaf parsley, for garnish

¼ cup (20 g) finely chopped green onions, for garnish

In New Orleans and all over South Louisiana, eating red beans and rice on Monday is an institution. The story goes like this: Red beans were cooked on Monday because it was laundry day. Laundry took a bit more time back in the old days, so starting a pot of beans and laundry at the same time meant they'd be done simultaneously. Now we celebrate red beans by eating them weekly and parading through the streets during Mardi Gras in costumes adorned with red beans and rice.

You can make this recipe simple, as given, or easily customize it. Lots of folks simmer their red beans with smoked sausage, a ham hock, or bacon. Choose one protein or a combination for extra flavor, or make your beans vegetarian by adding a chopped bell pepper or a couple stalks of celery. With or without meat, beans can be enhanced with a handful of herbs, such as thyme, sage, savory, basil, marjoram, or whatever you find or forage.

You'll need to soak your beans overnight: Put the beans in a large bowl and cover with 2 gallons (8 L) water. Cover the bowl and place it in the refrigerator.

In the morning, drain your beans and rinse them one more time.

Warm a heavy-bottomed 14-quart (13 L) soup pot over medium heat for 2 minutes, then add the oil and heat for 30 seconds. Add the salt pork and pork shank and cook, turning as needed to brown them on all sides, about 12 minutes.

Add the onions and stir to coat with the rendered fat from the pork. Cook, stirring often, until the onions are soft and translucent, about 15 minutes. Add the garlic and cook, stirring often, until the garlic is fragrant.

Add the beans, bay leaves, salt, black pepper, cayenne, hot sauce, and 3 quarts (3 L) water and stir to combine. Bring to a boil over high heat, then reduce the heat to medium-high and boil for 20 minutes. Reduce the heat to maintain a simmer (don't let the beans stop simmering, but don't keep things at a rolling boil). Cook, stirring frequently to avoid burning, until your beans are tender and the liquid has the consistency of gravy, about 2 hours. If the liquid seems too thick, add a bit more hot water (I like more liquid in my beans, as they tend to really thicken up after cooking).

When the beans are tender, mash some against the side of the pot and stir them into the liquid to make it creamier. Taste and adjust the seasoning.

Serve the beans over rice, garnished with the parsley and green onions.

NOTE: *Dried beans should wrinkle right when the water starts simmering; this means they are fresh and haven't been sitting on the shelf awhile.*

WHITE BEANS

SERVES 4 TO 6

2 tablespoons canola oil

½ pound (225 g) salt pork, homemade (see page 239) or store-bought, diced small

1 pound (455 g) onions, diced

1 celery stalk, diced

1 bay leaf (see Note, page 46)

1 pound (455 g) dried navy beans, rinsed with hot water and drained

2 teaspoons kosher salt

¼ teaspoon cracked black pepper

⅛ teaspoon cayenne pepper

Cooked rice (see page 209), for serving

2 tablespoons finely chopped fresh flat-leaf parsley, for garnish

2 tablespoons finely chopped green onion, for garnish

Of all beans, white beans are my favorite. There are so many different varieties that fall under the category. I prefer to cook with navy beans; they cook much faster than red beans and don't require an overnight soak. They are creamy and earthy and hold their shape even when cooked for long periods of time. They are the highest in fiber of all the white beans, too. There are four types of dried white beans that you can buy in any regular grocery store: navy beans, great northerns, cannellini, and baby limas (also called butter beans). I also love heirloom varieties like cranberry (borlotti) and Marcella beans (named after legendary cookbook author Marcella Hazan) from Rancho Gordo (see Resources, page 359). Any one of these white beans will work in this recipe.

Warm a heavy-bottomed 12-quart (11 L) pot over medium heat for 2 minutes, then add the oil and heat for 30 seconds. Add the salt pork and cook, turning as needed to brown on all sides, about 12 minutes.

Add the onions, celery, and bay leaf and stir to combine. Add the beans and 3½ quarts (3.5 L) water. Cover and bring to a boil over high heat. Reduce the heat to maintain a simmer and cook, uncovered, stirring often, until most of the water has boiled off or been absorbed and the beans are tender, 50 to 60 minutes. As the beans cool, they will absorb more liquid, so having some liquid left over is just fine; you don't want dry beans.

Mash some of the beans against the side of the pot and stir them into the liquid. Season with the salt, black pepper, and cayenne.

Serve the beans over rice, garnished with the parsley and green onion.

BUTTERY BABY LIMA BEANS

SERVES 4 TO 6

1 tablespoon canola oil

6 ounces (170 g) salt pork, homemade (see page 239) or store-bought, diced

1 pound (455 g) yellow onions, finely diced

1 bay leaf (see Note, page 46)

1 pound (455 g) fresh or thawed frozen lima beans

2 teaspoons kosher salt

½ teaspoon cracked black pepper

⅛ teaspoon cayenne pepper

1 tablespoon unsalted butter (optional)

Cooked rice (see page 209), for serving

¼ cup (13 g) finely chopped fresh flat-leaf parsley, for garnish

¼ cup (20 g) finely chopped green onions, for garnish

We cook lima beans fresh, along with crowder peas, purple hull peas, and some other Southern varieties. Limas are often called butter beans for their savory, rich, buttery flavor. I am so thankful that I can get a steady supply of fresh lima beans from the Indian Springs Farmers Association at the Crescent City Farmers Market. Fresh beans taste crisp and earthy. They have an unusually clean taste when plucked fresh from their shells, like they are telling a secret. Grow some lima beans in your own garden or find them at your local farmers' market in the spring and summer.

Fresh beans are ideal in this recipe, but you can use frozen if you must. Fresh beans soften in about thirty minutes and need only enough water to cover them. You can add any herbs you like, or perhaps garlic. The recipe calls for salt pork, but you can easily forge ahead without it and make this dish vegetarian.

Warm a heavy-bottomed 8-quart (8 L) soup pot over medium heat for 2 minutes, then add the oil and heat for 30 seconds. Add the salt pork and cook, turning as needed to brown it on all sides, about 12 minutes.

Add the onions and bay leaf and stir to coat with the rendered fat from the pork. Cook, stirring often, until the onions are soft and translucent, about 15 minutes.

Add the lima beans and enough water just to cover them. Bring to a simmer, then reduce the heat to low and simmer until the water has evaporated and the beans are tender and creamy, about 1 hour 30 minutes (this is a slow cook).

Season with the salt, black pepper, and cayenne. Add the butter (if using) and stir to melt and incorporate it.

Serve the beans over rice, garnished with the parsley and green onions.

SMOTHERED POTATOES

WITH SALT PORK AND PARSLEY

SERVES 4 TO 6

2 tablespoons canola oil

½ pound (225 g) salt pork, homemade (see page 239) or store-bought, cut into ½-inch (1.5 cm) cubes

2 pounds (910 g) yellow onions, finely diced

1 pound (455 g) red or new potatoes (8 to 12), scrubbed and cut into 2-inch (5 cm) chunks

½ teaspoon cracked black pepper, plus more for serving

⅛ teaspoon cayenne pepper, plus more as needed

½ teaspoon kosher salt, if needed

¼ cup (13 g) finely chopped fresh flat-leaf parsley, for garnish

¼ cup (20 g) finely chopped green onions, for garnish

Mr. Carol grows potatoes for families along Bayou Petit Caillou. When the potatoes are ready to harvest, everyone shows up to his house to collect their share. Then my mom and her sisters sit around, have coffee, and talk at length about how they are going to store their potatoes. The potatoes don't last long because we eat them so quick, but while we have them, they are the best.

Smothered potatoes (or *la sauce de patates*) is essentially a potato stew. Slowly smothering potatoes and salt pork over low heat gradually cooks down the potatoes and releases their starches. By adding water a little at a time, you create a stew that, when served over rice, will certainly fill you up. Starch on starch is something undoubtedly Cajun.

Warm a heavy-bottomed 10-quart (10 L) Dutch oven or soup pot over medium heat for 2 minutes, then add the oil and heat for 30 seconds. Add the salt pork and cook, turning as needed to brown it on all sides, about 12 minutes.

Add the onions and stir to coat with the rendered fat from the pork. Cook, stirring often, until the onions are soft and translucent, 10 to 15 minutes.

Add the potatoes, black pepper, and cayenne (use more cayenne if you really like heat) and stir to coat the potatoes with the fat. Reduce the heat to low, cover, and let the potatoes smother for 15 minutes. Lift the lid and add ¼ cup (60 ml) water, stir, and smother for 10 minutes more, then repeat, until the potatoes are broken down and the consistency of the stew is to your liking. You'll end up adding 1 to 2 cups (240 to 480 ml) water total, depending on how thick you want your stew, over 45 to 60 minutes. If the potatoes start to stick to the bottom of the pot and brown, that's okay—just use a wooden spoon to scrape up the bits from the bottom and stir everything together. Taste the stew and season with the salt, if needed.

Ladle the stew into bowls and garnish with the parsley and green onions. Top with more cracked black pepper and serve.

FIELD PEAS

SERVES 4 TO 6

2 tablespoons canola oil

½ pound (225 g) salt pork, homemade (see page 239) or store-bought, diced small

2 pounds (910 g) yellow onions, finely diced

⅓ cup (40 g) diced celery

3 bay leaves (see Note, page 46)

1 pound (455 g) dried field peas, rinsed with hot water and drained

1 tablespoon kosher salt

½ teaspoon cracked black pepper

⅛ teaspoon cayenne pepper

1 tablespoon hot sauce, preferably Original Louisiana Hot Sauce

Cooked rice (see page 209), for serving

¼ cup (13 g) finely chopped fresh flat-leaf parsley, for garnish

¼ cup (20 g) finely chopped green onions, for garnish

Hundreds of types of field peas grow in the South—all with different textures and flavors that range from nutty to earthy. Among the most well known are black-eyed peas, purple hulled peas, pink-eyed peas, and crowder peas. Even though they're called peas, they are technically legumes and also known as beans. Field peas were once grown in rice fields and cornfields to add nitrogen to the soil.

The messes of peas I pick up at roadside stands or farmers' markets rarely see heat because I usually eat them raw in the car on the way home. But if some of them *do* make it home, I cook them the same way I cook the lima beans on page 254. If I'm going to cook dried field peas, I use this recipe, which uses the same technique as the recipe for navy beans on page 253.

Warm a heavy-bottomed 8-quart (8 L) soup pot over medium heat for 2 minutes, then add the oil and heat for 30 seconds. Add the salt pork and cook, turning as needed to brown it on all sides, about 12 minutes.

Add the onions, celery, and bay leaves and stir to combine. Cook, stirring often, for about 5 minutes.

Add the field peas and 3 quarts (3 L) water. Bring to a boil over high heat, then reduce the heat to maintain a simmer and cook, stirring often, until most of the liquid has been absorbed and the peas are tender, 1 hour 30 minutes to 2 hours.

Mash some of the peas against the side of the pot and stir them into the liquid. Season with the salt, black pepper, cayenne, and hot sauce.

Serve the peas over rice, garnished with the parsley and green onions.

FISHERMEN'S DAUGHTERS

My mom and her five sisters grew up in a tiny green house down the bayou in Cocodrie, Louisiana. They all married fishermen, had children, and moved to Chauvin, up the bayou, away from the edge of the Gulf of Mexico. They built their houses side by side off Bayou Petit Caillou, where flood insurance wasn't required. This now seems preposterous in a place almost completely surrounded by water, but Chauvin had not yet experienced storm damage like it would in the coming years or the loss of so much land.

My aunts and my mom raised their kids in a rapidly changing time. They dealt with the pressures of the outside world, the draft, and wars. The simple life they knew growing up was cast in a new light. Many of their husbands had to leave the fishing industry because the price of shrimp hit an all-time low when foreign imports started flooding the markets. Most found new jobs in the oil industry (which itself had complicated the fishing industry); some signed on as deckhands, welders, or roustabouts on oil rigs, leaving their homes to work for seven to fourteen days at a time. The women were left alone to raise the children and run their households while also working outside the home. Managing a house this way was a full-time job with massive amounts of overtime.

My mom and aunts all cook a distinctive version of the traditional Cajun food they grew up eating—they're all great cooks—and they fed their families three meals a day. On top of that, they handled all the household tasks: sent the kids to school, got the baby changed and fed and put down for a nap, washed the clothes, cleaned the house, shopped for groceries, paid the bills, and prayed the rosary.

My aunts, mom, grandmother, and the women who came before them were responsible for the rhythm and heartbeat of their homes, but these women also ran shrimp docks and worked in grocery stores. They catered and took jobs arranging flowers. Some were master seamstresses and some were office and operations managers, helping to run businesses.

My mom raised six kids this way, and she never stopped working. Because my father left early and came home late from working his three or four jobs, my mom made breakfast and supper in two seatings: one for him and one for us kids. The kitchen was her office, and she ran it professionally, sustainably, resourcefully, successfully, and with pride.

She still does. And she is the first person I consult on just about everything, even if she exaggerates a bit. Just weeks after I delivered my eight-pound son with a midwife, she exclaimed that it's easier to deliver a baby than to make pecan candy. (I forgive her for that one.) I still call her. A lot. And she answers the phone 99 percent of the time. I learned the steps to cooking Cajun food on the phone with my mom, along with just about everything else that's important in life.

VEGETABLES

THERE IS A VEGETABLE FIELD ACROSS FROM

my childhood home. I watched the field get plowed and planted every year. I've watched it yield tons of vegetables. As the farmer aged, I watched the field grow wild and return to nature. The land was sold, and the new owners tried relentlessly to manicure the field. I laughed silently as nature mocked them: week after week, the field kept pushing vegetables, wild herbs, edible flowers, and even crawfish hidden in the soil. Louisiana's delta soil is magic and untamable.

As a kid, I used to walk across the field when it was planted with gardens: a healthy crop of okra, potatoes, peppers, tomatoes, green beans, eggplants, watermelons, and cucumbers. In the cooler months, there were rows of carrots, cabbages, mustard greens, squash, onions, parsley, and gigantic pumpkins for carving. I'd walk to the road and put my cash in a little "trust" box to pay for the vegetables. At five years old, I was already learning how to choose my vegetables. I still smell every tomato before I buy it. I examine cucumbers one by one for firmness. I check the stem ends of vegetables to make sure they were allowed to properly ripen on the vine. I knock on my watermelon and listen for a hollow sound to indicate that it's filled with water, and I check for the large yellow spot on the bottom that means the watermelon had enough time to properly grow and receive sun. But I'm not afraid of produce that doesn't look perfect—I am a huge fan of the bruised or ugly-looking seconds (you should be, too!).

Okra, commonly called lady fingers around the globe, grows well in our delta soil. My aunt grew the okra for our family. She kept a large garden right on Bayou Petit Caillou. Locating your garden on the bayou makes for easy irrigation, and the sweet brackish water means nutrient-injected soil. Great soil means great vegetables.

Every farmer on the bayou has rows and rows of sweet Texas Long-horns, an okra variety that is revered for its flavor and replanted every year with seeds from the season before. I remember my aunt Earline handing me a packet of okra seeds when I was a teen and feeling like I had just earned a notch in my belt. I was the keeper of the seeds and trusted to plant them. You need to file the seeds on a rough nail file before you plant them to ensure that they sprout. After your plant gets going, there's really nothing stopping its growth. Okra plants are sturdy, hearty plants. One of the things that separates a hobby gardener from a professional farmer is being able to keep up with the okra harvest once it gets going. Because if you don't have complete control over okra, things can go south quickly. I rely on the hard work of South Louisiana's farmers to provide me with okra that we base so many of our bayou meals on.

SMOTHERED OKRA

MAKES 1 QUART (980 G)

Canola oil

5 pounds (2.3 kg) okra, trimmed and cut into ¼-inch-thick (6 mm) rounds

1 small tomato, diced

Smothered okra is slow-cooked until it breaks down and thickens to a texture almost like that of creamed spinach. It's the base of other recipes in this book (see pages 171, 173, and 175) and can be added to soups and stews as a thickener. It's also a way to inject dishes with loads of nutrition.

Most folks are scared of okra's sticky, gelatinous texture, but you just need to know how to handle the slime. Yes, okra is very sticky when you cut it. Your hands and knife will be slimy. Stay with it—it will wash away. When cooking okra, you need to add acid to neutralize the slime and enhance the okra's flavor; in this recipe, that acid comes from a tomato.

Smothering okra is a slow process, so be sure you pick a day when you'll be home all day to try this recipe. Perhaps on a rainy day, or one set aside for cleaning the house. When Louisiana's heat is reaching its all-time high, I'll cozy up with a book, reorganize my spice cabinet, or clean my baseboards while smothering okra. Start with the amounts listed here to get the hang of it; then, if you want to do more, you can move on to smothering 10 pounds (4.5 kg) at a time.

Warm a heavy-bottomed pot large enough to hold all the okra over medium heat. Pour in oil to coat the bottom of the pot—just enough so the okra won't stick. Add the okra, reduce the heat to its lowest setting, and cover. Cook, stirring the okra every 15 to 20 minutes, for a total of 8 hours. The covered pot will create steam and the steam will drip into the okra, keeping it from sticking to the bottom of the pot. If you feel your pot is not creating enough steam, add a tablespoon of water when you stir.

After 7 hours, stir in the tomato.

After 8 hours, the final product should be a mess of dark swampy green okra and pale pink okra seeds. Let cool to room temperature, then transfer the okra to ziplock freezer bags and freeze to eat or use in gumbos or other meals. Okra holds its flavor and texture in the freezer for up to 1 year.

SMOTHERED OKRA WITH SHRIMP AND TOMATOES

SERVES 6 TO 8

2 cups (450 g) Smothered Okra (page 265)

1 tomato, coarsely chopped

1 tablespoon plus 1 teaspoon kosher salt, plus more as needed

¾ teaspoon cracked black pepper, plus more as needed

2½ pounds (1.2 kg) peeled and deveined small shrimp (see page 33)

⅛ teaspoon cayenne pepper, plus more as needed

1 tablespoon hot sauce, preferably Original Louisiana Hot Sauce, plus more as needed

Cooked rice (see page 209), for serving

¼ cup (13 g) finely chopped fresh flat-leaf parsley, for garnish

¼ cup (20 g) finely chopped green onions, for garnish

Pickles (see pages 300–303), for serving

This recipe is where land and sea meet, where the garden and the bayou marry. You can taste the brackish water in the sweet shrimp and the heat of summer in the okra and tomatoes. When we are putting up okra for the year, this is the dish we eat. It is Louisiana summertime in a pot.

This uncomplicated dish, a hash of sautéed okra, diced tomato, and shrimp, is delicious as is, but you can add to it, if you like. Caramelize onions before adding the okra, or throw in gumbo crabs or oysters along with the shrimp. Or you can simplify and remove the seafood—smothered okra and tomatoes is a favorite down the bayou.

Warm a heavy-bottomed 4-quart (4 L) pot or Dutch oven over low heat. Add the okra and tomato and season with 1 teaspoon of the salt and ¼ teaspoon of the black pepper. Cover and smother the vegetables for about 20 minutes.

Put the shrimp in a bowl and season with the remaining 1 tablespoon salt, the remaining ½ teaspoon black pepper, the cayenne, and the hot sauce. Add the shrimp to the pot and stir. Smother, covered, until the shrimp are pink and firm, not mushy, about 20 minutes. Taste and adjust the seasoning.

Serve the mixture over rice, garnished with the parsley and green onions, with a side of pickles.

FOR THE LOVE OF OKRA

My love for okra is deep. Okra plant blossoms are my favorite flower. Their beautiful, delicate, pale yellow petals open to meet the sun and reveal a vibrant maroon center. You can quickly tell that okra is related to the hibiscus family. In the age of nose-to-tail eating, okra is your veggie. You can eat the flowers, leaves, and stalks. You can roast and grind the seeds and steep them into a refreshing beverage that was once used as a substitute for coffee. And okra has many medicinal and nutritional benefits, including your daily dose of fiber.

SKILLET-ROASTED OKRA

SERVES 4 AS A SIDE DISH OR SNACK

2 tablespoons (60 ml) canola oil or clarified butter (see Note, page 89)

12 ounces (340 g) tender young okra pods (about 24), sliced lengthwise in half

⅛ teaspoon kosher salt

A couple turns of the pepper mill

Cayenne pepper

1 lemon wedge

Okra cooked in a skillet is a great side dish and simple to make. It requires no preparation ahead of time and, if done correctly, is a great accompaniment to just about anything. The key to bringing out the okra's natural deliciousness is to cook it hot and fast, so make sure your skillets are properly heated. Place two cast-iron skillets in the oven for at least 30 minutes before cooking. This quickly sears the okra on the outside but maintains a crisp center. Like fried okra (see page 270), the skillet version preserves the okra's unique flavor and color. Eat it with fresh summer fruit like peaches and plums; with corn, lime, and crème fraîche; and with boiled shrimp and crabs. It also works swimmingly next to fried or sautéed fish.

Preheat the oven to 425°F (220°C). Place two large cast-iron skillets in the oven to heat for 30 minutes. Line a baking sheet or platter with paper towels.

Carefully remove the hot pans from the oven and set them on the stovetop over medium-high heat. Keep the skillet handles covered to avoid burning your hands.

Add 1 tablespoon of the oil to each pan. Carefully place the okra in the pans in a single layer. Don't crowd them. Sear in the skillets until golden brown, about 3 minutes, then flip the okra and cook for an additional 2 minutes.

Transfer the okra to the paper towels to soak up any excess oil and use a paper towel or rag to carefully wipe out the excess oil from the skillets.

Toss the okra back into the skillets and season with the salt, some black pepper, a touch of cayenne, and a squeeze of lemon juice. Serve immediately.

FRIED OKRA

SERVES 4 AS A SIDE DISH OR SNACK

Peanut oil, for frying

4 egg yolks

⅛ teaspoon hot sauce, preferably Original Louisiana Hot Sauce

12 ounces (340 g) tender young okra pods (about 24), whole or sliced into 1-inch (2.5 cm) rounds

2 cups (360 g) cornmeal, preferably freshly milled

1 cup (130 g) cornstarch, preferably organic

2 teaspoons kosher salt, plus more as needed

½ teaspoon cracked black pepper, plus more as needed

¼ teaspoon cayenne pepper, plus more as needed

Simply put, fried okra is delish. I order it any time I see it on a menu, whether it's okra fries at Chai Pani in Asheville, North Carolina, or fried okra in restaurants all over New Orleans. I don't like the prepackaged frozen fried variety, but fresh fried okra pods are so fresh and tender. I'll eat them on their own or dip them in just about anything, from cocktail sauce to hummus to vinegar. I'm not too proud to try ranch or seafood dip (see page 306), or even just a little squeeze of lemon.

Look for small, young, tender okra at farmers' markets during the summer. These will fry the best. Be sure to coat your okra thoroughly with the cornmeal, and you'll end up with perfection.

Fill a large heavy-bottomed pot with 4 inches (10 cm) of peanut oil and heat the oil over medium-high heat to 350°F (180°C). (Alternatively, use a tabletop fryer; see page 25.)

In a medium bowl, whisk together the egg yolks and hot sauce. Add the okra and toss to coat well. In a shallow bowl, combine the cornmeal, cornstarch, salt, black pepper, and cayenne. When the oil reaches the right temperature, start dredging the okra: Working with 8 pods at a time, remove the okra from the egg and dredge it in the cornmeal mixture, coating it completely. Use tongs to carefully transfer the okra to the hot oil and fry until golden brown, about 4 minutes. Use tongs to transfer the okra to paper towels or brown paper bags to sop up the extra oil. Season the okra with salt, black pepper, and cayenne while it's hot. Repeat to fry the remaining okra.

Let fried okra cool for just a bit before eating, as the centers will be molten hot.

VARIATION

Naked Fried Okra

Cut the okra lengthwise into 2 or 4 pieces and add it to the hot oil, without any dredging. Cook as above. Toss the hot okra with salt and a touch of cayenne before serving.

OKRA SEASON

Each year when the okra harvest came in, my family gathered under the gazebo at my parents' house or nestled together in the garage to clean bushels of the lady fingers. We washed them in metal bowls large enough for a child to swim in, then chopped them into tiny rounds with paring knives. I remember being excited as a small girl when I was finally handed a knife so I could help. It seemed an impossible task, as the okra was piled so high on the table I could hardly see who was across from me. But together we cut all the okra and readied it for smothering.

I smother cut-down okra in a pot that is large enough for crawfish boils or even a bath. The pot can hold three cases of cut okra, about 60 pounds (27.5 kg); I cover the pot and smother the okra on the lowest heat possible for more than 16 hours. I might leave the house occasionally, but only for quick trips—I am at the mercy of the okra, and it needs me to keep stirring. I lift the lid once every 40 minutes or so to give the okra a stir and add a bit of water if need be. In the end, a case of okra will break down into 3 to 4 quarts (3 to 4 L) of finished product. I let it cool, then store it in ziplock freezer bags. I process about thirty-two cases and store them for gumbos to serve during the year at Mosquito Supper Club. Whenever people ask about my gumbo recipe, I explain that the cooking process starts during okra season.

SMOTHERED EGGPLANT AND SHRIMP

SERVES 4

3 tablespoons canola oil

1 pound (455 g) onions, finely diced

4 garlic cloves, crushed and chopped

1½ pounds (680 g) eggplant, peeled and cut into large chunks

1 bay leaf (see Note, page 46)

1 teaspoon kosher salt, plus more as needed

¼ teaspoon cracked black pepper, plus more as needed

1 pound (455 g) peeled and deveined small shrimp (see page 33)

⅛ teaspoon cayenne pepper, plus more as needed

1 teaspoon hot sauce, preferably Original Louisiana Hot Sauce, plus more as needed

2 tablespoons finely chopped fresh flat-leaf parsley, for garnish

2 tablespoons finely chopped green onion, for garnish

Eggplants are easy to grow in Louisiana and versatile in holding other flavors because of their subtle nature. Eggplant is sometimes boiled to remove some of its bitterness before it's combined with other ingredients. I skip this step and just smother everything together in one pot. Smothered eggplant and shrimp is served over rice with parsley and green onion, but I think it's also tasty on a piece of toasted country bread. It has the texture and consistency of a great tapenade—thicker than a stew, with enough structure to top rice or toast.

Warm a heavy-bottomed 8-quart (8 L) Dutch oven over medium heat for 2 minutes, then add 2 tablespoons of the oil and heat for 30 seconds. Add the onions and cook, stirring often, until soft and translucent, about 15 minutes.

Add the garlic to the onions and stir to combine. Reduce the heat to medium-low and cook, stirring, for 5 minutes.

Add the eggplant and bay leaf, then season with a pinch of salt and black pepper and stir to combine. Cover and let the vegetables smother together for 1 hour, or until the eggplant is falling apart, stirring every 10 minutes.

Meanwhile, put the shrimp in a large bowl and season with the salt, black pepper, cayenne, and hot sauce.

After the eggplant is smothered, warm a sauté pan over medium-high heat for a minute or two, then add the remaining 1 tablespoon oil and heat for 1 minute. Add the seasoned shrimp and sear for 2 minutes on each side, until they're just starting to brown, then transfer the shrimp to the pot with the eggplant and stir to combine. Reduce the heat to its lowest setting, cover, and let the shrimp and eggplant smother together for about 8 minutes. Taste and season again, if necessary.

Serve the shrimp and eggplant garnished with the parsley and green onion.

CORN SOUP WITH POTATOES, BELL PEPPER, AND TOMATOES

SERVES 8

1 tablespoon canola oil

½ pound (225 g) salt pork, homemade (see page 239) or store-bought, diced

1 pound (455 g) yellow onions, finely diced

⅓ cup (40 g) finely diced celery

¼ cup (35 g) finely diced green bell pepper

2½ teaspoons kosher salt, plus more as needed

½ teaspoon freshly ground black pepper, plus more as needed

6 to 8 ears corn, husked

2¼ pounds (1 kg) tomatoes, diced

½ teaspoon sugar

1 pound (455 g) red potatoes (about 8), scrubbed and cut into large chunks

⅛ teaspoon cayenne pepper (optional)

¼ cup (13 g) finely chopped fresh flat-leaf parsley, for garnish

¼ cup (20 g) finely chopped green onions, for garnish

When French settlers arrived in what would become Acadia, they met the Mi'kmaqs, one of Canada's many indigenous peoples. The natives taught them about the "three sisters": a companion planting of corn, beans, and squash. Acadians had corn for the first time after learning how to grow it from the Mi'kmaqs. They made soups with salt pork and corn. I don't know if they ever ate a soup like this one, but I imagine theirs wasn't far off.

This recipe calls for fresh tomatoes and fresh corn, but you can use canned or frozen tomatoes or corn if necessary. I learned from reading David Tanis's cookbook *Heart of the Artichoke* that tomatoes freeze well. When tomatoes are in season, put them on a baking sheet, freeze them whole for a couple of hours, then transfer them to ziplock freezer bags and store them in the freezer to use as you need them. When they defrost, the skins fall right off. Alternatively, can tomatoes when they are in season, or use store-bought canned tomatoes (I like San Marzano tomatoes). When corn is in season, try to put up as much as you can by freezing whole cobs or cutting the kernels off the cobs and canning or freezing them. If you must use store-bought canned corn, look for non-GMO, organic kernels.

Warm a heavy-bottomed 8-quart (8 L) soup pot over medium heat for 2 minutes, then add the oil and heat for 30 seconds. Add the salt pork and cook, turning as needed to brown it on all sides, about 12 minutes.

Add the onions and stir. Cook, stirring often, until the onions are soft and translucent, about 15 minutes.

Add the celery and bell pepper and stir to combine. Reduce the heat to low, cover, and cook until the celery and bell pepper are very soft, about 15 minutes. Season with a couple pinches of salt and a couple turns of a pepper mill.

Meanwhile, cut 3 cups (525 g) of corn kernels off the cobs (set aside a couple of ears with the kernels intact). A trick is to stand an ear of corn in the center of a Bundt pan, then use a sharp knife to slice the kernels off. They'll fall right into the pan. Once you've removed the kernels, take the dull side of the knife and run it up and down against the cob to release all the milk from the corn. Don't let a drop get away. Cut the reserved whole ears of corn into 2 or 3 pieces each.

Season the tomatoes with the salt and black pepper and add them to the pot, then add the sugar and stir. Cover and let everything smother together for 30 minutes.

Add the corn kernels and corn milk to the pot, stir, and smother together for 15 minutes. Add the potatoes, corn on the cob, and roughly 3 cups (750 ml) water. Raise the heat to medium to bring everything to a boil, then reduce the heat to low and simmer the soup for about 15 minutes, until the potatoes are tender and easily pierced with a fork. Turn off the heat. Taste the soup and season with more salt and black pepper. If you like heat, add the cayenne and let the soup sit for another 30 minutes before serving so all the flavors marry; soup is always better after it sits.

Ladle the soup into bowls and serve garnished with the parsley and green onions.

Women and
Their Kitchens

AS A FEMINIST, I don't gasp at the notion of a woman's place being in the kitchen. Kitchen work is hard work. Our knees hurt, our backs hurt, our arms are burned, our skin is oily, and we are tired but still standing guard at our prep tables and stoves and cooking through it. We are cooking through pain, suffering, anxiety, our divisive political climate, the struggle for gender equality, and oppression. We know we can be anything we want and we can do anything we want, and what we want to do is to cook.

For so long, kitchens were the singular place where women were in control. Women could communicate through food. Women had freedom to create. The kitchen is a sacred place where women could spend hours prepping and finding peace in their work. We cook with patience and fire. We cook with intention and love. We take a small list of ingredients and reimagine them over and over and over. We walk in the steps of the women who came before us. We ground ourselves in repetition and timing. We know intuitively when a dish is done by the aromas in the kitchen. We can cook our heart and pain into dishes, and we can cook our way back to ourselves. Back to a kitchen that nourishes and grounds us, a place that is ours.

Growing up, I was taken aback that the Cajun celebrity chefs were men. The Cajun kitchen, the one place that belongs to women, was being used as a springboard to once again put men on top. Those of us on the bayou know that women hold our cuisine, culture, and traditions together.

I keep a collection of spiral-bound Cajun cookbooks at the restaurant. These books were put together by women's church groups to share the information and knowledge passed down through generations of women. The cookbooks are timeless poetry and ambassadors for Cajun food. A place for women to record a piece of themselves. The recipes collected are a beautiful window into the soul of a woman and the soul of a place. From parish to parish, the books allow us to see time changing and food standing still, to see women passing on their knowledge and protecting the cuisine they built.

EGGPLANT FRITTERS

MAKES 24 FRITTERS

1 large eggplant or 3 small Fairy Tale eggplants

Peanut oil, for frying

1 cup (125 g) all-purpose flour

½ cup (65 g) freshly milled red wheat flour (see sidebar, page 319)

¼ cup (45 g) raw unrefined sugar

1½ teaspoons baking powder

½ teaspoon kosher salt

1 large egg

1 cup (240 ml) whole milk

½ teaspoon pure vanilla extract

Cane syrup, for serving

Wilma Dusenbery ran a Sunday supper club in Chauvin from 1980 to 2005. The restaurant was called La Trouvaille, French for "lucky find." She would invite folks into her home, play Cajun music, and share an authentic bayou dining experience. Her restaurant was a living, breathing objet d'art, and this recipe is inspired by hers.

Eat the fritters hot, with cane syrup for dipping, or dust them with powdered sugar, if you want a sweeter version.

Preheat the oven to 375°F (190°C).

Place the eggplant on a baking sheet and bake until the flesh is soft, the skin is papery and tearing, and the eggplant is cracking open, about 1 hour 30 minutes. Remove from the oven and let cool slightly.

Place a strainer over a bowl and scrape the flesh of the eggplant into the strainer; discard the skins. Using your hands, squeeze the eggplant flesh to remove the excess liquid, then let it sit in the strainer to drain for 30 minutes. Mash the eggplant with a fork to push out yet more liquid, then set aside while you make the batter.

Fill a large heavy-bottomed pot with 4 inches (10 cm) of peanut oil and heat the oil over medium-high heat to 375°F (190°C). (Alternatively, use a tabletop fryer; see page 25.)

In a medium bowl, sift together the flours, sugar, baking powder, and salt. Form a well in the center and crack the egg into it. Put the eggplant flesh on top of the egg and pour the milk and vanilla onto the eggplant. Use a fork to just slightly bring the mixture together—this should take about 10 calculated blends with a fork. You do not want to overmix.

Working in batches, drop the batter by tablespoons (or use a #100 cookie scoop) into the hot oil, forming 8 to 12 fritters per batch, and fry until golden brown on both sides, about 5 minutes. Use a slotted spoon to pull a fritter out and split it open to make sure it's cooked in the center, then transfer all the fritters to paper towels to absorb excess oil. Repeat to fry the remaining batter.

Serve the fritters with cane syrup alongside for dipping.

A MESS OF GREENS

SERVES 4

2 tablespoons canola oil

4 ounces (115 g) salt pork, homemade (see page 239) or store-bought, diced

2 pounds (910 g) yellow onions, finely diced

1 pound (455 g) mustard greens, chopped

1 teaspoon kosher salt, plus more as needed

½ teaspoon cracked black pepper, plus more as needed

You can cook this recipe with just about any dark leafy greens—or any vegetables, for that matter. My mom mostly cooked mustard greens this way; that's what was growing on the bayou. The sweet salt pork mellows out the greens' bitterness during their long simmer. Nowadays, I often cook greens hot and fast, but when I have time to slow-cook mustard greens in a cast-iron pot, this is the method I use.

Warm a heavy-bottomed 8-quart (8 L) pot over medium heat for 2 minutes, then add the oil and heat for 30 seconds. Add the salt pork and cook, turning as needed until golden on all sides, about 12 minutes.

Add the onions and cook, stirring often, until they start to caramelize, about 30 minutes. Add the mustard greens, salt, and pepper and stir to combine. Reduce the heat to low and smother, covered, for 60 to 90 minutes, until all the greens are completely cooked through and tender. Taste and adjust the seasoning before serving.

POTATO SALAD

SERVES 6 TO 8

4 teaspoons kosher salt, plus more as needed

1 pound (455 g) red potatoes (about 8), scrubbed

6 large eggs

1 cup (240 ml) homemade mayonnaise (see page 306)

1 tablespoon Dijon mustard

1 tablespoon hot sauce, preferably Original Louisiana Hot Sauce, plus more as needed

⅛ teaspoon freshly ground black pepper, plus more as needed

Pinch of cayenne pepper, plus more as needed

Here is the rule for the potato salad I grew up eating: There should be no relish or any other green things in the mix. Although I've never met a potato salad I didn't like, I stand by this rule. This is a quick and easy potato salad to serve with gumbo. Whether you put your potato salad *in* your gumbo or eat it on the side is a matter of preference. It doesn't mean you're from Baton Rouge or any other place. Just like some folks like their gravy on their mashed potatoes and others prefer it on their meat and still others like it on both, it's simply about eating it the way you like.

In a medium pot, bring 4 quarts (4 L) water to a boil over high heat and add 1 tablespoon of the salt. Add the potatoes and boil until they are fork-tender, about 10 minutes. Drain.

Meanwhile, in another medium pot, bring 2 quarts (2 L) water to a boil over high heat. Once the water is boiling, carefully lower in the eggs and boil for 8 minutes. Drain the eggs and rinse under cold water or transfer to a bowl filled with ice and water until the eggs are cool enough to handle. Peel the eggs and cut them in half, separating the yolks and whites.

In a medium bowl, whisk together the mayonnaise, mustard, and hot sauce until it is smooth. Use your hands to break apart the potatoes and add the pieces to the bowl. Zest the egg yolks into the bowl using a Microplane, then break the egg whites into small pieces with your hands and put them in the bowl, too (you could also use a fork to mash them, if you'd rather).

Add the remaining 1 teaspoon salt, the black pepper, and the cayenne. Use a fork to mash all the ingredients together. Taste and adjust the seasoning before serving.

CUCUMBER AND TOMATO SALAD

SERVES 6 TO 8

4 tomatoes (2 pounds/
910 g), cut into wedges

4 cucumbers, sliced into
rounds ½ inch (1.5 cm) thick

2 tablespoons cane vinegar,
preferably Steen's (see
Resources, page 359),
or apple cider vinegar,
champagne vinegar, or
white vinegar

1 teaspoon kosher salt

¼ teaspoon freshly ground
black pepper

You might want to eat this salad every day, but you have to wait to eat it during the high days of summer. That's when you get the very best cucumbers and tomatoes. When both vegetables are vine ripened from the heat of the sun, this salad is at its best. Use tomatoes and cucumbers you grew yourself, or buy some directly from a farmer or another reputable source. You can pair the salad with sliced red onions and sweet peas, or toss in fresh green beans or freshly hulled purple hull peas. I often add whole parsley leaves, too, because I have a slight addiction to parsley. There's not much that won't pair with this simple salad.

Put the tomato wedges and cucumber slices in a medium bowl. Toss with the vinegar, then season with the salt and pepper. Eat immediately.

THISTLE SALAD

SERVES 2

1 thistle plant

1 tablespoon cane vinegar, preferably Steen's (see Resources, page 359), or white vinegar or apple cider vinegar

½ teaspoon kosher salt

¼ teaspoon freshly cracked black pepper

Pinch of cayenne pepper

In the springtime, milk thistle can be found in any field and throughout the woods of South Louisiana. There is something incredibly nostalgic about seeing these plants pop up; I am immediately transported to being five years old and carefully cutting down thistles, trimming their sharp prickly thorns, peeling them, and slicing them into rounds for a simple salad of thistle, salt, black pepper, vinegar, and cayenne.

I never knew how healthy thistle was, only that it's delicious. But milk thistle promotes liver detoxification, is great for keeping arteries clear, and lowers cholesterol. It's good for your skin and reduces inflammation, too. So when you see milk thistle lining fields during the spring, do yourself a favor and stop to get some. You want to find a young thistle plant—one that is about 1½ feet tall with a beautiful, healthy flower. The taller they get, the tougher they are.

Carefully use a knife to trim off all the thistle's thorns. You eat just the stalk of the thistle; it is similar to celery or a cardoon. Once you've trimmed off the top prickly flower and thorns (discard these), use a sharp knife to peel away the outer layer of the thistle, in the same way you would peel a stalk of celery of its tougher outer skin.

Slice the thistle into ¼-inch-thick rounds and toss in a bowl with the vinegar; then sprinkle the salt, black pepper, and cayenne on top. Enjoy.

MOSQUITOS!

The question I am asked most often at Mosquito Supper Club is "Why the name 'Mosquito'?" With all the different variations of Cajun life and Cajun food, the one thing all Cajuns have in common is mosquitos. Mosquito Supper Club is the Cajun life as I experienced it. My brother helped me name Mosquito Supper Club; it was inspired by a recording of my grandmother saying, "Maxine, mosquitos!" She is talking about the number of mosquitos that were present when she was growing up, and she says "mosquitos" in a very long Cajun French drawl, accenting each syllable, reassuring my mom that there were certainly a lot of mosquitos back then.

The supper club started very organically, and I had no idea how it would take shape. I knew I wanted a space where I could use food to tell stories and share images of Cajun life, illustrating the beauty of present-day Cajuns, and to capture what is real Cajun and what is contrived, what is true and what is "commercialized." I wanted to cook for intimate groups of people and talk about the food, dispel some myths about Cajuns, and describe what it truly meant to grow up in the Cajun tradition on Bayou Petit Caillou. In one seating per night, so guests don't feel rushed, I wanted to re-create the feeling of lingering over a table at home.

The supper club started as an experiment to see if strangers could sit together and pass around platters of Cajun food as if it were an old-fashioned family meal. Maybe these folks would want to listen to some tales about what it means to grow up Cajun in Terrebonne Parish. Maybe they'd even hear some stories about the grim status of Louisiana's coastline and leave with more awareness of the situation. Most important, I wanted the food to be made up of the very best ingredients. These ingredients are a story in and of themselves and celebrate the bounty produced by our local fishermen, farmers, butchers, bakers, and millers. I wanted a staff that felt like family. I wanted to create a stage for food, activism, art, music, and sustainability. I chose tables for the stage.

I went to the hardware store with a friend and spent $200 I didn't have on supplies; over the course of one weekend, he and I fashioned two family-style tables out of new and salvaged wood. He did the building and I did the sanding and staining. I chose a blue paint that reminded me of water and sea glass. The tables fit twelve people each, and I had enough plates and glasses to serve that many folks. I pulled together some benches and random chairs for seating.

I rented a hip multipurpose space in the Ninth Ward of New Orleans; the owner offered it for $200 a night plus some work trade. I created an Instagram account and built a website.

The dinners were to be prepaid so I'd know exactly how many people I was feeding

and could eliminate food waste. I created my own online ticketing system for dinners using a Squarespace retail shopping cart and made an old-fashioned reservation book with spreadsheets.

From the beginning, I offered one Cajun tasting menu per night and set some boundaries. I cooked only the food I grew up eating—the style of food that my grandmothers, mom, and aunts cooked. It was a style of food I never came across in New Orleans—subtle, full of flavor, and stripped down. I wanted to elevate the cuisine of the women in my life. They were my muses, and I intended to carry on their recipes and share

them with whoever wanted to have a seat at the table.

I posted my first few pictures on Instagram: a shot of the newly built tables, a shot of the space I rented on Royal and Clouet Streets, and a shot of me walking down a tiny street in Cocodrie toward Lake Boudreaux, flanked on both sides by tall wild Roseau cane, a thick cane grass used for duck-hunting blinds that grows like bamboo in these parts. The picture shows Lake Boudreaux really close to Highway 56. There was once almost a half mile of land between the roadside and the lake. Cattle and pigs roamed freely. Water now laps right at the side of the road.

Continued →

Mosquito Supper Club was never a club, and it is never exclusive. Anyone is welcome to reserve a seat at our dinners. I have never turned a person away for monetary reasons. My first dinner was a five-course Cajun meal that cost $25, and drinks were BYOB. The basics for the business were outlined and defined in that first dinner, and they remain unchanged.

That was April 2014, and we've been in operation ever since. We've grown from a twice-a-month pop-up supper club to a fully permitted restaurant and bar. We open our restaurant four days a week and run service the same way we did the first night. We overcame some serious obstacles on our journey, but the initial core values and philosophy are still in place: working with local farmers and fishermen to tighten the net of community and sustainability and put the best possible ingredients into dishes that are indicative of the food I grew up eating on the bayou.

We have a saying at the supper club: "Hot rolls wait for no one." We want guests seated when the rolls come out of the oven. We start the rolls precisely three hours before guests are to be seated at 7:35 p.m. We serve piping-hot cast-iron pots of seafood gumbo, potato salad, fried shrimp boulettes, lagniappe rolls with a cane syrup–laced compound butter, and platters of overstuffed crabs—to name a few of our most popular dishes. The exact menu depends on the day and how we're feeling as a team. Each dish has a story, and we tell it at our tables and through our food.

In 2017, we decided it was time to refashion the original supper club tables. They'd seen a lot of use and had some water damage, and we needed to retire them with honor. We were nervous about changing the tables. After all, they were at the center of everything. We made the new tables smaller and painted them a color I remembered from my grandfather's net shop—a beautiful muddy green that resembles an old schoolhouse chalkboard. They are rustic and seem vintage. The new tables are perfect. I look at them now and think, *If these tables could talk . . .*

Mosquito Supper Club and those tables were built by a team, with love; they have been at the center of a growing business. Thousands of people have sat at them, and thousands of people have been fed sustainable food from South Louisiana on them. They have been the platform on which a community of growers come together on a plate and make a difference as a whole. They have been the stage for the theater that is Mosquito Supper Club. We have told our stories on this stage, and have laughed and cried on this stage. We have dealt with the death of a parent, a cousin, and friends at this table. We have dealt with my own outrageously painful divorce and the realities of raising a transgender teenager in a world evolving too fast for humankind. We have lost friends—good friends—and gained new ones at these tables. We have had people turn their noses up at our project and our food, and we have had people thank us endlessly for the experience. These refurbished tables are the heart of Mosquito Supper Club.

PANTRY

SOUTH LOUISIANA SHARES IN THE TRADITION

of canning and putting up fruits and vegetables throughout the summer. It means we can enjoy our seasonal fruits all year long. Just like we use our freezer as a larder to hold seafood, we do the same with blackberry compote (see page 299), fig compote (see page 294), and muscadine compote (see page 296). We eat almost all our dishes with pickles, and put up jars of okra, beets, and a variety of different peppers. Your option is to can these fruits and vegetables or just make a tiny batch for your icebox or freezer.

I remember being at my aunt's house watching cauldrons of blackberries simmering away on outdoor propane burners, waiting to be canned. Blackberry jam was always a favorite for the biscuits we ate daily. And if you have a stash in the winter, you can also spread the fruit preserve between layers of cakes. Do the same when figs are in season.

With so many citrus trees lining the bayou, it's hard to believe they aren't native to South Louisiana. Our citrus originates from Asia, but South Louisiana has a climate and geography that are perfect for growing citrus. Citrus may have come to North America via Columbus and his voyages, but it's probably the Spanish who brought over the bulk of Louisiana's citrus trees, and we have the Jesuits to thank for satsumas. They brought them to Louisiana from their pilgrimages to and from Asia. By the 1800s, satsuma trees were planted up and down the Mississippi River. The cold-hardy crop adapted like an indigenous fruit. We eat satsumas one by one and in salads, and I like to turn them into marmalade to slather on sweet potato biscuits (see page 326).

When your favorite produce is in season, cooking fruit in sugar or preserving vegetables in salt is a great way to keep them on your table through the year.

SATSUMA MARMALADE

MAKES 1 QUART (1 L)

2½ pounds (1.2 kg) satsumas or Seville oranges, mandarins, or grapefruit

1 lemon, zested and quartered, seeds removed

3 cups (625 g) raw unrefined sugar

Satsumas make a fine marmalade. The pith in the citrus peel is packed full of natural pectins that thicken the preserve into a honey-like spread.

Marmalade is a delicious topping for biscuits, scones, English muffins, and toast. Spread it between cookie layers or roll it up in cinnamon roll dough. You can also warm it and use it as a glaze for roasted chicken.

Place a couple of small plates in the freezer to chill.

Peel the satsumas and cut the skin into strips about 4 inches (10 cm) long. Set aside.

Separate the satsuma segments, remove any seeds, and coarsely chop the flesh. (You can put it in a food processor and pulse a couple of times to chop it, or just use a knife.)

In a heavy-bottomed pot, combine the satsuma peels and 2 cups (480 ml) water and bring to a boil over medium-high heat. Reduce the heat to medium and simmer for 20 minutes, until the peels are soft, then add the satsuma segments, lemon zest, lemon quarters, and sugar and clip a candy thermometer to the side of the pot.

Bring the mixture back up to a boil over medium-high heat, stirring with a wooden spoon to ensure that the sugar dissolves. When the marmalade reaches 220°F (105°C), boil for 5 minutes, then check the marmalade's thickness and viscosity with what's called a plate test (see Note): Remove one of the plates from the freezer and drop 1 tablespoon of the marmalade onto it. Draw your fingertip through the marmalade: if the indentation stays put, without the marmalade immediately running back onto itself, it's done. If the marmalade is still runny, cook it for 5 minutes more, then repeat the plate test.

Turn off the heat and let the marmalade cool. Once cool, the marmalade can be transferred to sterilized jars and canned, refrigerated, or frozen. The marmalade will keep in the refrigerator for up to 3 months and in the freezer for up to 1 year.

NOTE: *The amount of pectin and juice in fruit varies, which means you may need a little more time for your marmalade to set. Make a note of how long this batch takes to cook and use it as a guideline the next time you make marmalade.*

FIG COMPOTE

MAKES 2 CUPS (480 ML)

2 cups (415 g) raw unrefined sugar

Juice of 1 lemon

1 pound (455 g) fresh figs
(see Note)

Fig season in Louisiana can be daunting because it's you against the birds. But if you take the time to cover your fig trees with a net, you will have many more figs for yourself. Skip this step, and you need to be ready to pick every fig as soon as it reaches peak ripeness, or else the birds will win. It's tough to put figs away for the season when you just want to eat them right then and there. If you have some figs to save, make a fig compote. It's a bit thicker than jam and goes well with almost anything. Put it on sweet treats, stuff it into hand pies, use it as a side for cheese plates, or sandwich it between two Pillowcase Cookies (page 330).

In a heavy-bottomed small pot, warm the sugar and lemon juice over medium heat until the sugar is melting, about 5 minutes, stirring frequently. Add the figs, clip a candy thermometer to the side of the pot, and cook for about 20 minutes, until the mixture reaches 220°F (105°C).

Turn off the heat and let the compote cool. Transfer it to a clean lidded jar and store in the refrigerator for about 6 months or in the freezer for up to 1 year.

NOTE: *The figs stay whole in this recipe. If you'd rather smother your preserves, you can chop the figs first.*

MUSCADINE COMPOTE

MAKES 2 CUPS (480 ML)

1 pound (455 g) muscadines

2 cups (415 g) raw unrefined
sugar

Juice of 1 lemon

Muscadines are Louisiana's native grapes. We pluck muscadines off the vine and eat them on the porch. From there, it's easy to spit the seeds into the garden. You can chop up muscadines and put them in a salad, or use them to make this compote, a favorite on biscuits or as a glaze for poultry or pork (see Note).

Juice the muscadines in a juicer or with a hand press. Discard the solids.

In a heavy-bottomed small pot, bring 2 cups (480 ml) of the muscadine juice to a boil over medium-high heat and cook for about 20 minutes.

In another small pan, warm the sugar and lemon juice over medium heat until the sugar is starting to melt, about 5 minutes, stirring often. Add the sugar mixture to the juice and cook for 20 minutes more, until the compote has thickened and reached 220°F (105°C). Remove from the heat and let cool.

Transfer the compote to a clean lidded jar and store in the refrigerator for about 1 month or in the freezer for up to 1 year.

NOTE: *I warm the compote before using to loosen it up.*

STEEN'S BUTTER

MAKES 1 CUP (240 ML)

½ pound (2 sticks/225 g) unsalted butter, at room temperature

⅓ cup (90 ml) cane syrup, preferably Steen's (see Resources, page 359)

Maldon or other coarse salt, for serving

I serve this simple compound butter with cane syrup every night at my supper club. Folks love it on our Lagniappe Bread Rolls (page 315), but you can put it on anything you'd spread butter on. Before service, our staff likes to snack on the butter slathered between two saltine crackers. They call it the Cajun Oreo.

In the bowl of a stand mixer fitted with the paddle attachment or in a large bowl using a handheld mixer, beat the butter and cane syrup on medium speed until thoroughly combined.

Transfer the butter to a quart-size (1 L) container with a lid. Store the butter in the refrigerator for up to 6 months or in the freezer for up to 1 year. Sprinkle it with coarse salt when serving.

BLACKBERRY AND BAY LEAF COMPOTE

MAKES 1 QUART (1 L)

1 pound (455 g) blackberries

1 cup (250 g) raw unrefined sugar

Juice of 1 lemon

1 bay leaf (see Note, page 46)

Blackberries have a quick season in Louisiana. They don't grow like strawberries. In three to four weeks, they are here and then gone. If you have the time during the summer to pick wild berries of any kind, you're in for a treat, but I'm partial to blackberries.

This jam is a quick compote that has a sweet and savory flavor. It works in all baked goods, between layers of cakes, and as a cookie filling, and is a great addition to savory dishes like pork chops, too. It also pairs well with ice cream.

In a large bowl, combine the blackberries, 1 cup (250 g) of the sugar, and the lemon juice and let macerate at room temperature for at least 2 hours or up to overnight.

Transfer the blackberries to a large heavy-bottomed pot and add the remaining 1 cup (250 g) sugar, the bay leaf, and 1 cup (240 ml) water. Mash the berries with your hands or a potato masher. Bring to a boil over medium-high heat, stirring with a wooden spoon, then cook for 20 minutes more, maintaining a hard simmer over medium heat; the liquid will reduce and the mixture will thicken. Remove from the heat and let cool.

Transfer the jam to a clean lidded jar and store in the refrigerator for up to 6 months or in the freezer for up to 1 year.

PICKLED OKRA

MAKES ONE 1-QUART (1 L) JAR

12 ounces (340 g) tender young okra pods (about 24)

3 cups (720 ml) white vinegar

¼ cup (75 g) kosher salt

3 tablespoons raw unrefined sugar

½ teaspoon red pepper flakes, or 1 fresh hot cayenne pepper

At my table, a meal is not a meal unless it has a vinegar component, and that often comes in the form of pickles. I usually pickle at the end of the summer and stretch the pickles so they last all year.

This is a quick way to pickle okra without having to can it. You can use this recipe to pickle anything—beets, peppers, carrots, radishes, cucumbers, you name it. You can add any spice or herb to this pickling liquid.

Pack the okra into a clean 1-quart (1 L) jar (you should be able to fit all the okra).

In a large saucepan, combine the vinegar, salt, sugar, red pepper flakes, and ½ cup (125 ml) water. Bring to a boil over medium heat, then reduce the heat to low and simmer for 15 minutes.

Pour the hot liquid into the jar over the okra. Let cool at room temperature, then seal the jar. Let the okra pickle in the refrigerator for 2 to 4 weeks before you dig in.

The pickled okra will keep in the refrigerator for 6 to 8 months as long as it is covered in vinegar. When you want to enjoy an okra, use a clean fork—not your fingers—to remove it from the jar, to keep the okra in the jar sterile.

PICKLED BANANA PEPPERS

MAKES ONE 1-QUART (1 L) JAR

½ pound (225 g) banana peppers

2½ cups (600 ml) cane vinegar, preferably Steen's (see Resources, page 359), or apple cider vinegar or white vinegar

¼ cup (50 g) raw unrefined sugar

2 tablespoons plus 2 teaspoons kosher salt

1 bay leaf (see Note, page 46)

Pickles are an important part of the Louisiana diet. In early times, we pickled to preserve our harvest. Nowadays we just love salty, briny pickles as a complement to our food. I grew up with mostly pickled banana peppers and pickled cayenne peppers, but you can use this method to pickle any pepper you'd like. I can't eat gumbo or jambalaya without a side of pickles; to me, the combination is as natural as French fries and ketchup.

Slice the banana peppers into rings or leave them whole. Pack them into a clean 1-quart (1 L) jar.

In a small saucepan, combine the vinegar, sugar, salt, bay leaf, and ½ cup (120 ml) water and bring to a boil over medium-high heat.

Pour the hot liquid into the jar over the peppers, making sure all the peppers are covered. Let cool, then seal the jar and store in the refrigerator for up to 1 year. You can eat them immediately or wait longer for the peppers to really absorb the vinegary flavor.

PICKLED BEETS

MAKES ONE 1-QUART (1 L) JAR

2 medium beets (1 pound/ 455 g)

2 cups (480 ml) cane vinegar, preferably Steen's (see Resources, page 359), or apple cider vinegar or white vinegar

1 tablespoon plus 1 teaspoon kosher salt

2 teaspoons raw unrefined sugar

1 bay leaf (see Note, page 46)

Pickled beets are sweet, briny, and vibrant in color. They pair well with bitter green salads and complement jambalaya and fried fish. They are a staple of the Cajun pantry. You can use any variety of beets for this recipe. I'm partial to the deep dark red ones with a small to medium-size bulb. Pickled beets are also great to dice up and serve with a cheese plate, which is not very Cajun but is very delicious.

Remove the greens if they are still attached (discard or reserve for another use). Scrub and peel the beets, then slice into rounds or cut into cubes. Pack the beets into a clean 1-quart (1 L) jar or other container with a lid.

In a small saucepan, combine the vinegar, salt, sugar, bay leaf, and ¼ cup (60 ml) water and bring to a boil over medium-high heat.

Pour the hot liquid into the jar over the beets, making sure all the beets are covered. Let cool, then seal the jar or put a lid on the container and store in the refrigerator. After about a week, the pickles will be ready to eat; they will last for 6 to 8 months.

CHICKEN STOCK

MAKES 1 GALLON (4 L)

4 pounds (1.8 kg) chicken scraps, preferably backs and necks

3 pounds (1.35 kg) yellow onions, coarsely chopped

3 celery stalks, coarsely chopped

2 green bell peppers, coarsely chopped

Stems from 1 bunch parsley

1 bay leaf (see Note, page 46)

Pinch of kosher salt

I like cooking with chicken stock best, as it adds richness and balance to a dish without overpowering the flavor of the other ingredients. If I want to infuse a dish with more shrimp, crawfish, or crab flavor, I make those stocks by simply adding those shellfish to a chicken stock base.

Making stock is a great way to utilize your cooking scraps. For chicken stock, save all the parts from butchering chicken or leftovers from a meal of baked chicken. Just put the bones in a freezer bag, along with any onion, celery, bell pepper, parsley, and green onion scraps. When you have two gallon-size freezer bags full of scraps and bones, make stock. Of course, you can start stock from scratch, too, and procure all the ingredients from your grocer before you begin.

Preheat the oven to 400°F (200°C).

Put the chicken in a stockpot and add the onions, celery, bell peppers, parsley stems, and bay leaf. Cover with cold water; the amount of water should be double that of vegetables and chicken—more water than solids. So, if you have 1 gallon (4 L) chicken and vegetables, add 2 gallons (8 L) water.

Bring to a boil over high heat, then reduce the heat to maintain a low simmer and cook until flavorful, 4 to 6 hours. Ladle a bit of the stock into a cup, season with the salt, and sip. Does it have enough flavor? Have the vegetables given up all their goodness? Should it cook longer? If you could easily add potatoes, pepper, parsley, and green onions and have a delicious soup, it's ready. If you think it needs more flavor, simmer for another 30 minutes and taste again.

Strain the stock through a fine-mesh sieve and discard the solids. Use the stock immediately, or let cool to room temperature, then transfer to airtight containers and freeze for up to 6 months to use in many meal adventures.

NOTE: *Stocks are best stored in the freezer, as it maintains their clarity. Stocks left in the refrigerator get cloudy quick.*

VARIATIONS ——————————————————————

Duck Stock

Substitute duck scraps for the chicken scraps.

Shrimp or Crawfish Stock

For this stock, you add the heads of shrimp or crawfish in the last couple hours (rather than start with them as you do with chicken). You wait until the vegetables have developed flavor, then add the heads. The heads can't cook all day like chicken bones or beef bones; they start to break down, so you really just want to simmer them for a couple hours.

Start with all the vegetables in a stockpot, cover them with water, and bring to a boil. Let simmer for 2 hours so the stock develops full flavor, then add the crawfish heads if you're making crawfish stock or shrimp heads if you're making shrimp stock. Simmer the heads in the stock for another 1½ to 2 hours over low heat. You want to draw all the flavor out of the heads but not get to the point that the shells are starting to break down into the stock.

MAYONNAISE

MAKES 2 CUPS (480 ML)

1 large egg, at room temperature

½ teaspoon kosher salt

¼ teaspoon cracked black pepper

Juice of ½ lemon

Pinch of cayenne pepper

1½ cups (360 ml) canola oil

Mayonnaise is so easy to make, everyone should try it—especially anyone who likes mayonnaise as much as my dad. He eats fried seafood, French fries, tomatoes, cucumbers, and so many other things with it.

Be sure to let your egg come to room temperature before you make this recipe to ensure that the mayonnaise doesn't break.

Put the egg in a food processor and season with the salt, black pepper, lemon juice, and cayenne. With the food processor running, very slowly drizzle in the oil until the mixture has the consistency of mayonnaise. (You may think, as you're adding the oil, that using more will make it thinner, but this is not the case—the oil emulsifies with the egg, and as you add more, the mayonnaise thickens.) Transfer the mayonnaise to a container or jar with a lid and store in the refrigerator for up to 2 weeks.

MARIA'S SEAFOOD DIP

MAKES 3 CUPS (720 ML)

2 cups (480 ml) homemade mayonnaise (above)

1 cup (240 ml) ketchup

½ yellow onion, finely diced

1 teaspoon yellow mustard

1 teaspoon hot sauce, preferably Original Louisiana Hot Sauce

⅛ teaspoon kosher salt

Pinch of freshly ground black pepper

The dip to eat with boiled shrimp, crawfish, and crab is a simple combination of mayonnaise, ketchup, and seasonings. It seems like many different cuisines have a Thousand Island dressing–like combination such as this.

Mix all the ingredients in a bowl until well combined. This dip will keep in an airtight container in the refrigerator for up to 3 months.

COCKTAIL SAUCE

MAKES 1½ CUPS (360 ML)

1 cup (240 ml) ketchup (I like to use Heinz made without corn syrup)

¼ cup (60 ml) fresh lemon juice, plus more as needed

1 tablespoon hot sauce, preferably Original Louisiana Hot Sauce, plus more as needed

2½ tablespoons prepared horseradish, preferably Bubbies, plus more as needed

¼ teaspoon kosher salt, plus more as needed

¼ teaspoon freshly ground black pepper, plus more as needed

To make cocktail sauce, start by looking for prepared horseradish with only vinegar, salt, and sugar in the ingredients list and no extra fillers or corn syrup. Better yet, grate your own horseradish fresh from a horseradish root. Look for one that does not have any soft spots, peel the skin off with a sharp paring knife, and grate it on the smallest holes of a box grater or with a Microplane (this may make your eyes water like when dicing onions). If you love horseradish, use as much as you can handle in this recipe.

Mix all the ingredients in a bowl until well combined. Taste and adjust the seasoning. Store in an airtight container in the refrigerator for up to 6 months.

STEEN'S VINEGAR MIGNONETTE

MAKES 1 CUP (240 ML)

1 cup (240 ml) Steen's cane vinegar (see Resources, page 359)

1 tablespoon finely chopped shallot

1 tablespoon finely chopped green onion whites

1 tablespoon finely chopped fresh flat-leaf parsley stems

¼ teaspoon finely ground black pepper

We never had mignonette growing up on the bayou, but after spending some time on the West Coast, I realized how well it goes with oysters. The vinegar lends an extra bite to the sweet, salty oyster.

Combine all the ingredients in a small serving bowl and keep chilled until ready to serve.

SNOWING SUGAR

Summer is brutal in South Louisiana. The temperature stays in the high nineties most of the summer months, and the weight of the humidity is unforgiving. September means the start of fall weather in most parts of the United States, but on the bayou, we are sweating until the end of October. This fever, this temperature, is prime for growing tropical sugarcane. For centuries, sugarcane has silhouetted the bayou landscape, economy, and rhythm of life. The upside to stifling heat is sugar.

Sugar, one of the world's oldest commodities, was once so valuable that folks locked it up like gold in a "sugar safe." Sugar has affected human civilization on every possible front. It has built and destroyed empires. Tropical cane or sugarcane came to Louisiana from the Caribbean. It took thousands of years before the crop made its way to South Louisiana, but when it did, it stuck.

Sugarcane was established in Louisiana when a young planter figured out which variety of cane was prolific. Étienne de Boré, then mayor of New Orleans, mortgaged his life and his young wife's fortune to be one of the first successful planters. He traded Louisiana's cash crop, indigo, for sugarcane. Sugarcane production was dependent on slaves for labor, and the whole industry was based on coercion and torture of the worst

kind. Up and down the Mississippi River, slaves planted, harvested, transported, and milled sugar, then they boiled cane juice, scooped molasses, and broke down bricks of sugar. Frederick Douglass described working in Louisiana's sugar industry as a "life of living death." Norbert Rillieux, a free man of color, is credited with revolutionizing the sugar process. He aided early planters in developing a system that would make sugar truly marketable.

Sugarcane is the most successful crop in the history of Louisiana and is in its third century of production. It's a colossal industry spread out over twenty-two parishes, and eleven sugarcane processing plants exist today to do the mammoth work of turning cane into granulated sugar. In the land of sugar, Terrebonne Parish was ground zero for sugarcane research and production. Sugarcane was grown on every possible acre available, and the fields stretched all over the parish and meandered up and down the bayou. Terrebonne Parish still grows a tremendous amount of sugarcane, but processing has been moved to large refineries. Gone are the smaller factories; co-ops gave way to larger factories as the industry became "efficient." The refinery closest to my childhood home was shuttered in 1979 and sold its mill to an operation in Guatemala.

When fall comes, sugarcane towers twenty to twenty-five feet tall along the roadside. The crop blankets Highway 90 on any available land that sugar planters can acquire; the only place cane is not planted is in neighborhoods and on water. It's a beautiful sight when the crop is peaking; the landscape and horizon are a sea of sugar.

When I was young, sugarcane harvesting was a magical time. The fields all over South Louisiana are methodically burned, scenting the air with a smoky s'mores aroma, and pieces of sugarcane refuse float through the air, creating an atmosphere of snowing sugarcane. For kids like me who never experienced snow falling from the sky, this was as close to it as we could get. My pulse still quickens when trucks filled with cane are moving in and out of town, when a field is set aflame, and when the first sugar of the season makes its way to my tongue. The pure sugar jogs memories of running through fields of cane and playing hide-and-seek as a teen, of sneaking a stalk of cane to chew on, of an elementary school playground filling with sugarcane snow.

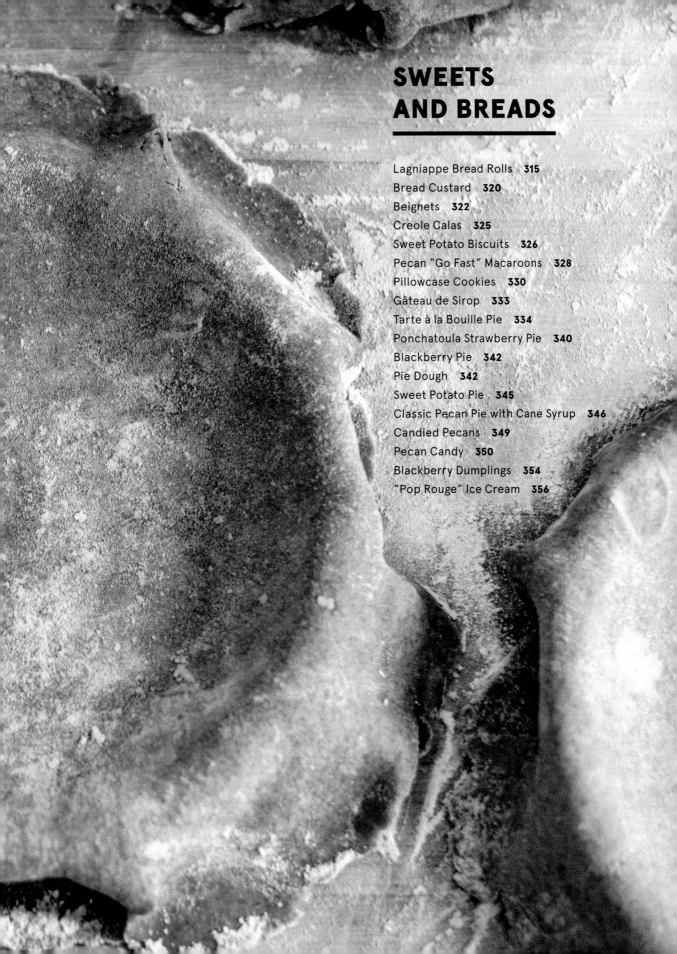

SWEETS AND BREADS

MY MOM SAID, "DON'T BRING A KING CAKE

from New Orleans." It was Mardi Gras, and she was warning me that she had already baked two cakes and made blackberry dumplings; my aunts had also baked cakes and were sharing. This number of desserts is typical for a Sunday on the bayou. When visiting, you must brace yourself for what you know will be a day of discipline and restraint or falling off the wagon. A credo in Chauvin and across many Cajun tables is that you always need to have a sweet treat and strong coffee.

I learned to make beignets and dinner rolls growing up. A dough that starts with flour, yeast, and water can be easily made into a multitude of different baked treats. Different ratios of butter, honey, milk, or eggs and a few different cooking techniques can quickly change minimal ingredients into multiple creations.

When my mom brews a pot of Community Coffee at five a.m., ten a.m., and two p.m., I'm game. There is always a sugary treat to go with her dark brew. If there isn't anything freshly baked, something seems wrong, and we discuss how to rectify it. What should we bake? What do we feel like eating? Are we going to make a cake from scratch or pimp a Duncan Hines box of yellow cake mix? Cajun ladies are known to take a box of cake mix and turn it into something you would never recognize. Growing up with this practice, I was perplexed; why wouldn't you make a cake from scratch? There was an uproar recently on the bayou when Duncan Hines recalled their cake mixes right before a big holiday. (We survived.)

Sugar is the basis for all our sweet treats. We use sugar in our pies, cookies, cakes, jams, and ice creams. Sugar mixed with a combination of flour, eggs, baking powder, and fat can yield a multitude of desserts, from cookies and cakes to pies to breads. Coupled with fruit or nuts in season, a sweet treat is only a mixing bowl, an oven, and a couple of hours away.

Sweet treats laden with sugar are served on our breakfast, lunch, and dinner tables. We make pecan cakes, cookies, and pies until we run out of pecans, and blackberry dumplings until we run out of blackberries. Sweet potatoes keep well in a cool place, which means you can make sweet potato pies all year round. Coffee cakes are on constant rotation, as are biscuits. We make *tarte à la bouille* pies during the holidays. Bread custard is enjoyed year-round. Beignets are a breakfast, lunch, or dinner treat and are always served with cane syrup for dipping.

The recipes shared in this chapter are some of my favorite breads and desserts, the ones served on the bayou and in my restaurant kitchen. It should go without saying that all these recipes should be paired with a cup of strong coffee brewed with love and intention, and shared with family and friends.

LAGNIAPPE BREAD ROLLS

MAKES 2 DOZEN ROLLS

3 cups (720 ml) warm water (105° to 110°F/40° to 45°C)

¼ cup (60 ml) local honey

3 tablespoons active dry yeast

¼ cup (60 g) leaf lard, plus more for greasing

1 tablespoon sea salt or kosher salt

5 cups (625 g) bread flour or all-purpose flour, preferably King Arthur

1 cup (150 g) freshly milled whole wheat flour (see sidebar, page 319), plus more for dusting

1 egg yolk

Splash of heavy cream

Coarse sea salt, for sprinkling

Timing is everything in both life and cooking. Maybe that's why I like kitchens and baking: on a good day, you can control the ingredients, process, and technique—the mixing of water and yeast, watching the dough rise and shaping it right before the fall, then finishing it in a precisely heated oven. These are my simple pleasures, yet it's a simple process mocked by the weather. In October, when the heat in Louisiana breaks, we call this weather "lagniappe weather" (*lagniappe* means a little something extra). It's when the humidity ceases to exist and dough can rise at a tempered pace. In the hot summer months, a sixty-minute dough rise time is easily shortened to thirty minutes. And if you're not ready to bake, you have to put your dough in the icebox to slow down the rising process.

No matter the weather, these rolls are very forgiving. They are the rolls that remind me of my childhood. They are the rolls that are on my aunts' tables on Sunday. Everyone makes them slightly different, but the end product is the same. This slightly sweet soft dinner roll can be eaten with everything from cane syrup to fried oyster sliders.

Place the warm water in a large bowl, add the honey and yeast, and stir to combine. Let stand for 5 minutes to allow the yeast to bloom.

Add the lard and salt and stir to combine.

Add the flours and stir to combine until the dough comes together and forms a manageable ball.

Turn the dough out onto a clean, lightly floured surface and begin kneading, adding flour a little at a time as needed so the dough doesn't stick to the surface. Incorporate the least amount of flour that you need to manage the dough. I like to knead my dough for 10 minutes (or three songs on my current favorite playlist). Let the dough sit for a minute while you wash and dry the bowl. Grease the bowl.

Put the dough in the greased bowl, cover with plastic wrap or a clean dish towel, and set it in a warm, draft-free spot to rise for 1 hour or until doubled in size. Depending on the weather and strength of your yeast, this can happen way quicker than an hour. Watch that your dough does not rise too much and fall in on itself.

Preheat the oven to 375°F (190°C).

Continued →

Turn the dough out of the bowl onto a lightly floured surface. Using a bench scraper, divide the dough into 20 to 24 balls, about 1½ ounces (40 g) of dough per ball. You can weigh them if you want them all to be exactly the same, but I usually just eyeball it.

Take one piece of dough and gently roll it into a ball, using a circular motion with the side of your hand. It's important not to have an overly floured surface or you won't have any resistance when rolling dough, and you need some resistance in order to give the dough shape. I use the sides of my hands flat on the surface with thumbs up and a circular motion to guide the dough ball toward my body. I never use the palm of my hand because that flattens the dough. The bottom of the ball should spiral inward, creating a tight seal. Repeat with the remaining pieces of dough.

Place the rolls in two cast-iron skillets or two 9-inch (23 cm) square baking pans or casserole dishes of comparable size. The rolls should be touching each other. They will help each other rise. Set aside in a warm, draft-free spot to rise until doubled in size, 20 minutes to 1 hour.

Make an egg wash by mixing the egg yolk, heavy cream, and sea salt in a small bowl. Brush the wash on top of the rolls.

Bake immediately for 45 to 50 minutes, until the tops are golden brown. Pull the rolls from the oven, cover with a clean dish towel, and let rest for 5 minutes before serving.

FRESHLY MILLED GRAINS

The first thing you'll notice when using freshly milled grains is their flavor. Commercially processed white flour is stripped completely of its bran and germ, nutritional value, and taste. Grains that are milled with a stone mill retain their nutritional value and flavor. Freshly milling grains turns back the clock on the industrialization of wheat. Slow-moving stones caress the grains, which allows them to retain their natural oils, making the resulting flour silky and flavorful, the nuances of each variety revealing themselves. There was a time when a mill and miller existed in every town in proximity to wheat fields. Folks baked only with freshly milled grains from a variety of different wheats. Then wheat took a hard hit with the industrialization of agriculture. Now with freshly milled flours, bakers are taking back ancient and heirloom grains, supporting a new generation of millers and growers, and baking up bread and sweet treats with integrity and flavor.

When Bellegarde Bakery started milling grains in New Orleans, they were immediately available to me, but I wasn't sure how to use them. There weren't a lot of books available with supporting recipes, so I took a baking workshop in Walnut, North Carolina, with Tara Jensen of Smoke Signals. Tara quickly became a great friend and opened my eyes to the possibility of baking and going all in with freshly milled grains. I left that workshop with a new outlook on bread and pastries, a new palette of paints, and a fresh canvas for the art of baking. Now I bake with grains from Bellegarde Bakery or from Carolina Ground in North Carolina. You can order from both these mills and others around the country online (see Resources, page 359); check to see if there's a mill local to you first before you branch out and order online.

Turkey Red and Ruby Lee wheat are two of my favorite grains to use in rolls, pies, cakes, and cookies. But I also bake with Red Fife from the Pacific Northwest, Oklahoma whole wheat, Kansas white wheat, Abruzzi rye, and anything the mills near me are milling. I encourage you to experiment. You will taste the difference and figure out which flours you like the best. Use softer wheats for pastry, or look for a pastry blend. Harder wheats are for making bread. You will be able to feel if you need more water or less and get to know the way the grains feel in your hands. Some will be coarse and some silky, but all will be delicious after baking.

BREAD CUSTARD

**MAKES 12 LARGE OR
24 SMALL SQUARES**

3 large eggs

¾ cup (150 g) sugar

2 (12-ounce/354 ml) cans
evaporated milk

1 tablespoon pure vanilla
extract

½ loaf stale or two-day-
old white bread or about
12 white bread rolls, broken
into 1- to 2-inch (2.5 to
5 cm) pieces

2 tablespoons unsalted
butter

There are many different versions and endless preparations of bread pudding in New Orleans. This bread custard is my mom's recipe, and it uses soft breads; beautiful sourdoughs with a heavy crust won't work here.

I like the simplicity of the recipe and the delicious custardy way it sets: not like a wet bread pudding but rather a denser flan. It is not too sweet, perfect to serve with fruit or ice cream.

You can make this bread custard with stale bread, but leftover Lagniappe Bread Rolls (page 315) from the day before are my go-to.

Preheat the oven at 375°F (190°C) for at least 15 minutes.

In a large bowl, whisk together the eggs and sugar until well combined, then mix in the evaporated milk and vanilla. Add the bread pieces and press all pieces under the liquid. Let the egg mixture soak into the bread for at least 30 minutes.

Put the butter in a 9-inch (23 cm) square glass or ceramic casserole dish and set it in the preheated oven. Once the butter has melted, carefully remove the dish from the oven and use a pastry brush to coat the sides of the dish with the melted butter.

Pour the bread mixture into the prepared dish and bake for about 45 minutes, until the pudding is set and a sharp knife inserted into the center comes out clean. The top will puff up like a soufflé before it's done. Remove from the oven and let cool, then cut into small squares.

We eat bread custard plain, picking up little pieces and popping them into our mouths.

BEIGNETS

**MAKES 16 LARGE OR
32 SMALL BEIGNETS**

¾ cup (190 ml) warm water
(105° to 110°F/40° to 45°C)

¼ cup (60 g) raw unrefined
sugar

1½ tablespoons active dry
yeast

½ cup (120 ml) milk

1 large egg, beaten

½ teaspoon kosher salt

2½ cups (370 g) all-purpose
flour, plus more for dusting

½ cup (65 g) freshly milled
flour, preferably Ruby Lee
(see Resources, page 359)

2 tablespoons leaf lard
or shortening, at room
temperature, plus more
for the bowl

Peanut oil, for frying

Powdered sugar or cane
syrup, for serving

Eating beignets never gets old; we have them for breakfast on the bayou, but also as an afternoon treat. In New Orleans, sitting and eating beignets with a piping-hot cup of chicory coffee in the French Quarter during a rainstorm or at 3:00 a.m. is one of the great pleasures of living in our old city. We eat our beignets with cane syrup on the bayou and with powdered sugar in the city.

Put the warm water in a large bowl and stir in the raw sugar and yeast. Let stand for 2 minutes to allow the yeast to bloom.

Add the milk, egg, and salt and stir to combine.

In a medium bowl, stir the flours together. Stir half the flour mixture into the milk mixture, then add the lard. Add the remaining flour mixture and use a fork or your clean hands to bring the dough together.

Turn the dough out onto a floured work surface and knead until smooth, about 8 minutes. Grease a large bowl and put the dough in the bowl. Cover with a clean dish towel and set aside in a warm, draft-free spot until doubled in size, 30 minutes to 1 hour, depending on where you live.

Turn the dough out onto a floured surface and roll it into a 10 × 10-inch (25 × 25 cm) square. Using a pizza cutter, cut out 1- or 2-inch (2.5 or 5 cm) squares. If you have the space, you can let them rise on your counter; if not, transfer them to a baking sheet lined with parchment or a silicone baking mat. Dust the squares lightly with flour, cover with a clean dish towel, and let rise until doubled in size, about 45 minutes.

Fill a cast-iron skillet with 4 inches (10 cm) of peanut oil and heat the oil over medium-high heat to 370°F (185°C). (Alternatively, use a tabletop fryer; see page 25.)

Working in batches, add the squares of dough to the hot oil and fry until golden brown, 3 to 5 minutes. Use tongs to transfer the beignets to paper towels to absorb excess oil.

Serve warm beignets dusted with powdered sugar or with cane syrup for dipping.

STRONG COFFEE

Coffee is an important part of bayou culture. Coffee is to folks on the bayou as wine is to folks in Burgundy, France. We take it very seriously. In the past, people would parch or roast their own beans daily or weekly for brewing. They brewed coffee in beautiful enameled French drip pots. They drank it strong, and during harder times, they added chicory to stretch their beans. Foreigners often thought Louisianans were poisoning them when they tried our bitter, chicory-laced brew.

Even today, coffee never makes an exit in the rhythms of daily bayou life. Freshly ground and brewed coffee beans trigger nostalgia and an emotional response, and coffee is omnipresent, whether you take it black, *au lait*, with chicory, or with cream and sugar. It's brewed at home, but also on boats. No fancy pour-overs are favored, just simple dark-roast drip coffee for hardworking women and men. It is brewed artfully with fresh cold water, perfectly measured grounds, and a clean coffee-brewing apparatus, with raw sugar and cream waiting to join. Coffee is served hot, and we drink it hot even if it's ninety degrees outside! No one messes with any iced coffee down the bayou. To us, coffee is both a ritual and an art form.

CREOLE CALAS

MAKES 2 DOZEN CALAS

½ cup (120 ml) milk

1 tablespoon active dry yeast

½ cup (125 g) raw unrefined sugar

1½ cups (290 g) cooked rice (see page 209; I prefer brown rice)

3 large eggs

1 cup (130 g) all-purpose flour

½ cup (65 g) freshly milled flour, preferably Ruby Lee (see Resources, page 359)

1 teaspoon pure vanilla extract

½ teaspoon kosher salt

Pinch of freshly grated nutmeg

Peanut oil, for frying

Powdered sugar or cane syrup, for serving

Before Café Du Monde and Morning Call were the go-to dessert spots in New Orleans, Creoles were pushing carts around the French Quarter and selling *calas*—fried doughnuts made with leftover rice. I learned this recipe from the Hermann-Grima museum when they exhibited it at the New Orleans Jazz Festival. I've adjusted it to include freshly milled flours and a little less sugar. The yeasted dough is better after it sits for a while and can be held in the refrigerator for up to a week before frying. Be sure to put it in a container with a lot of space for it to rise and grow. Fry it up when you need a treat and serve with a café au lait or strong black coffee.

In a small saucepan, warm the milk over low heat just until lukewarm or baby-bottle temperature. Remove from the heat and stir in the yeast and raw sugar. Let stand for 2 minutes to allow the yeast to bloom.

Combine the milk mixture, rice, eggs, flours, vanilla, salt, and nutmeg and whisk to combine. Cover with a kitchen towel and let rise for 30 minutes in a warm, draft-free spot.

Meanwhile, fill a large heavy-bottomed pot with 4 inches (10 cm) of peanut oil and heat the oil over medium-high heat to 375°F (190°C). (Alternatively, use a tabletop fryer; see page 25.)

Using two spoons or a small (#100) cookie scoop, carefully drop balls of the batter into the hot oil. Drop about 12 calas at a time and fry until golden brown, 3 to 5 minutes. Use tongs to transfer the calas to paper towels to absorb excess oil.

Serve the warm calas dusted with powdered sugar or drizzled with cane syrup.

SWEET POTATO BISCUITS

MAKES 12 TO 15 LARGE BISCUITS

3 cups (390 g) all-purpose flour, plus more for dusting

1 cup (150 g) freshly milled flour, preferably Ruby Lee (see Resources, page 359)

2 tablespoons baking powder

2 teaspoons kosher salt

6 tablespoons (85 g) unsalted butter, cut into small pieces

6 tablespoons (85 g) leaf lard, cut into small pieces

½ cup (150 g) mashed cooked sweet potato, chilled

2½ cups (600 ml) buttermilk

Heavy cream and raw unrefined sugar, for topping

A good biscuit is a work of art. This variation uses the sweet potatoes that are always available in Louisiana. When making biscuits, you will know if the dough is good from the way it feels between your fingers. If it feels light and airy while you're mixing it, then you're on the right path.

If you have a baking stone in your oven, your biscuits will turn out even better. Put the stone in the oven when you turn it on to preheat. Let it get hot for at least an hour. If you don't have a baking stone, put a couple of cast-iron skillets in the oven instead. They make great biscuits, too.

Keep your ingredients cold. You want to just barely bring the dry ingredients together with the buttermilk, then bake them hot and fast.

Preheat the oven to 425°F (220°C; if your oven runs hot, go for 375° to 400°F/190° to 200°C). Put a pizza stone (or a couple of cast-iron skillets) in the oven and let it preheat for 1 hour or so—you want it superhot.

In a large bowl, sift together the flours, baking powder, and salt. Add the butter and leaf lard and cut it in with your fingers until the mixture is crumbly and resembles coarse sand. Some big chunks of butter are fine. Put the bowl in the freezer for 10 minutes.

Remove the bowl from the freezer and cut in the mashed sweet potatoes with a fork until just incorporated. The mixture will be lumpy.

Make a well in the center of the mixture and add the buttermilk. Mix together with your fingers just until the dough comes together. Do not overmix—you are not looking for a highly cohesive, smooth dough.

Transfer the dough to a floured work surface and use your hands to shape it roughly into an 8 × 8-inch (20 × 20 cm) square about 2 inches (5 cm) thick (do not knead or fold the dough). Use a 2½-inch (6.5 cm) biscuit cutter to cut out rounds of dough. Place the biscuits on a baking sheet and freeze for 5 minutes.

Remove the baking sheet from the freezer. Transfer the biscuits to the preheated pizza stone (or cast-iron pans). Brush the tops with heavy cream and raw sugar. Bake for about 1 hour, or until the tops are browned. Remove from the oven and let the biscuits rest, covered, for 5 minutes before serving.

PECAN "GO FAST" MACAROONS

MAKES 12 TO 15 COOKIES

1 cup (110 g) pecans

1 cup (120 g) powdered sugar, sifted

Dash of fine salt

1 egg white (40 g)

Pinch of cream of tartar

1 teaspoon pure vanilla extract

These macaroons are called "go fast" because they disappear soon after you make them. They are also easy to make, light, and gluten-free.

When whisking the egg whites, always make sure your bowl is clean, dry, and free of oils. Be sure your oven is preheated to the exact temperature. Whipped egg whites will hold their shape for only a short amount of time, and a changing temperature and humidity are not your friends. Be sure to sift your powdered sugar and salt together, too. You want to use a fine salt for this recipe.

Preheat the oven to 350°F (180°C). Line a baking sheet with parchment paper or a silicone baking mat.

Put the pecans in a food processor and pulse to coarsely grind them.

In a medium bowl, sift together the powdered sugar and salt.

In a large bowl, whip the egg white and cream of tartar until the egg white holds medium peaks, then add the vanilla. Using a wooden spoon or silicone spatula, fold in the ground pecans and powdered sugar-salt mixture just until combined, barely mixing everything together.

Use a tablespoon or a small (#100) cookie scoop to place the cookies on the prepared pan. Bake for 15 to 18 minutes, turning the pan halfway through baking, until they lighten in color (to almost white) and crack on top. Remove from the oven and let cool completely on the pan. They'll continue to set as they cool.

Store in a cookie jar or airtight container at room temperature for up to 1 week.

MAKING THE VEILLÉE

"Making the veillée" is a social stop for Cajun folks. *Veillée* translates to "vigil," but to Cajun folks, it means taking a moment to enjoy some downtime, relax, sit a spell, and catch up with friends and family. And it usually includes a sweet and some coffee. If folks come by to make the veillée, you don't offer them an old pot of coffee—you immediately brew a fresh one. You might even offer apologies that you didn't magically know the exact time they were arriving so the coffee could've been brewed to miraculously finish as soon as they arrived. If you don't have a sweet treat to offer with the coffee, you are embarrassed and a little ashamed. So you pull out the blackberries you put away from the season and mix up a quick batch of dumplings (see page 354), or you make a quick batch of Pecan "Go Fast" Macaroons (opposite).

These rituals are of utmost importance in Cajun society, and are taken seriously. In Chauvin when I was growing up, making the veillée was done under a gazebo on cypress swings. No matter what was going on in people's lives, sisters and brothers, mothers and fathers, kids and cousins made their way to the gazebo to spend the afternoon connecting.

PILLOWCASE COOKIES

MAKES 2 DOZEN COOKIES

2 cups (255 g) all-purpose flour, preferably Carolina Ground (see Resources, page 359)

1 cup (250 g) raw unrefined sugar

1 tablespoon baking powder

½ teaspoon kosher salt

½ cup (1 stick/115 g) unsalted butter

2 large eggs

1 teaspoon pure vanilla extract

Alzina Toups is a muse on Bayou Lafourche in Louisiana, where she cooks and shares the Cajun food she grew up with. This recipe is adapted from one of hers. Alzina's mother was of Portuguese descent, and her father was from a line of Nova Scotia fur trappers. Alzina learned to hunt, trap, and prepare all the delicacies of South Louisiana. She was a trawler with her husband for years before she started cooking for small parties in her son's machine shop. People from all over the world make the pilgrimage to Alzina's to taste her version of Cajun food.

According to Alzina, the story of these cookies began with oyster fishermen. They worked during the cold winter and could be on the water for weeks at a time. They brought cookies onto the boats in a pillowcase, to remind them of the warmth of the homes they would soon return to. These cookies are slightly sweet and puffy, like a cross between hardtack and a sugar cookie.

In a food processor, combine the flour, sugar, baking powder, and salt. Pulse, pulse, pulse. Add the butter and pulse for 30 seconds. Add the eggs and vanilla and pulse until the dough comes together. Wrap in plastic wrap and refrigerate for 30 minutes.

Position an oven rack in the center of the oven and preheat the oven to 375°F (190°C). Line two baking sheets with silicone baking mats or parchment paper.

Transfer the dough to a clean, lightly floured work surface. Using a rolling pin, roll out the dough to a ¼-inch (.5 cm) thickness and cut it into whatever shape you desire (I like to use an alligator-shaped cookie cutter). Dip the cookie cutter in flour first, then press it into the dough. Use an offset spatula to transfer the cookies from your work surface to the prepared baking sheets.

Bake for about 15 minutes, until the edges are golden brown. Remove from the oven and let cool on the pan for 2 minutes, then transfer to a wire rack and let them cool completely. These cookies taste great for up to a week; store them in an airtight container at room temperature.

GÂTEAU DE SIROP

SERVES 12 TO 14

1¼ cups (225 g) leaf lard, plus more for the pan

1 cup (250 g) raw unrefined sugar, plus more for the pan

3 large eggs

1 cup (240 ml) cane syrup

1 tablespoon pure vanilla extract

1½ cups (190 g) all-purpose flour

1 cup (130 g) freshly milled flour (see sidebar, page 319)

1 teaspoon kosher salt

2 teaspoons baking soda

Cane syrup or powdered sugar, for serving (optional)

A classic cane-syrup cake is the perfect coffee cake. It even gets better after a day or two. Despite its name, *gâteau de sirop* is not overly sweet and needs just a simple dusting of powdered sugar or a drizzle of cane syrup to finish it off. Enjoy this cake with a nice piping-hot cup of coffee to accompany it.

When you're making a Bundt cake, be sure to take special care when oiling and sugaring your pan. You want this cake to come out of the pan in one piece, without sticking, and that starts with greasing and sugaring.

I love the old-school cake method of adding baking soda to boiling water. I'm glad the method is making its way back into rotation. I noticed it in the famed Violet Bakery's perfect chocolate cake recipe and in many old recipes from church cookbooks. The boiling water ensures that the baking soda is completely dissolved and is activated.

Preheat the oven to 350°F (180°C). Heavily coat a Bundt pan with lard or nonstick cooking spray, then sprinkle sugar over the entire pan to coat, tapping out any excess. (Be liberal with both the lard and the sugar—this will make it easier to remove the cake from the pan.)

In a large bowl using a handheld mixer, or in the bowl of a stand mixer fitted with the whisk attachment, cream together the lard and sugar for 2 minutes on high. Add the eggs one at a time, stopping frequently to scrape the sides and bottom of the bowl. Add the cane syrup and mix until combined. Add the vanilla and mix to incorporate.

In a medium bowl, sift together the flours and salt. Add the flour mixture to the lard mixture and mix until just combined.

In a small pan, bring 1 cup (250 ml) water to a boil over high heat. Remove from the heat, add the baking soda, and immediately pour the mixture into the cake batter. Mix until combined, about 30 seconds.

Pour the batter into the prepared pan. Bake for 45 to 50 minutes, until a cake tester inserted into the center comes out clean. Remove from the oven and let cool in the pan for 15 minutes. Run a flexible metal spatula around the edges of the cake pan to loosen any stuck-on cake, then turn the cake out onto a parchment paper–lined cake stand. Top with cane syrup or powdered sugar before serving, if desired.

TARTE À LA BOUILLE PIE

MAKES 1 PIE

For the Dough

2½ cups (320 g) all-purpose flour

2½ teaspoons baking powder

1 cup (200 g) raw unrefined sugar

½ cup (1 stick/115 g) unsalted butter, cut into cubes and chilled

2 large eggs

¼ cup (60 ml) whole milk

1 teaspoon pure vanilla extract

For the Custard

3 cups (720 ml) whole milk

4 egg yolks

1½ cups (300 g) raw unrefined sugar

½ cup (65 g) cornstarch, preferably organic

½ teaspoon kosher salt

½ cup (1 stick/115 g) unsalted butter, cut into 4 pieces and chilled

2 tablespoons pure vanilla extract

In Chauvin, Thanksgiving and Christmas mean one thing for certain—bouille pies. In French, *tarte à la bouille* means a tart or pie filled with burnt milk. A simple milk custard fills a sweet shell of goodness. The recipe has been in my family for generations. I can remember watching my mom and her sisters crowd into our kitchen and bake more than forty pies to eat and share with family and friends. I would watch in amazement as they churned out pies and placed them on every available surface to cool. It was the first time I saw kitchen production in unison: my mom, Maxine, stirred the custard; Brenda made the crust; Linda rolled the dough; Christine floated from station to station; and each of them peered into the oven from time to time to determine if the pies were done.

My mother would keep us kids occupied with bowls of bouille custard and raw sweet dough, which we ate until our stomachs grew sour. We practiced our rolling skills with extra pie dough and cut out Christmas trees, snowmen, and angels using the same cookie cutters each year.

Once, I was hired to bake forty bouille pies as Christmas gifts. I knew there was only one place to make this happen, so on a Friday evening, after scrubbing my commercial kitchen in New Orleans (which had two convection ovens and two commercial ovens, mind you), I headed to Chauvin. My mother waited with our stations set up. I made the dough for each pie, one at a time, in a food processor. I rolled the dough and placed it in pie tins while my mother made the custard filling. After each pie shell was filled, we rolled out strips of dough to make a quick lattice and crimped the edges. In three hours, we had all the pies in tins awaiting their turn to bake. We baked them, four at a time, in her vintage yellow Roper oven. We cleared the dining room table, dropped the thermostat, and lined them up to cool as they emerged from the oven. We fought to keep our eyes open while waiting for the last pies to bake. In the morning, we boxed up all forty pies and I drove them back to the city. Before I left, my mom said to me, "We should start a pie company." I replied, "We just did."

Make the dough: In a food processor, combine the flour, baking powder, and sugar and hold down the pulse button for about 10 seconds to combine. Add the butter and hold down the pulse button for another 30 seconds to cut it into the flour. Add the eggs, milk, and vanilla and process until the dough comes together and forms a ball, about 20 seconds.

Remove the dough from the food processor, divide it in half, and form each half into a disk. Wrap each disk in plastic wrap and set aside in a cool place or in the refrigerator while you make the custard.

Preheat the oven to 350°F (180°C).

Make the custard: In a heavy-bottomed medium pot, heat the milk over medium heat, stirring often so it doesn't scorch on the bottom, until it comes to a boil.

Meanwhile, in a medium bowl using a handheld mixer or a whisk, whisk the egg yolks until frothy, slightly thickened, and pale in color. Add the sugar and mix well. Add the cornstarch and mix well. Add the salt and mix well.

While whisking continuously, slowly pour ¼ cup (60 ml) of the hot milk into the egg mixture and whisk until incorporated to temper the egg (this prevents the egg from scrambling when you add it to the hot pan later). Repeat three times, whisking in ¼ cup (60 ml) of the hot milk each time.

Bring the milk remaining in the pot to a rolling boil over medium-high heat. As soon as it reaches a rolling boil and wants to creep up the pan and boil over, add the tempered egg mixture to the pot and continue to cook, immediately whisking continuously, for 5 minutes, until the custard is thick. (This is when a handheld mixer really is handy. If you don't have one, work your arm muscles.) Remove the pot from the heat and, while whisking continuously, add the butter one piece at a time, mixing, then add the vanilla.

Assemble the pie: Roll out one disk of dough into a 15-inch (38 cm) round that is ¼ inch (.5 cm) thick. The dough should be very soft and pliable, and you will need to work fast—if it gets too crackly and crumbly, form it into a disk again and let rest before attempting to roll it again. Transfer the dough to an 8- or 9½-inch (20 or 24 cm) pie pan. It should have an overhang of about 2 inches (5 cm). Tuck the overhang under the dough on the rim of the pie pan to create a thick outer crust.

Continued →

(When I do my top crust strips, I let them go past the rim and then I tuck those pieces under the rim crust, too.) It's okay if the dough cracks a bit—just piece it together or patch it with a scrap of dough. Roll out the second disk of dough and cut it into 6 strips 12 inches (30.5 cm) long and 1 to 2 inches (2.5 to 5 cm) wide.

Fill the bottom crust with 3 cups (750 ml) of the warm custard filling. Arrange the strips of dough over the top to form a wide lattice. I don't create a proper lattice on a bouille pie because the dough sticks to the bouille. So just lay out the strips in a lattice pattern. After you're finished with the top strips, use your hands to pull in the sides of the pie slightly off the rim. While baking, it will increase in size and want to fall off the rim, so it helps to slightly squeeze it together.

Bake the pie immediately, until golden brown on top, about 30 minutes. Remove from the oven and let cool for about 1 hour before serving. If you plan to eat the pie the next day, put the pie in the refrigerator. It is delicious cold.

Cane Syrup

FOLKS ON THE bayou and in the prairies once grew small patches of cane for home use. Old sugarcane boiling pots can be found in yards up and down the bayou from the time when folks made their own cane syrup. The pots weigh more than 500 pounds (225 kg) and can hold 100 gallons (380 L) of juice. Now they are sometimes used to hold plants or serve as man-made ponds. But back then, families joined together to juice cane and boil the juice to make syrup. They shared the syrup, then traded with other farmers for things they needed: rice or flour, potatoes or corn. As life sped up, fewer people had time to grow and process their own cane.

Those who didn't process their own sugarcane could drive to the local mill and pick up raw sugar or a gallon of hot syrup ladled straight into a jar. Folks would have to ride home with this piping-hot glass jar balanced between their feet to avoid burning their legs. When they made it home, they poured the syrup into a bowl and sopped it up with warm French bread or beignets.

Charles Poirier of Poirier's Cane Syrup (see Resources, page 359) lives in Youngsville, Louisiana, and harvests ribbon cane the old-fashioned way. He is in a class of his own for preserving and carrying on this tradition. Helping people reclaim and preserve the art of processing cane brings him joy. He takes pride in fielding calls from young folks who want to learn from him. Visiting Mr. Poirier, you learn that processing cane is a family affair. His kids push cane stalks through an old-fashioned juicer and the juice flows straight into propane-fired black cast-iron pots. Mr. Poirier boils the cane juice all day long until the syrup thickens up and is a dark rich amber color.

Although hundreds of acres of sugarcane fields in south Terrebonne Parish are gone, underwater now, sugar is still a vibrant, important industry in South Louisiana. Thanks to Mr. Poirier and others, micro-batch cane production is fueling a resurgence of backyard cane production, too.

PONCHATOULA STRAWBERRY PIE

MAKES 1 PIE

3 pints (2¼ pounds/1 kg) strawberries

1 cup (200 g) raw unrefined sugar, plus more for topping (see headnote)

¼ cup (30 g) tapioca starch

1 tablespoon lemon juice

2 disks Pie Dough (recipe follows)

1 egg yolk

Splash of heavy cream

Vanilla ice cream, for serving

This pie is named for a region in Louisiana famous for its strawberries. *Ponchatoula* is a native word referring to the beauty of this place: it is an area famous for its agriculture and produces most of Louisiana's strawberries in a season that lasts practically six months!

When you get strawberries, taste them to determine how much sugar you should add to the pie. If they're at the height of their sweetness, hold back on some of the sugar. The sugar should enhance the flavor, not overwhelm the berries.

Preheat the oven to 425°F (220°C).

Wash and dry the strawberries, then hull and slice them.

In a large bowl, combine the strawberries and sugar. Use your hands to crush the berries a bit. Let stand for 1 hour (this will draw out some of the liquid and make for a firmer filling).

Pour off any liquid that has collected in the bowl (and save for another use), then add the tapioca and lemon juice and mix until just combined.

On a lightly floured work surface, roll out one disk of the dough into a 14-inch (35 cm) round about ¼ inch (.5 cm) thick and transfer it to a 9-inch (23 cm), 1-inch-deep (2.5 cm) pie pan. Roll out the second disk of dough and cut it into 1- to 2-inch-wide (2.5 to 5 cm) strips that are 12 inches (30 cm) long.

Fill the bottom crust with the strawberries, then arrange the strips of dough over the top to form an open lattice. (I roll out my lattice with wide strips that are about ¼ inch (.5 cm) thick because I think the pie dough is one of the best parts of a pie.) Cut off any excess, leaving a 1-inch (2.5 cm) overhang for both the bottom crust and the lattice strips. Tuck the overhang of both under the crust around the rim.

In a small bowl, whisk together the egg yolk and cream to make an egg wash. Brush the pie dough with the egg wash and sprinkle with raw sugar.

Place the pie on a baking sheet (this will catch any drips) and slide it into the oven. Bake for about 1 hour 20 minutes, until the crust is

browned and the filling is bubbling. Remove from the oven and let cool completely before slicing.

Serve with a scoop of vanilla ice cream.

NOTE: *You don't want to cover the top of the pie completely. Berries have a lot of liquid in them, and you don't want to trap the liquid in the pie while it's baking; a lattice top allows the liquid to evaporate as it cooks, rather than cause the crust to get soggy.*

VARIATION ────────────────────────────────────

Blackberry Pie

Wash and dry 3 pints (2¼ pounds/1 kg) blackberries. Follow the method for the strawberry pie, using the blackberries in place of the strawberries.

PIE DOUGH

MAKES FOUR 12-OUNCE (340 G) DISKS OF DOUGH, ENOUGH FOR 2 DOUBLE-CRUST OR 4 SINGLE-CRUST PIES

5 cups (640 g) freshly milled flour (see sidebar, page 319)

2 teaspoons kosher salt

1 pound (4 sticks/455 g) unsalted European-style or other high-fat butter, cut into ½-inch (1.5 cm) cubes and chilled

I've made pie dough many different ways, but I tend to come back to this classic recipe of freshly milled grains, butter, salt, and water. I learned the technique from Tara Jensen of Smoke Signals Baking. She taught me to smudge the butter rather than cut it in. When you press the butter and flour through your fingers, the two ingredients are slightly combined and ready to merge with just a little hydration (water). Tara taught me how to roll the dough out first into a long strip so it can be folded up into a neat little stack to get layers of flakiness in the pie dough. With this technique, you will see large pieces of butter streaked throughout a rustic flaky piecrust.

────────────────────────────────────

Put 2 cups (480 ml) water in the freezer to chill.

In a large bowl, sift together the flour and salt. Add the butter to the flour mixture and smudge it in with your fingers. Take the water out of the freezer and work it into the flour mixture 2 tablespoons at a time until the dough comes together (you may not need all the water).

Divide the dough into four equal-size disks. Put two disks in a large bowl, cover with a clean dish towel, and refrigerate for at least 1 hour

before using. Wrap the other two disks well in plastic wrap and freeze for another baking adventure (they will keep for up to 6 months in the freezer).

When you are ready to roll out the dough, take the disks out of the refrigerator and transfer to a floured work surface. Pat the dough into a very long cylinder, then roll it into a piece of dough 2 feet (60 cm) long by 4 inches (10 cm) wide. Starting at one end, fold the dough 4 inches (10 cm) at a time, until you have a stack of folded dough (this will help distribute the butter in streaks and makes for a flakier crust). Do this with both disks. Let the dough rest for about 5 minutes, then roll out into a circle per the pie directions.

NOTE: *With white flour, it's easy to overmix the dough, causing it to lose flakiness and become dense. With freshly milled flours, you can really work the dough, squeezing it and making sure it is hydrated all the way through.*

SWEET POTATO PIE

MAKES 1 PIE

1 disk Pie Dough (see page 342)

4 tablespoons (½ stick/56 g) butter

1 cup (200 g) cooked sweet potato flesh (1 large or 2 small sweet potatoes)

1 cup (250 g) raw unrefined sugar

¾ cup (180 ml) heavy cream

1 teaspoon pure vanilla extract

1 teaspoon ground cinnamon

½ teaspoon kosher or sea salt

2 large eggs

Pinch of ground allspice

Pinch of freshly grated nutmeg

Sweet potato pie was brought to the United States by enslaved Africans, but the original recipes were made with yams. We are blessed with sweet potatoes and yams all year round in Louisiana, because they can be easily stored for twelve months, but this pie is a specialty for fall and the holidays. Most recipes call for evaporated milk, but I like to make it with a local heavy cream to keep it as sustainable as possible and use a rustic piecrust.

Preheat the oven to 350°F (180°C).

On a lightly floured work surface, roll out the disk of dough into a 12-inch (30 cm) round and transfer it to a 9-inch (23 cm) pie pan. Trim the overhanging dough to 1 inch (2.5 cm) past the rim, then tuck the overhang under the crust. Crimp it with your thumbs and fingers, or use a fork or spoon to create a design around the rim. Line the dough with parchment paper or cheesecloth and fill it with pie weights or uncooked beans. (I use dry coffee beans, but red beans, rice, or lentils will work.) Place the crust in the freezer for 5 minutes to chill, then bake for 20 minutes, until it starts setting and stiffening and the bottom is cooked. (This is called blind baking.)

Meanwhile, in a small saucepan, melt the butter, unless you are adding it directly to sweet potatoes that just emerged from the oven. In the bowl of a stand mixer fitted with the whisk attachment or with an immersion hand blender, add the sugar, cream, vanilla, cinnamon, salt, eggs, allspice, and nutmeg to the sweet potatoes and butter and blend or whisk until smooth. This will take about 5 minutes on high speed in the stand mixer or about 3 minutes with an immersion blender.

Pour the filling into the piecrust and bake for 1 hour, until the filling is set. Use a sharp knife to check that the center is set before you remove it from the oven; it should come out clean. Let cool for a couple of hours before slicing and serving.

You will not be sorry about the aroma this pie leaves in your kitchen. Eat a slice with some whipped cream or ice cream. It's delicious cold, too. The pie will keep for up to 1 week in the refrigerator.

CLASSIC PECAN PIE WITH CANE SYRUP

MAKES 1 PIE

1 disk Pie Dough (see page 342)

4 large eggs

½ cup (125 g) raw unrefined sugar

1 cup (240 ml) cane syrup

2 tablespoons unsalted butter, melted and cooled

1 teaspoon kosher salt

1 teaspoon pure vanilla extract, or 1 vanilla bean, split lengthwise and seeds scraped out

2 cups (230 g) whole pecans

½ teaspoon coarse salt (see Note)

Vanilla ice cream, for serving

This classic pecan pie uses cane syrup instead of the traditional corn syrup. When I am fortunate enough to get my hands on Charles Poirier's micro-batch cane syrup (see page 339), I use it in this recipe. But you can substitute Steen's or another cane syrup. Of course, try to make this pie with whole Louisiana pecans. If you are in South Louisiana, you can procure all these ingredients (except the vanilla) from local brands or producers.

Preheat the oven to 350°F (180°C).

On a lightly floured work surface, roll out the disk of dough into a 12-inch (30 cm) round and transfer it to a 9-inch (23 cm) pie pan. Trim the overhanging dough to 1 inch (2.5 cm) past the rim, then tuck the overhang under the crust. Crimp it with your thumbs and fingers or use a fork or spoon to create a design around the rim. Line the dough with parchment paper or cheesecloth and fill it with pie weights or uncooked beans (I use dry coffee beans, but red beans, rice, or lentils will work). Bake the crust for 15 minutes, until it starts setting and stiffening and the bottom is cooked. (This is called blind baking.)

Meanwhile, in the bowl of a stand mixer fitted with the whisk attachment or in a medium bowl using a whisk, beat the eggs on high speed until frothy, slightly thickened, and pale in color. Add the sugar and mix until combined. Add the cane syrup, melted butter, salt, and vanilla and mix until combined.

Arrange the pecans in the piecrust. I like to place them one by one in a specific pattern, but this really doesn't do anything for the flavor; it's just a feast for the eyes. Pour the egg mixture over the pecans and sprinkle the pecans with the coarse salt.

Bake for about 45 minutes, until the filling is set; there should be some resistance if you press down. If you notice the crust starting to get too brown during baking, cover the edges with aluminum foil. The pie will set more once it's cooled. Remove from the oven and let cool completely for a couple of hours before serving.

Serve with a scoop of vanilla ice cream.

NOTE: *This pie is so sweet that the salt is necessary to balance out the sweetness.*

CANDIED PECANS

MAKES 2 CUPS (230 G)

¼ cup (60 g) raw unrefined sugar

2 cups (230 g) whole pecans

Pinch of sea salt

Candied pecans are tasty on salads, folded into cookie dough, or eaten by the handful as a snack. They make a great little gift, too, when packaged up in a pretty container. There are many different ways to candy pecans: some folks toss their pecans in sugar and cinnamon, then in frothy egg whites before baking them. Others want shiny pecans or sugared pecans.

This simple method makes pecans that are slightly sweet and candied with fewer ingredients. The key is to add the simple syrup to a hot skillet so it immediately starts bubbling and reducing. You don't want too much liquid, and you don't need a lot to coat the nuts. You'll find the balance once you make the recipe a couple of times. Too much liquid will make your nuts too sticky; the perfect amount will adhere to the pecans, coating them in enough simple syrup to candy them but not overwhelm them.

Preheat the oven to 250°F (120°C). Line a baking sheet with parchment paper or a silicone baking mat.

In a small saucepan, combine the sugar and ¼ cup (60 ml) water and bring to a boil over medium-high heat, stirring. Boil the syrup for 1 minute.

Set a large skillet over medium-high heat and pour the sugar syrup into the pan. When the syrup starts furiously boiling, add the pecans and toss to coat them in the liquid. Season with the salt. Let any extra liquid boil away, then pour the pecans onto the prepared baking sheet in a single layer. Bake for 15 minutes. This helps dry the pecans. Let cool before eating, then store in an airtight container. They will stay fresh for a couple of weeks.

NOTE: *If you want the pecans to have a sugared appearance, toss them in sugar before you put them in the oven.*

PECAN CANDY

**MAKES 15 SMALL
SQUARES**

2 cups (200 g) sugar

1 (14-ounce/396 g) can
condensed milk

1¼ cups (125 g) pecan pieces

2 tablespoons unsalted
butter

1 teaspoon pure vanilla
extract

⅛ teaspoon coarse salt

The ladies who taught me to make pecan candy made hundreds of batches
to sell at the Lagniappe on the Bayou fair in my hometown. They make
the candy using their intuition. They never use a candy thermometer. I
remember watching my mother and these amazing women churn out batch
after batch of the sweet stuff, making my home smell like a candy factory.

This recipe is dependent on a thermometer and the outside
temperature. The candy will set better when the humidity is low. A cool and
crisp day is perfect, but if you live in a place that is hot and humid, I would
suggest making the candy first thing in the morning before your kitchen
heats up.

Butter an 8 × 10-inch (20 × 25 cm) glass baking dish.

In a heavy-bottomed small saucepan, combine the sugar and ½ cup
(120 ml) water, clip a candy thermometer to the side of the pan, and
cook the sugar-water mixture over medium-high heat until it's at
a rolling boil and starting to thicken and the temperature reaches
275°F (135°C), about 15 minutes.

Add the condensed milk and cook, continuously stirring with a wooden
spoon, for 10 minutes. The color will change to light brown and the
temperature will increase to 300°F (150°C). Keep stirring as the mixture
thickens, maintaining the temperature, for another 5 minutes.

Remove the pan from the heat, add the pecans, butter, vanilla, and salt.
and beat with a wooden spoon for 5 to 7 minutes. There will be a point
in stirring that the cooling mixture will start to thicken. Immediately
pour the batter into the buttered pan and allow it to set and cool
completely. Cut the pecan candy into squares for sharing. If there are
any left, wrap them in plastic wrap and store for up to 2 weeks.

BLACKBERRY DUMPLINGS

MAKES 24 DUMPLINGS

For the Blackberry Stew

2 pints (6 cups/750 g) blackberries

2 cups (500 g) raw unrefined sugar

1 bay leaf (see Note, page 46)

For the Dumplings

1½ cups (190 g) all-purpose flour, plus a little more for the top

½ cup (65 g) freshly milled flour, preferably Ruby Lee wheat (see Resources, page 359)

1 tablespoon baking powder

1 tablespoon kosher salt

2 tablespoons leaf lard

4 large eggs

1 cup (240 ml) whole milk

Ice cream, for serving (optional)

Blackberries come into season at the beginning of April, so that's when I start checking the waterline on the back bayou of my grandparents' land in Cocodrie to see how the crop looks. My dad and I love the unripe blackberries for salads and garnishes; they have a slight bitterness. When blackberries are in full season, we'll pick as many as we can so we can make blackberry dumplings throughout the year. Pair any flavored dumplings with a scoop of "Pop Rouge" Ice Cream (page 356) or vanilla ice cream.

Make the blackberry stew: In a large bowl, combine the blackberries and sugar; add the bay leaf. Let sit at room temperature for a couple of hours.

Pour the blackberries and 2 cups (480 ml) water into a wide, heavy-bottomed 8-quart (8 L) pot and bring to a simmer over medium heat. Reduce the heat to maintain a simmer and cook for about 45 minutes.

Make the dumplings: In a medium bowl, sift together the flours, baking powder, and salt. Add the lard and cut it in with your fingers or a fork.

Make a well in the center of the mixture and crack the eggs into it. Add the milk to the well, then use a fork to whisk the eggs and milk into the flour mixture. Just bring the ingredients together—don't overmix. Sprinkle a little flour over the batter to cover it. This also helps coat the scoop with flour when you go in to scoop up the dough. Let sit for 5 minutes.

Working in batches, use two spoons or a small (#100) cookie scoop to drop the dough into the simmering blackberry stew (see Note) and cook, basting the dumplings frequently with the blackberry mixture, until they are set and cooked through, about 6 minutes, then carefully flip the dumplings over and cook, basting frequently, for 5 to 6 minutes more. The dumplings will stiffen and be easy to handle with a slotted spoon. If the batter is still gooey and falling apart, then the dumplings are not cooked yet. Once they are cooked, remove the dumplings with a slotted spoon to a plate. Repeat with the remaining batter.

Eat the dumplings warm as is or serve with a scoop of ice cream.

NOTE: *When cooking the second round of dumplings, you may need to add a little boiling water to the blackberry stew to thin it out.*

"POP ROUGE" ICE CREAM

MAKES 1 GALLON (4 L)

1 large egg

2 (14-ounce/396 g) cans
condensed milk

3 (12-ounce/354 ml) cans
evaporated milk

1 teaspoon kosher salt

3 (12-ounce/354 ml) cans
strawberry soda, such as
Fanta

1 tablespoon pure vanilla
extract

Pop Rouge was a strawberry soda (*pop rouge* means "red soda" in French) popular on the bayou. When it was discontinued sometime in the late 1980s, it caused an uproar in my family. What would we possibly use to replace it at our yearly pop-up ice cream stand at the Lagniappe on the Bayou fair? We tried a couple of different brands of red pop through the years—Barq's red creme soda, strawberry Sunkist, strawberry Fanta. Things got even hairier when soda companies started using corn syrup to sweeten their sodas instead of sugar, changing the flavor profile even more.

Presently lots of companies are making boutique strawberry sodas, and I'm always sampling as many as I can, chasing the original Pop Rouge flavor. I have also tried to re-create Pop Rouge with macerated strawberry juice and fizzy water, but the closest I can come to the flavor I remember is Mexican Fanta, known for using real sugar and sometimes a percentage of actual fruit juice. Strawberry Fanta is the best option to use in this ice cream I remember from my childhood. You'll need an ice cream machine to make this recipe.

In a large bowl, whisk the egg until it is light in color and frothy. Add the condensed milk, then fill one empty can with water and add the water to the bowl. Add the evaporated milk and stir to combine. Add the salt, strawberry soda, and vanilla. Whisk for 1 minute, then transfer the mixture to an ice cream maker and churn according to the manufacturer's instructions.

Meanwhile, find a 4-inch-deep 10 × 10-inch (10 × 25 × 25 cm) pan or container large enough to hold 1 gallon (4 L) of ice cream and chill it in the freezer.

Transfer the ice cream to the chilled pan, cover, and freeze for at least 4 hours before serving. The ice cream will keep for weeks. But the consistency is always best the same day it is spun.

RESOURCES

INGREDIENTS

Beans

L.H. Hayward and Company
(Camellia Brand beans)
camelliabrand.com

Rancho Gordo
(heirloom beans)
ranchogordo.com

Filé

Penzeys
penzeys.com

Freshly Milled Cornmeal and Flour

Anson Mills
ansonmills.com

Bellegarde Bakery
(Ruby Lee flour)
bellegardebakery.com

Carolina Ground
carolinaground.com

Hot Sauce

Original Louisiana
Hot Sauce
louisiana-brand.com

Leaf Lard

Fannie and Flo
fannieandflo.net

Louisiana Cane Syrup and Cane Vinegar

Poirier's Cane Syrup
realcanesyrup.com

Steen's Syrup
steenssyrup.com

Louisiana Raw Sugar

Three Brothers Farm
threebrothersfarm.com

Louisiana Rice

Baker Farms
campbellfarms.com

Stansel's Gourmet Rice
stanselrice.com

Louisiana Seafood

Anna Marie Shrimp (shrimp)
annamarieshrimp.com

Louisiana Crawfish Co.
(crabs, crawfish, shrimp)
lacrawfish.com

Louisiana Direct Seafood
(crabs, fish, oysters, shrimp)
louisianadirectseafood.com

Sea to Table (fish, shrimp)
sea2table.com

Salt Pork

Wellshire
wellshirefarms.com

EQUIPMENT

Crawfish Boilers

Bayou Classic Depot
bayouclassicdepot.com

Skillets and Pots

Cajun Cast Iron
(McWare products)
cajuncastiron.com

Lodge Cast Iron
lodgemfg.com

Seasoned (Magnalite
cookware)
seasonednola.com

ACKNOWLEDGMENTS

To the fishermen, the farmers, and all the people working to provide real sustainable food for human consumption, and to the immigrants and refugees who are a large part of that equation.

First and foremost, I'd like to thank Denny Culbert for his endless hours of work, for honoring the quest to shoot what I was feeling on any given day. I am forever grateful for choosing you to shoot this book and forever appreciative of the time you took away from your wife and wild child to make it right. I loved sharing the intimacy of Chauvin with you.

To my mom and dad, who let me live in Chauvin for three months while I was writing so I could immerse myself in the rhythms of bayou life. I survived on my mom's endless pots of coffee, sweet treats, and Scrabble games. Thanks to my dad, the fish whisperer, for launching the boat every time I needed the serenity of the water to ground myself.

To my family on Blaise Street in Chauvin who raised me and fed me, you know who you are. You are my muses, and I am forever grateful, especially to Lance and Heidi Authement for all your help and perfectly fished shrimp.

Thank you to all my Mosquito Supper Club captains of the ship, present and past: Ellen C. Durand, Ellis Douglas, Misha Heil, Donelle Williams, and Maritza Howard.

To Keira Watt for taking MSC's food seriously. This book was possible because of your dedication, hard work, and professionalism. I am completely in awe of your courage and talents.

To the folks who come and go but make a restaurant successful, especially Christina Balzebre, Betsy Lindell, Regina Parkinson, Mikaela Grantham, Loriana Perschall, and Nikki Simard. Thank you.

To anyone who has ever dined at Mosquito Supper Club, thank you.

I'd like to thank my agent, Leslie Stoker, for listening and having faith in me. Thank you, Leslie. And thanks to Artisan Books for taking a chance on me. Especially my editor, Judy Pray, for bringing the *Mosquito Supper Club* cookbook to life; Nina Simoneaux for the design; and all the other folks at Artisan who made this book possible, including Sibylle Kazeroid and Nancy Murray. I also owe thanks to Mimi Assad for recipe testing this entire book and Amanda Medgser for styling on the photo shoots.

A sincere thanks to my son, Lucien, who grew up with a mom struggling to be a chef, struggling to run restaurants, and struggling to find her way in life. You are everything; I love you.

Finally, to Ryan and Iskra, thanks for eating meals at a table with me. And, I love you.

INDEX

Note: Page numbers in *italics* refer to illustrations.

MELISSA M. MARTIN grew up on the Louisiana coast and has lived in New Orleans for twenty years. After Hurricane Katrina, she relocated to Northern California and worked at some of the top Napa Valley restaurants, honing her self-taught culinary skills. Upon returning to New Orleans, she helped to open Satsuma Café, a casual farm-to-table restaurant, and worked at Café Hope, a non-profit restaurant, teaching at-risk youth to cook. In 2014, she opened Mosquito Supper Club, where she serves a family-style Cajun dinner with a glimpse into life on the bayou. She's made it her life's work to support local fishermen and farmers and to run a sustainable restaurant. Find her on Instagram @mosquitosupperclub.